SO YOU WANT TO
SING SACRED MUSIC

So You Want to Sing

Guides for Performers and Professionals

Project of the National Association of Teachers of Singing

So You Want to Sing: Guides for Performers and Professionals is a series of works devoted to providing a complete survey of what it means to sing within a particular genre. Each contribution functions as a touchstone work for not only professional singers, but students and teachers of singing. Titles in the series offer a common set of topics so readers can navigate easily the various genres addressed in each volume. This series is produced under the direction of the National Association of Teachers of Singing, the leading professional organization devoted to the science and art of singing.

So You Want to Sing Music Theater: A Guide for Professionals, by Karen S. Hall, 2013.

So You Want to Sing Rock 'n' Roll: A Guide for Professionals, by Matthew Edwards, 2014.

So You Want to Sing Jazz: A Guide for Professionals, by Jan Shapiro, 2015.

So You Want to Sing Country: A Guide for Performers, by Kelly K. Garner, 2016

So You Want to Sing Gospel: A Guide for Performers, by Trineice Robinson-Martin, 2016

So You Want to Sing Sacred Music: A Guide for Performers, edited by Matthew Hoch, 2017

SO YOU WANT TO SING SACRED MUSIC

A Guide for Performers

Edited by
Matthew Hoch

Allen Henderson
Executive Editor, NATS

Matthew Hoch
Series Editor

A Project of the National Association of
Teachers of Singing

ROWMAN & LITTLEFIELD
Lanham • Boulder • New York • London

Published by Rowman & Littlefield
A wholly owned subsidiary of The Rowman & Littlefield Publishing Group, Inc.
4501 Forbes Boulevard, Suite 200, Lanham, Maryland 20706
www.rowman.com

Unit A, Whitacre Mews, 26-34 Stannary Street, London SE11 4AB

Copyright © 2017 by Rowman & Littlefield

All rights reserved. No part of this book may be reproduced in any form or by any electronic or mechanical means, including information storage and retrieval systems, without written permission from the publisher, except by a reviewer who may quote passages in a review.

British Library Cataloguing in Publication Information Available

Library of Congress Cataloging-in-Publication Data

Names: Hoch, Matthew, 1975–
Title: So you want to sing sacred music : a guide for performers / edited by Matthew Hoch.
Description: Lanham : Rowman & Littlefield, [2017] | "A project of the National Association of Teachers of Singing." | Includes bibliographical references and index.
Identifiers: LCCN 2016039953 (print) | LCCN 2016040563 (ebook) | ISBN 9781442256996 (pbk. : alk. paper) | ISBN 9781442257009 (electronic)
Subjects: LCSH: Singing—Instruction and study. | Sacred music—Instruction and study.
Classification: LCC MT820.S699 2017 (print) | LCC MT820 (ebook) | DDC 782.2/2143—dc23
LC record available at https://lccn.loc.gov/2016039953

∞™ The paper used in this publication meets the minimum requirements of American National Standard for Information Sciences—Permanence of Paper for Printed Library Materials, ANSI/NISO Z39.48-1992.

Printed in the United States of America

CONTENTS

Foreword *Allen Henderson*	xi
Acknowledgments	xiii
Introduction: Singing Sacred Music *Matthew Hoch*	xv
Online Supplement Note	xix

1 Jewish Traditions   *Evan Kent* 1
   Liturgical Origins 2
      Music in the Bible 2
      Beyond Biblical Times 3
      The Modern Cantor 4
   Musical Characteristics 5
      What Is Cantorial Music? 5
      Three Categories of Music 5
      Three Major Ethnic Groups 6
   Training Requirements 7
      The Basics of Cantorial Education 7
      Admissions: General Information 7
      Some First Steps 8

Seminaries Offering Cantorial Education	9
General Course of Study for Cantorial Education	9
Training Programs for Cantors: The Six Seminaries	10
Non-Cantorial Opportunities to Sing Jewish Music	16
Repertoire and Resources	17
Online Sound Archives	17
Jewish Music Publishers	18
Basic Repertoire Suggestions	19
Final Thoughts	20

2 Gregorian Chant and Polyphony   *Anthony Ruff*   23

Liturgical Origins	24
Textbox: Key Dates in the Development of the Liturgy and Its Chant	25
Textbox: The Liturgical Calendar	26
Textbox: Some Basic Liturgy Terms	29
Textbox: Names of the Offices	32
Table: Structure of the Mass	34
Musical Characteristics	40
Modality	41
Treatment of Text	45
Training Requirements	46
Vocal Technique	47
Interpretation	47
Pronunciation	48
Translation	48
Tempo, Note Lengthening, and Breathing	49
Men and Women Singing Together	50
Conducting	50
Repertoire and Resources	51
Introductory and Scholarly Books about Gregorian Chant	52
Final Thoughts	52

3 Contemporary Catholic Directions   *Anthony Ruff*   55

Liturgical Origins	55
From Trent to Vatican II	55
The Catholic Reformation and the Birth of the Baroque	56
Two Streams of Catholic Sacred Choral Music	57
A Catholic Ethos of Sacred Music?	59

Musical Characteristics and Repertoire	61
Navigating the Choral Repertoire	61
Musical Performance within the Liturgy	61
The Mass	62
The Requiem	63
Liturgy of the Hours (Office)	64
Sacred Choral Music alongside the Liturgy	65
High Mass, Low Mass, and Vernacular Hymnody	66
Sacred Music in Concert	67
The Second Vatican Council (1962–1965)	69
The Liturgy Constitution: *Sacrosanctum Concilium*	72
Chapter VI of the Liturgy Constitution	74
The Liturgy of the Second Vatican Council	75
Sing to the Lord: Basic Orientation	77
Sacred Music, Liturgical Music, or Pastoral Music?	77
Congregation versus Choir?	78
Schools of Thought in Catholic Liturgical Music	80
A Step into the Past: *Summorum Pontificum* and the "Extraordinary Form"	83
Performance Skills for Music in the Liturgy	84
Structures and Organizations	86
Repertoire and Resources	87
Official Church Documents and Studies of Them	87
History and Theory of Worship Music	88
Practical Guides	88
Final Thoughts	89
4 Sacred Choral Traditions *Matthew Hoch*	91
Liturgical Origins, Musical Characteristics, and Repertoire	92
Historical Overview	92
Protestant Choral Genres	94
Liturgical Considerations	96
The Organ	96
Training Requirements and Choral Technique	98
Training to Be a Professional Chorister	98
Technical and Stylistic Differences between Choral and Solo Singing	100
Some Thoughts on Vibrato	103
Sight Reading and Musicianship	105

	Diction and Language	106
	Coping with Vocal Fatigue	107
	Church Jobs: Securing Work as a Professional Chorister	107
	Auditioning	107
	Practical Skills: It's Not Just about How Well You Sing!	109
	Diversify Your Skill Set	111
	Do I Have to Be Religious?	112
	Summer Work: Where to Sing (and Make Money) When Choirs Aren't in Session	113
	Additional Resources	114
	Listening to Church Music	114
	Where to Experience Sacred Choral Music	115
	Professional Organizations	115
	Further Reading	116
	Final Thoughts	116
5	Contemporary Christian Music *Sharon L. Radionoff*	119
	Liturgical Origins	122
	Historical Context	122
	Group 1: 1940–1960	123
	Textbox: Ralph Carmichael	124
	Group 2: 1961–1989	127
	Group 3: 1990–present	128
	Textbox: Bill Gaither	129
	Megachurches	131
	Table: American Megachurches	131
	Houseplant Churches	132
	Mainstream Rock	134
	Musical Characteristics	134
	Training Requirements	135
	Vocal Technique and Contemporary Christian Music	136
	Repertoire and Resources	139
	Final Thoughts	142
6	Singing and Voice Science *Scott McCoy*	145
	Pulmonary System: The Power Source of Your Voice	146
	Larynx: The Vibrator of Your Voice	151
	Vocal Tract: Your Source of Resonance	156

CONTENTS

	Mouth, Lips, and Tongue: Your Articulators	160
	Final Thoughts	162
7	Vocal Health and the Singer of Sacred Music *Wendy LeBorgne*	163
	General Physical Well-Being	163
	Considerations for Whole Body Wellness	164
	Nutrition	164
	Hydration	165
	Tea, Honey, and Gargle to Keep the Throat Healthy	168
	Medications and the Voice	169
	Reflux and the Voice	170
	Physical Exercise	171
	Mental Wellness	172
	Vocal Wellness: Injury Prevention	174
	Train Like an Athlete for Vocal Longevity	174
	Vocal Fitness Program	175
	Speak Well, Sing Well	176
	Avoid Environmental Irritants: Alcohol, Smoking, Drugs	178
	Smart Practice Strategies for Skill Development and Voice Conservation	178
	Practice Your Mental Focus	179
	Specific Vocal Wellness Concerns for the Sacred Music Vocalist	180
	Vocal Wellness Tips for Traditional Worship	180
	Contemporary Christian Singers	181
	Final Thoughts	182
8	Using Audio Enhancement Technology *Matthew Edwards*	185
	The Fundamentals of Sound	186
	Frequency	186
	Amplitude	186
	Harmonics	187
	Resonance	187
	Signal Chain	188
	Microphones	189
	Equalization (EQ)	196
	Compression	199
	Reverb	201

    Delay   202
    Auto-Tune   203
    Digital Voice Processors   204
  The Basics of Live Sound Systems   204
  Microphone Technique   206
  Final Thoughts   207

Glossary   209

Index   215

About the Editor and Contributors   229

FOREWORD

This is the first volume in the "So You Want to Sing" series that is an edited volume featuring contributions from several content authors. Due to the breadth of traditions represented, it is a perfect opportunity to assemble knowledgeable authorities on these various traditions and provide expert perspective as you the reader seek to broaden your knowledge of various traditions of sacred music. Series editor Matthew Hoch has edited this volume as well as authored some of the content. It is often the case that singers of no faith at all or who have a background in a certain faith tradition join a choir or are paid to sing in a choir of another faith tradition. While this volume does not cover the music of all faith traditions, it should help you navigate some of the major faith traditions of today. This volume is also filled with practical advice for the aspiring singer on negotiating the day-to-day activities and responsibilities of a professional, semiprofessional, or amateur singer in the sacred space.

In addition, we continue the tradition of including several chapters found in other volumes in the series on voice science, vocal health, and audio enhancement. These are provided so that there is consistency on these universal topics of concern to all who seek to sing authentically in a variety of styles. The collected volumes of the "So You Want to Sing" series provide valuable resources for the amateur as well as professional singer or teacher who wants to broaden the skills set necessary to sing or teach in our diverse industry.

Allen Henderson
Executive Editor, NATS

ACKNOWLEDGMENTS

The authors are indebted to Rowman & Littlefield and NATS for their sponsorship and support of this project. Special thanks to Natalie Mandziuk, associate editor at Rowman & Littlefield, and Allen Henderson, executive director of NATS, for their leadership throughout the process. Matthew Hoch is grateful to all of the contributing authors for their expertise, excellent work, efficient correspondence, and patience throughout the lengthy writing and publication timeline. Evan Kent would like to thank his students at Hebrew Union College and all the future cantors who will grace our synagogues with inspiring song and uplifting worship. Anthony Ruff expresses his gratitude to NATS and the staff of Rowman & Littlefield for the opportunity to be involved in this project. Sharon Radionoff wishes to thank Len Radionoff for his editorial assistance and Lee Poquette for his extensive historical guidance.

INTRODUCTION

Singing Sacred Music
Matthew Hoch

God made so many different kinds of people. Why would he allow only one way to serve him?

—Martin Buber (1878–1965)

In virtually all religions, music plays an integral role in worship. The earliest accounts of recorded history affirm that this has probably always been true. In the Bible, the Psalms of David describe lyres, harps, and cymbals all being used to accompany singing. It is safe to say that the human voice, the most primal of all instruments, has been used to glorify God for millennia. In addition, each religion has developed its own unique musical traditions, and—in recent centuries—denominational traditions have emerged as well, each with its own distinctive singing style and genres. The world of sacred vocal music has continued to diversify as time has marched onward.

Does one "perform" sacred music? On an obvious level, of course, but for many this term is too trivial to describe what is a sacred offering of great spiritual significance. Music is an outgrowth of the liturgy, and to sing a passage from the Torah, the Lord's Prayer, or an anthem at the right moment of the service heightens that moment in a way that speaking cannot. For many, music completes the worship experience and is an integral part of the spiritual journey. The chapters in this book tell the story of sacred singing from this perspective, placing the repertoire within its specific religious and liturgical context, without which it cannot exist.

Early blueprints of this book were ambitious, looking to cover the wide variety of sacred singing styles that exist across the globe, including Muslim, Buddhist, Hindu, and other world music traditions. This would have made for fascinating reading, and these are certainly important topics that deserve to be covered. Ultimately, however, the scope was narrowed to focus on the Judeo-Christian traditions in which American and Canadian singers are most likely to find singing opportunities and employment. Even with this more focused approach, it was difficult to cover these diverse topics within the confines of single chapters. For this reason, each chapter points the way to further resources so that the singer can further explore these respective traditions and repertoires.

So You Want to Sing Sacred Music is the first book of the "So You Want to Sing" series that is an edited work by multiple authors. It would have been impractical (and perhaps impossible) for a single author to address the wide breadth of styles covered in these pages. Each of the distinguished scholars engaged for this project brings decades of practical experience as well as scholarly expertise to his or her respective topic. The book is roughly organized along a historical timeline, beginning with Jewish traditions before proceeding chronologically through Christian ones. Like other books in the series, supplemental chapters on voice science and vocal health by Scott McCoy and Wendy LeBorgne reappear in this volume. This book also includes Matthew Edwards's chapter on audio enhancement technology, important information for the performer of contemporary sacred styles.

Perhaps most important, each chapter goes beyond historical context and repertoire by also addressing *how* to sing the style being discussed as well as how to pursue further training. This is perhaps the most valuable feature of this book. Many singers earn four-year degrees studying classical voice, but these curricula are not probably not enough to help the student become a successful Jewish cantor, professional choral singer, or contemporary worship leader. After fifteen years of college-level teaching, I have yet to encounter a voice program that allows Gre-

INTRODUCTION

gorian chant to be sung in the studio or on a voice jury. That's why this book is so important.

On a personal note, I feel the need to confess that this project was a complete labor of love for me. While my day job as a singing teacher is deeply fulfilling, singing in a sacred context has always been my sustaining joy and passion. I am delighted that there is now a resource available to help singers explore the rich world of sacred music and that I had the opportunity to be a part of its creation.

ONLINE SUPPLEMENT NOTE

So You Want to Sing Sacred Music features an online supplement courtesy of the National Association of Teachers of Singing. Visit the link below to discover additional exercises and examples, as well as links to recordings of the songs referenced in this book.

http://www.nats.org/So_You_Want_To_Sing_Book_Series.html

A musical note symbol ♪ in this book will mark every instance of corresponding online supplement material.

1

JEWISH TRADITIONS

Evan Kent

What does a Jewish cantor do? The job is rich and varied and extends beyond singing in the synagogue sanctuary. The following three vignettes illustrate the variety of the cantor's vocation.

> Vignette 1: It is the evening of Yom Kippur—the holiest evening in the Jewish year—and the synagogue sanctuary is filled to capacity. Cantor Michael Bernstein, a newly ordained cantor who has just completed his seminary education, begins chanting the Kol Nidre prayer—one of the oldest and most revered prayers in the entire Jewish liturgy. On this most solemn night of the calendar, Michael shares with the congregation liturgy and melody that are part of Judaism's sacred tradition and are hundreds of years old.

> Vignette 2: On Friday morning, when Cantor Karen Newman walks into the preschool classroom, with her guitar slung over her back, the children all look up from their art project and immediately call out her name, "Cantor Karen! Cantor Karen!" The children all form a big circle, and she leads them in the Shabbat blessings over the candles, grape juice, and challah (the special twisted egg-bread specially baked for Shabbat).

Vignette 3: Late Wednesday evening, Cantor Scott Shapiro sits in Beverly Hirsch's hospital room. Beverly is blessed to have her four children, grandchildren, and even great-grandchildren surrounding her. Beverly has struggled with cancer for almost two years, and she has been through many courses of treatment. She and her family know that her death is imminent. Cantor Scott—along with Beverly's doctors—is at the hospital to provide the family with comfort and solace as Beverly approaches death. The cantor sings verses from the psalms; aids Beverly in reciting the words of one of Judaism's most central prayers, Shema Yisrael; and is with the family as Beverly takes her last breath.

These three brief illustrations demonstrate the variety and complexity of the vocation of the modern synagogue cantor—or *hazzan* as the role is known in Hebrew and in certain communities. In order to fully understand the role of the cantor and how this role developed through Jewish communal life, it is important to have some understanding of the development of Jewish musical life from biblical times until the present and how the role of the cantorate developed and rose to prominence.

The next part of this chapter will take a look at the variety of Jewish music and the various cultural streams. Following this, I will examine the requirements for entry into cantorial school and what you can do to prepare yourself for admission. After that, I will present the current programs and highlights of their curriculums. This chapter concludes with recommendations for online resources, where you can purchase music, and the basics of a cantorial library.

LITURGICAL ORIGINS

Music in the Bible

The Bible is filled with many instances of music making. For example, Moses and the Israelites sing as they cross the Red Sea at the moment of the Exodus (Exodus 15:1–18). The Book of Psalms also provides insight into the musical life of the Israelites. Some psalms indicate stage directions or perhaps provide instruction on how the psalm was to be sung.

JEWISH TRADITIONS

Others, like Psalm 150, give us insight into what the music in the ancient temple might have sounded like. The psalm says:

> *Hallelujah.*
> *Praise God in his sanctuary; praise Him in the sky, his stronghold.*
> *Praise Him for His mighty acts; praise Him for His exceeding greatness.*
> *Praise Him with blasts of the horn; praise Him with harp and lyre.*
> *Praise Him with timbrel and dance; praise Him with lute and pipe.*
> *Praise Him with resounding cymbals; praise Him with loud-clashing cymbals.*
> *Let all that breathes praise the LORD.*
> *Hallelujah.*[1]

The Book of Chronicles describes the splendor of the Temple in Jerusalem in great detail. For example, in I Chronicles 15:16–28, we are told that the orchestra in the Temple in Jerusalem was composed of 288 instrumentalists, and rich description is provided, telling us of the instruments that were played and that hundreds of vocalists forming tremendous choirs were also employed as functionaries to enhance the services of the time that featured the ritual sacrifice of animals as a form of worship. Since ancient times, music has played a great role in Jewish ritual and liturgy.

Beyond Biblical Times

With the destruction of the Temple in 70 CE, and as the Jews of Israel dispersed, the entire sacrificial structure came to an end, and in place of the Temple in Jerusalem, the localized synagogue developed. The cultic worship of the Temple was replaced by personal prayers, and it was determined that prayer was most effective "if it was communal, rather than private, and sung rather than spoken."[2] By around the year 600 CE, the function of the *hazzan* began to solidify. As many people could not read or understand Hebrew, the need for someone who could read Hebrew and interpret the prayers in a manner that would convey meaning, as well as understand an increasingly complex liturgy, developed. This man—and only men functioned as cantors until the late twentieth century—was essentially a liturgical messenger of the congregation (in Hebrew a *shaliach tzibur*). The cantor led the prayers, and the congregation only had to offer the appropriate responses. In his book *A Voice Still Heard*, musicologist Eric Werner described the early relationship between cantor and congregation:

> The individual worshipper needed only listen carefully and attentively to the precentor and by saying the prescribed responses, and especially the "Amen" at the end of each benediction, he fulfilled all his obligations. This is easily understood when one realizes that the writing down of prayers was not permitted until the eighth century.[3]

As the role of the cantor developed, the requirements for any man wishing to serve in this capacity in a synagogue were codified. A compendium of Jewish law written in the sixteenth century called the *Shulchan Aruch* provided guidelines for who may become a cantor. This book of laws determined that a cantor should be pure in spirit and without sin, be modest in his behavior, have a pleasant voice, and be the most pious and learned in the congregation. The *Shulchan Aruch* further specified that the cantor should sing sweetly and beautifully:

> The one dedicated to lead the congregation in prayer must be a worthy person. He should be one who has a good reputation and is not known as a transgressor, even as a youth. He should be modest and agreeable to the congregation. His voice should be pleasant, melodious, and appealing. He should of course be conversant with the payers and the order of the service. (*Shulchan Aruch*, Orech Chayim 53:4–14)[4]

The Modern Cantor

In his 1955 essay entitled "The Vocation of the Cantor," rabbi and philosopher Abraham Joshua Heschel acknowledged that the role of the cantor goes beyond the requirements set forth in the 1500s. According to Heschel, the cantor's role is to bring a group of individuals together so that they form a praying, liturgical community. He acknowledged, however, that this is often difficult:

> The call to prayer often falls against an iron wall. The congregation is not always open and ready to worship. The cantor has to pierce the armor of indifference. He has to fight for a response. He has to conquer them in order to speak for them. Often he must first be one who awakens those who slumber, before he can claim to be a *sheliah tsibbur*.[5]

Ultimately, the role of the cantor, according to Heschel, is to stand before God, with deep humility, as a messenger of the congregation. He wrote:

> He will learn to realize that his task is not to entertain but to represent the people Israel. He will be carried away into moments in which he will forget the world, ignore the congregation, and be overcome by the awareness of him in whose presence he stands. The congregation then will hear and sense that the cantor is not giving a recital but worshiping God, that to pray does not mean to listen to a singer but to identify oneself with what is being proclaimed in their name.[6]

For the cantor in the twenty-first century, Heschel's vision of the cantorate remains true. At the center of the vocation of being a cantor is the desire to serve the Jewish community by connecting with the holy through sacred text and music. But as was illustrated above, the cantor's vocation extends beyond singing in the synagogue. Today's cantor is a full member of the clergy team in the synagogue and not only is expected to participate in liturgy and worship but should be prepared to share in educational programs, cultural ventures, hospital visitation, and pastoral counseling.

MUSICAL CHARACTERISTICS

What Is Cantorial Music?

By definition, cantorial music is a specific genre of Jewish music that is reserved for the synagogue. In the contemporary synagogue, music that is sung by cantors encompasses a wide variety of styles and traditions. In order to better understand the music that cantors sing, a brief outline of the many types of Jewish music is helpful.

Three Categories of Music

Jewish music can be grouped into three general categories: *devotional music*, *celebration music*, and *music for entertainment*. Devotional music includes music reserved for communal prayer and ritual. In Judaism, this would include music used in the synagogue to celebrate the Sabbath, festivals, and other holidays. This music also encompasses music reserved for rituals and rites outside of the synagogue. These might include music for rituals at home, like the Passover Seder or wedding ceremonies or funerals. Jewish music can also be employed for celebration. This could include *bar* and *bat mitzvah* parties, weddings, social events, and anniversaries. Finally, Jewish music can also be used for entertainment. This music ranges from music reserved for symphonic or choral performances ("art" music) on Jewish subjects, themes, ideas, or stories to Jewish-themed opera or musical theater or even music used for folk dancing. These categories are very general and of course there is much overlap between them.

Three Major Ethnic Groups

Jewish music also comes from a variety of geographic and ethnic sources. Three major ethnic groups can be identified: *Ashkenazic, Ladino,* and *Mizrahi.* This section will give a general overview of these three ethnic groups and their influence upon Jewish music.

Jewish music that originated in Eastern Europe is referred to as music having Ashkenazic roots or origins. This music style eventually spread to Western Europe and traveled to North America with the waves of Jewish immigration that took place at the end of the nineteenth century and the beginning of the twentieth century. Much of klezmer music and music sung in Yiddish can find its roots in the communities of Eastern Europe, Western Europe, and the Balkans. Yiddish is a form of German that combined German and Hebrew. The language is written with Hebrew alphabet characters.

In 1492, when the expulsion of Jews from Spain took place, many of the members from these Jewish communities took their musical traditions with them to newfound homes in North Africa, Turkey, Greece, Egypt, and other locations around northern Africa and the Mediterranean. Jews from these countries often spoke and sang in a language known as Ladino, which is a form of Spanish that over time integrated many Hebrew words. Like Yiddish, Ladino is also written using the Hebrew alphabet.

The third stream of Jewish culture is referred to as Mizrahi (or "Eastern"). This stream of Jewish practice, culture, and music refers to Jews from Turkey, Asia, Persia, and the Arabian Peninsula. This encompasses the countries of Israel, Jordan, Iran, Iraq, Yemen, and Egypt. Mizrahi music often utilizes rhythms, melodies, modes, and melodic progressions that reflect these regions. Just as Jews from Europe spoke Yiddish, Jews from these countries often spoke a version of Hebrew-Arabic.

When many people think of cantorial music, they often think of a style of music that is based in the Eastern European tradition that is called *chazzanut*. This is music that employs sacred text and the traditional Ashkenazic Jewish prayer modes or melodies and is often florid, melismatic, and virtuosic in style. This music was popularized in the late nineteenth century and early twentieth century by cantorial luminaries who had come to the United States and promoted this genre of music. But in today's synagogue—especially in Reform or Conservative synagogues—a variety of types of music and styles is utilized.

TRAINING REQUIREMENTS

The Basics of Cantorial Education

The decision to become a cantor is not one that should be taken lightly nor made hastily. Becoming a cantor implies a life of dedication to the Jewish community and being a continual proponent of Jewish music. The education for cantors—like all clergy—is a long process, and cantorial education at any of the leading seminaries in the United States is filled with many rigorous academic, religious, and musical requirements. In addition to the requisite coursework, seminaries also provide ample opportunity for exploring issues of personal growth and spiritual development through student congregations, internships, mentor programs, and performance opportunities.

Admissions: General Information

There is no one definitive path to the cantorate. Cantors serving congregations come from an enormous variety of academic fields, professions, and backgrounds. Many cantors do have undergraduate degrees in music, but many also have degrees in Jewish studies, religious studies, literature, education, and even business and engineering. All cantorial applicants do share one thing in common: the desire to serve the Jewish religious community and glorify the presence of God in our lives through the medium of song.

There was a time when the sacred profession of the *hazzan* or cantor was limited to men. This is no longer the case. In 1975, Barbara Ostfeld became the first female graduate of the Hebrew Union College–Jewish Institute of Religion. Since that date, many women have become cantors and all Jewish seminaries (with the exception of Yeshiva University) admit women to their cantorial programs.

Students of all ages are also accepted for cantorial training. Although many students in cantorial programs are recent college graduates, the cantorate is a profession that welcomes those who are seeking a second (or even third) career. The life experience a more mature candidate offers is often seen as very complementary to being a cantor. Many cantorial programs also accept gay and lesbian applicants into their programs.

Some First Steps

If you are thinking of becoming a cantor, there are some preliminary steps you should undertake to begin the process. It is always beneficial to find a mentor cantor in the community. This might be your cantor from the synagogue in which you grew up. If you are away at college, ask your hometown cantor to refer you to one of his or her colleagues. You could even contact the local synagogue and speak to the cantor there. If you are at college, having an honest discussion with the director of the campus Hillel is also advisable. Cantors working in your community will certainly welcome you and share their experiences with you and are often quite pleased that you have reached out to them. It is also helpful to spend a few days or even weeks "shadowing" a cantorial mentor. This might entail following the cantor around through a typical workday so you can gain an understanding of the depth, complexity, and variety of the profession. You should also contact one of the institutions that offer cantorial training to discuss the steps necessary for admission.

Most of the programs discussed here ask that you set up a preliminary interview with a representative from the seminary. If you live near the seminary, you might be able to visit with a member of the faculty or the administration. Often, if you live a great distance from the campus, the school will arrange for you to meet with a graduate of the program who is living in or near your community. This meeting is designed for you to obtain more information about the cantorate as a career, to find out more about the specific graduate program, and to help you determine if a career as a cantor is appropriate.

After this preliminary meeting, you will begin the written application process. The questions on the application vary from institution to institution, but in general they will serve to assess your previous experience in the Jewish community, your understanding of the profession, your prior Jewish musical experience, and your previous musical involvement in a Jewish setting. Often, the questions on the application will consider your personal religious philosophy. You will be asked for transcripts from the institutions and programs you have previously attended. For cantorial programs that are graduate programs, you will probably be asked to take the GRE or another graduate admittance exam.

In addition to the written application, there will be a series of tests and exams that will serve to evaluate your knowledge of Judaica, Hebrew, and basic Jewish concepts. There will also be an audition to assess your vocal abilities. Some of the programs discussed here also request that potential candidates take part in a psychological evaluation that may include a variety of evaluative tests as well as an interview.

SEMINARIES OFFERING CANTORIAL EDUCATION

General Course of Study for Cantorial Education

All cantorial programs require their students to take classes in Hebrew language, Bible, historic and modern Jewish and Rabbinic texts, as well as multiple courses in Jewish liturgy. Cantorial students are also required to study biblical, ancient, and modern Jewish history as well as Jewish music history. Most cantorial programs also require their graduates to be proficient in Western music theory, harmony, conducting, piano (and often guitar), and arranging. Cantorial students also study Jewish music theory. This subject area encompasses an understanding of the Jewish musical modal system, the harmonization of these modes, and how these modes are utilized in traditional Jewish prayer services during weekday worship, celebration of the Sabbath, festivals, and high holidays. The training for cantors also includes the study of the cantillation (chanting) of the Torah, the prophetic books, and other texts (*megillot*) that are read on the holidays of Sukkot, Purim, Passover, Shavuot, and Tisha B'Av.

Many of the programs feature a required yearly "practicum"—a program that is similar to a recital but features the presentation of a selection from one of the prayer services or a life-cycle event. Master's-level programs also require students to complete a thesis and, in some cases, present a final recital.

Although the programs are somewhat similar in their approach to the education of cantors, each program does organize its courses and materials differently and many have distinct features (such as Hebrew Union College's well-established year in Israel program or Boston Hebrew College's three-year accelerated program). The following is a summary of core courses, curriculum strategy, and particular attributes of each program.

Training Programs for Cantors: The Six Seminaries

Training to be a cantor is a highly specialized endeavor. Currently, there are only six American institutions offering cantorial education. They are the following:

Hebrew Union College–Jewish Institute of Religion (HUC-JIR)
Debbie Friedman School of Sacred Music
New York, New York

Academy for Jewish Religion (AJR)
Yonkers, New York

Academy for Jewish Religion California (AJRCA)
Los Angeles, California

Jewish Theological Seminary (JTS)
H. L. Miller Cantorial School
New York, New York

Hebrew College
School of Jewish Music
Newton Centre, Massachusetts

Yeshiva University
Belz School of Jewish Music
New York, New York

The curricula offered by these institutions share some common characteristics as well as some unique features. After an initial discussion of the general course of study for cantorial training, an overview of each individual program will be discussed. Website links to these institutions are available on the book companion page on the NATS website.

Hebrew Union College–Jewish Institute of Religion The Debbie Friedman School of Music, located on the New York campus of the Hebrew Union College–Jewish Institute of Religion (HUC-JIR), is the oldest and largest cantorial program in the United States. The school is sponsored by the Reform movement of Judaism, and a very high percentage of the school's graduates serve Reform Jewish congregations throughout North America.

The program at HUC-JIR is a five-year course of study with the first year of coursework taking place on the Jerusalem, Israel, campus of the college and the next four years of classes in New York. In Jerusalem, students spend the year in intensive classes in modern Hebrew, biblical Hebrew, and grammar, learning the basics of the Jewish modal music system and the appropriate chanting of the Torah, prophetic readings, and the other scrolls chanted on the various festivals. Students also spend time exploring Israel through field trips, weekly excursions, and lectures that examine the diversity of Israeli society. Cantorial students also study Jewish liturgy and ancient history with their rabbinic counterparts.

When students return to the United States, the next four years are devoted to four core areas of study: liturgical music, general music, Judaica, and professional development. Upon graduation, students receive a master's degree in sacred music and cantorial ordination and become members of the American Conference of Cantors.

The study of liturgical music encompasses the largest section of the curriculum. Traditional music for Shabbat, the Jewish festivals, and the high holidays are learned alongside contemporary music in a fully integrated curriculum in which liturgy and associated music are fully explored. In these classes, appropriate prayer modes (*nusach*) are learned and students gain appreciation for traditional musical elements as well as more contemporary prayer settings. Hebrew Union College also trains its students to be top-notch musicians. Throughout the course of study, general musicianship is stressed with courses in sight-singing, piano, guitar, harmony, conducting, arranging, and composition. Each year students present a "practicum"—essentially a mini-recital—in which they explore a portion of one of the services in depth and present it to the entire student body. In the fifth year, each student completes a master's thesis on an aspect of Jewish music and presents a recital based on the same material. Cantorial students also study the Bible, rabbinic texts, Jewish philosophy, and biblical and modern Jewish history. The goal is to be conversant in and knowledgeable of a wide variety of historic and contemporary texts and literature.

As part of a curriculum in professional development, cantorial students are assigned to part-time pulpits throughout their years at Hebrew Union College. All students receive mentoring and critical assessment as part of this process. Students all take classes in interpersonal communications, family systems psychology, and clergy counseling, and many students also choose to study hospital chaplaincy. HUC-JIR also emphasizes community, and students are required to attend weekly prayer services, participate in a campus-wide choir, and participate in student body retreats. The faculty also considers vocal growth to be a significant part of the cantorial student's education. To this end, continued private vocal study is also required for all students at HUC-JIR. ♪

Academy for Jewish Religion (New York) The Academy for Jewish Religion (New York) was founded in 1956 and presents potential cantorial students with a pluralistic approach to the training to enter the cantorate. AJR New York's students and faculty cross denominational lines and represent the wide spectrum of the Jewish community. The AJR cantorial curriculum also is designed to provide an education that will assist cantors who not only are musical leaders and experts in the sanctuary but are leaders of their community.

The cantorial program at AJR New York takes five years of full-time study to complete, and the AJR weekly schedule is organized with classes taking place only on Mondays through Wednesdays. Students in this program are required to take voice lessons and cantorial coaching each week. As well, each student must present a cantorial "practicum" every year. In this program, the student presents a section from one of the services for the student body and faculty.

Similar to other cantorial programs, the study of traditional *nusach* and *chazzanut* is stressed in the AJR New York curriculum. Through the study of *nusach*, cantorial students are exposed to the traditional melodies used in synagogue for Shabbat, high holidays, festivals, and weekday prayer services. A feature of the AJR New York curriculum is that all *nusach* classes meet twice weekly: the first session is a lecture and the second session a lab or coaching session. Contemporary synagogue music is explored through a four-class sequence that surveys music for Shabbat (morning and evening) and the high holidays. Students also learn the appropriate chanting for Torah, Haftarah (prophetic books), and the festival scrolls. Additionally, cantorial students are expected to be proficient in Hebrew, liturgy, and basic rabbinic texts.

As part of a sequence of classes in professional development, students are exposed to educational theory and concepts, counseling techniques, techniques for congregational singing, and musicianship skills. ♪

Academy for Jewish Religion California The Academy for Jewish Religion in California (not affiliated with the Academy for Jewish Religion in New York) prides itself on being a transdenominational and pluralistic institution that trains rabbis and cantors for the ever-evolving needs of the twenty-first-century Jewish community. The curriculum emphasizes the cantor's historical links to the past and strives to make sure that cantors are well prepared for the future. The program at AJR California can be completed in five years of full-time study, with a part-time option available. AJR recommends (but does not require) study in Israel, and many AJR students indeed spend summers studying there. Prior to graduation, AJR cantorial students must complete a master's thesis and present a public recital.

The study of *chazzanut* (cantorial music) constitutes the largest area of study at AJR. Students learn *nusach* for weekday services, Shabbat, the festivals, and the high holidays. Students also learn music for life-cycle ceremonies and cantillation of Torah, prophetic books, and the other scrolls. Before graduation, students also must demonstrate competency in music theory, conducting, song leading, and guitar.

All students must complete up to twenty-four units of Hebrew language instruction. Where students begin in this sequence is determined by their placement exam. Upon graduation from AJR, students are expected to be able to translate biblical texts as well as understand and translate appropriate liturgical texts and applicable rabbinic texts. In addition to the study of Hebrew language, cantorial students are required to take a wide range of courses that include an introductory to the Bible and biblical literature, liturgy, rabbinic literature, Jewish history, and courses in Chassidic text and mysticism.

As part of the sequence in professional development, students at AJR take courses in professional ethics, clinical pastoral education, counseling, and fundamentals of Jewish education. Students also receive extensive supervision in the student pulpits and internships.

Cantorial candidates are required to take electives to complete the 150 credits necessary for graduation. The AJR faculty administration strongly recommends that students take electives in Jewish Bible or rabbinic literature, Jewish education, or interreligious studies. ♪

Jewish Theological Seminary, H. L. Miller Cantorial School The Jewish Theological Seminary (JTS) was established in the late nineteenth century and has been responsible for the training of generations of rabbis and cantors for the Conservative movement of Judaism. Students enrolled in the JTS cantorial program can be expected to complete the program in three to five years of full-time study. The school's focus is on the evolving role of the *hazzan* in the contemporary American synagogue, and upon completion of the program, students receive cantorial investiture and a master's degree in sacred music and are inducted into the Cantor's Assembly, the professional organization for cantors serving Conservative movement synagogues.

The curriculum at H. L. Miller consists of four core areas: Hebrew language studies, Jewish and general music, Jewish studies, and professional skills. The JTS curriculum requires that cantorial students spend at least one semester studying in Israel.

As in the other programs, the cantorial curriculum emphasizes the study of *hazzanut* and *nusach*. This sequence of study is four yearlong classes. A notable feature of these classes is that they are team taught and consist of an integrated approach that includes Jewish musical theory, classroom practice, and individual coaching. General music classes in ear training, Western music theory, choral conducting, and piano are also mandated, and each year students present a practicum in a synagogue-like atmosphere. The cantorial students at JTS are also required to study the Bible, the Talmud, and the history and philosophy of Conservative Judaism.

JTS requests that students continue their private vocal training throughout their studies in the seminary. Students are also required to attend weekly religious services and adhere to a religiously mandated code of conduct. Additionally, as part of the professional skills sequence, students are expected to participate in a range of summer activities including attendance at the North American Jewish Choral Festival and a summer unit of pastoral education (chaplaincy) and work at a Jewish summer camp. In their fifth year of study, students enroll in two seminars: a semester-long course with the director of the cantorial school and a yearlong seminar with rabbinic students also in their final year of study. ♪

Hebrew College, School of Jewish Music   Hebrew College's School of Jewish Music trains cantors through a deep education of liturgy, text studies, and a blend of creativity that respects the hallowed cantorial tradition. One of the distinguishing features of Hebrew College's program leading to cantorial ordination is that it is a three-year program (as compared to five-year programs at other institutions). The program is a full-year intensive program that requires students to also be in residence during two summer sessions. Hebrew College is a pluralistic and multidenominational school.

Upon completion of the Hebrew College program, students receive a master's degree in Jewish education and ordination and are eligible for membership in either the American Conference of Cantors or the Cantor's Assembly. Hebrew College also provides extensive mentoring, guidance, and supervision for students in their first placement post-ordination.

The Hebrew College curriculum varies from other schools in that the three-year curriculum includes very intensive summer sessions during which much of the *nusach* learning and other musical education takes place. During the academic years, students take courses in cantillation, educational methods, intensive Hebrew language, basic *nusach*, Jewish music history, rabbinic texts, and pastoral counseling. During the summer sessions, students take classes that aid them in building a foundation as prayer leaders. These classes include in-depth *nusach* study, choral conducting, composition, arranging, and continued studies in liturgy. ♪

Yeshiva University, Belz School of Music   The Belz School of Music is a division of Yeshiva University's Rabbi Elchanah Theological Seminary. It was established in 1954 and is devoted to preparing *hazzanim* (cantors), music educators, and lay prayer leaders for the community of Orthodox synagogues. Yeshiva offers the only undergraduate cantorial program in the United States. As an Orthodox institution, admission to the Belz School is limited only to men. Participants in the program may receive a cantorial diploma or an associate cantorial certificate.

The school provides opportunities for students to become professional cantors, *ba'alei tefillah* (prayer leaders), and music teachers. The course of study includes *nusach ha-tefillah*, cantillation of sacred books and scrolls, piano instruction, general music theory and Jewish modal music theory, history of Jewish music, liturgy, Hebrew calligraphy, and Sephardic music. ♪

NON-CANTORIAL OPPORTUNITIES TO SING JEWISH MUSIC

You do not need to be a cantor to explore the vast variety and depth of Jewish music. There are many programs and events in which you can take part. If you are interested in singing Jewish choral music, you should contact the local synagogue and see if the synagogue has a volunteer choir that you could join. Even if you are not Jewish, many choirs will welcome your participation. Many synagogue choirs rehearse practically every week and sing through the year and even at special events in the community. Other synagogue choral organizations may just sing for the Jewish high holidays of Rosh Hashanah and Yom Kippur. There are many Jewish community choirs that you might consider joining. The largest gathering of Jewish choral singers is the North American Jewish Choral Festival (NAJCF). The five-day festival affords participants the opportunity to study with master conductors, hear new choral works, and socialize with others who truly enjoy the art of singing choral music.

The Union for Reform Judaism (URJ) also sponsors two worthwhile programs for those interested in pursuing their interest in present-day Jewish music. Hava NaShira (meaning "Come let us sing!") is a five-day intensive workshop held at the Oling-Sang-Ruby Union Institute (OSRUI) Camp in Wisconsin in which participants are taught by the leading creators and innovators in contemporary Jewish music. There is ample opportunity for group singing, learning from your peers, and experiencing the joy of Jewish song.

JEWISH TRADITIONS

The URJ, in conjunction with the American Conference of Cantors and the Guild of Temple Musicians (GTM), sponsors Mifgash Musicale (literally "musical meeting") during the summer on the Cincinnati campus of Hebrew Union College. This five-day program is designed for those who already have some experience with synagogue music and is geared to synagogue accompanists, choral directors, cantorial soloists, and music directors. Those attending the workshop will have ample opportunity to learn alongside some of the leading figures in the Reform movement.

REPERTOIRE AND RESOURCES

Online Sound Archives

The world of Jewish music in general—and cantorial music specifically—is vast. One of the best ways to acquaint yourself with this fascinating and extensive repertoire is to listen to as much as you can. The following online collections are quite large and should provide hours of listening and learning. Please see the book companion page on the NATS website for links to these resources.

Judaic Sound Archives This compendium of recorded music is a project of Florida Atlantic University (FAU) and is one of the most comprehensive online libraries of recorded Jewish and cantorial music. The cantorial section of the FAU sound archive allows listeners to hear the voices of cantorial legends from the turn of the twentieth century to today's most prominent cantors from around the world. ♪

The Milken Archive of Jewish Music Established in 1990, the Milken Archive of Jewish Music is devoted to preserving, disseminating, and capturing the music of the American Jewish experience. They have recorded the works of more than two hundred composers and through their recorded works have shared music previously unavailable with thousands. The online collection features recordings by notable cantors. Although only short samples are available online, all of the music is available for purchase. ♪

Hebrew University Jewish Music Centre Founded in 1964, the Hebrew University Jewish Music Research Center (JMRC) is dedicated to preserving and documenting music from Jewish communities around the globe. This tremendous online resource provides many scholarly articles but also provides biographies and sound clips of many cantorial luminaries. ♪

Jewish Music Publishers

There are many music publishers that have Jewish music as part of their collection. The publishers below only publish Jewish printed music, sound files, and cantorial educational materials.

Transcontinental Music Transcontinental Music Publications is the largest publisher of Jewish music in the world and is a division of the American Conference of Cantors, the organization of Reform cantors worldwide (www.accantors.org). Their catalog contains thousands of titles with musical selections ranging from solo cantorial works to Jewish-themed orchestral works. The TMP site also features downloadable sound files, as well as downloadable sheet music.

Tara Publications Tara Publications was founded in 1971 by Velvel Pasternack, a noted Jewish musicologist. The publisher's earliest collections were compilations of Hasidic songs. Since that time, Tara has become one of the largest resources of Jewish music. They are an especially good resource for Jewish music anthologies, fake books, Israeli music, and children's music. All of their printed publications are available as electronic books, and their very large collection of recordings are downloadable as MP3s.

OySongs OySongs is sort of like the Jewish version of iTunes, except that the company also sells sheet music from selected composers. OySongs was created in 2006 and has thousands titles in their digital sound catalogs. OySongs' system of organization by genre and subcategories makes finding music easy. OySongs also has a large selection of specialized digital songbooks organized by composer, Jewish holiday, and specific occasion.

Cantors Assembly   The Cantors Assembly (CA) is the professional organization affiliated with the Conservative movement of Judaism. The CA publishes the *Journal of Synagogue Music* (which is available online) as well as a large assortment of printed cantorial music available through the Assembly's online store. The CA music catalog includes printed music for Shabbat, festivals, and life-cycle events as well as collections dedicated to the opus of cantorial luminaries.

Basic Repertoire Suggestions

The universe of cantorial music is quite vast. There are some basic resources that every cantor (and cantorial student) should include in his or her library. This list presents a comprehensive overview of materials that are deemed valuable and are readily available.

- Joel N. Eglash, ed., *The Complete Shireinu: 350 Fully Notated Jewish Songs* (Schaunberg, IL: Transcontinental Music Publications, 2003). This volume is a wonderful addition to any cantorial student's library. It contains hundreds of songs used in school settings, Jewish summer camps, youth groups, and synagogue worship.
- Joel N. Eglash and Jonathan B. Hall, eds., *Shabbat Anthology*, six volumes (New York: Hal Leonard, 2003–2012). This very popular series presents the most contemporary music for congregational use. It features settings of prayers and blessings by both established and emerging composers and arrangers. Each volume contains approximately thirty selections, all notated for piano, guitar, and voice.
- Charles Davidson, ed., *Gates of Song–Shaarei Shirah* (Schaunberg, IL: Transcontinental Music Publications, 1987). This volume of music was designed as a supplement to *Gates of Prayer*, a Reform Jewish prayer book. Although the book was first published in 1987, it is quite useful and has great settings of many prayers used in contemporary synagogue worship.
- J. Mark Dunn, Joel N. Eglash, Alane S. Katzew, and Steve Richards, eds., *The Complete Jewish Songbook for Children*, two volumes (New York: Hal Leonard, 2002–2004). This wide-ranging and diverse collection of music appropriate for children for both worship and play is a good addition to any cantorial library. It presents music based on grade level, holiday, and purpose.

Moshe Nathanson, *Zamru Lo*, three volumes (Fairlawn, OH: Cantors Assembly, 1974). These massive volumes contain numerous settings of prayers and blessings designed for congregational worship. Volume 1 features music for Friday night and Saturday morning Shabbat services. Volume 2 has a complete assortment of music for the high holidays—both Rosh Hashanah and Yom Kippur. Volume 3 features music for the Jewish festivals of Sukkot, Passover, and Shavuot.

Marshall Portnoy and Josee Wolfe, eds., *The Art of Cantillation: A Step-by-Step Guide to Chanting Torah*, two volumes (Springfield, NJ: Behrman House Publishing, 2000–2002). One of the skills every cantor must have is the ability to chant Torah (the Five Books of Moses) and the Haftarah (the prophet readings). These two volumes give you clear, step-by-step instructions on how to learn this successfully. Each volume comes with an accompanying CD that corresponds to exercises in the book.

FINAL THOUGHTS

I served Temple Isaiah in Los Angeles as its cantor from the time of my ordination from Hebrew Union College in 1988 until 2013 when I migrated to Israel. It was an amazing and glorious time in my life. Through my work in the congregation, I met thousands upon thousands of people and made some of my closest friends. We celebrated together: the birth of children, weddings, and *bar* and *bat mitzvah*. We also consoled and cared for each other through illness, death, divorce, and separation. The adult volunteer choir I directed, HaSharim (the singers), was like a second family—we literally danced at each other's weddings and held each other closely in moments of misfortune and sadness. Children that I sang with in preschool classrooms are now married with children of their own. Some of those preschoolers are now students studying to become rabbis and cantors. The hours were long; the work at times was exhausting physically, emotionally, and spiritually. Each day was unique; no prayer service was ever the same, and each moment as a part of the clergy of the synagogue was a sincere gift. If you decide to pursue the cantorate as a career, you will be rewarded on a daily basis by a vocation that is continually changing and amazingly dynamic and allows you to explore the richness of the Jewish faith and cultural tradition.

I hope my words have helped to place you upon a path toward a life in Jewish music. If you have questions, please speak to the cantor in your local congregation or contact me. I'm happy to answer your inquiries. May your pathway to Jewish vocal music always be blessed by beauty of voice, an open heart, and an appreciation of a thousands-year-old tradition.

NOTES

1. Translation: Jewish Publication Society of America.
2. Mark Slobin, *Chosen Voices: The Story of the American Cantorate* (Urbana: University of Illinois Press, 2002), 4.
3. Eric Werner, *A Voice Still Heard: The Sacred Songs of the Ashkenazic Jews* (University Park: University of Pennsylvania Press, 1976), 10.
4. Rabbi Gershon Appel, *The Concise Code of Jewish Law: Compiled from Kitzur Shulchan Aruch and Traditional Sources* (New York: KTAV Publishing, 1977).
5. Abraham Joshua Heschel, *The Insecurity of Freedom: Essays on Human Existence* (New York: Farrar, Straus, and Giroux, 1963), 244.
6. Abraham Joshua Heschel, *Moral Grandeur and Spiritual Audacity: Essays* (New York: MacMillan, 1997), 122.

2

GREGORIAN CHANT AND POLYPHONY

Anthony Ruff

Gregorian chant is "in," and it has been for several decades now. Many monasteries have issued high-selling CD recordings of chant. Many other choirs, ranging from the highly professional to the more amateur, have also issued popular recordings. Small but increasing numbers of Catholic parishes are celebrating Mass in Latin with Gregorian chant or using more Latin chant in vernacular worship services. The Internet allows one to hear an enormously great variety of examples of Gregorian chant from around the world. Movies use excerpts of Gregorian chant for special effect.

All this would no doubt surprise Christians of the early centuries of the Church or the first Benedictine monks of the sixth century. These Christians and monks didn't know the term "Gregorian chant," for that label came only later. They didn't see Gregorian chant as a special kind of music in worship contrasting with music for organ or piano or music sung in harmony—Gregorian chant was the *only* music used in worship. They didn't see Gregorian chant as sacred and otherworldly because it is in an ancient, foreign language—Latin was the language they spoke in daily life. They had no reason to use terms such as "sacred music" or "chant," and it never occurred to them that there was a treasury of Latin chant repertoire to cherish and cultivate. They took for granted that texts in worship should be sung, not spoken, for they were a singing people who naturally sang the liturgy. (The idea of reciting the liturgy arose only much later in the course of the first millennium.) When Christians and monks first sang what we now call "Gregorian chant," they simply thought they were worshipping God by expressing sacred texts in song.

And it is there, in the worship of God, that one should start in order to understand what we now call Gregorian chant. For Gregorian chant was born in the liturgy. Or more precisely, Gregorian chant *was* the liturgy—the liturgy had its prayers and Bible readings, and these were prayed and proclaimed by being chanted.

LITURGICAL ORIGINS

What is liturgy? Literally, based on Greek roots, the word means "work of the people." (By the way, the earliest Christian liturgy in Rome was celebrated in Greek, the language of the first Christians there, and the language shifted to Latin in the third and fourth centuries because that was increasingly the language spoken by the people.) The liturgy is a whole mix of ceremonies and rituals and symbols and texts and songs, rather like a Broadway musical or an opera—though that comparison risks misunderstanding the purpose, for the liturgy is about spirituality and worship of God, not entertainment or cultural edification.

The structures of the liturgy grew up gradually. At first, the prayers were improvised by the leader, and letters and stories (which gradually became the New Testament) were sung by lectors (i.e., readers). Communities selected on their own which psalms to sing, and song leaders improvised verses to alternate with refrains sung by the whole community. It all must have been rather spirited and expressive and uninhibited, if a bit unorganized. But as is true of improvisation today (think of jazz singers or rock instrumentalists), there must have been patterns and formulas that soon developed for the singer to draw upon. And early on, in both liturgy and music, organization increasingly set in. Greater organization and expansion of ceremonial music was much more possible after the Peace of Constantine in 313, when the liturgy moved from being underground and the Christian religion was officially tolerated in the Roman Empire.

By about the sixth century, the structures of the liturgy had developed to a state rather similar to what one finds today in a Catholic or Lutheran

KEY DATES IN THE DEVELOPMENT OF THE LITURGY AND ITS CHANT

c. 30: death and resurrection of Jesus Christ
Early to mid-second century: writing of the last books of the New Testament
313: Peace of Constantine, the decree allowing the Christian church to worship publicly
fourth century: beginnings of the Middle Ages
c. 543: death of St. Benedict, author of the *Rule* for monasteries
590–604: reign of Pope Gregory the Great
mid-seventh century on: founding of choir schools across Europe
eighth century: evolution of Mass propers to the melodic form still used today
eighth century: earliest polyphony, known as organum
ninth century: beginnings of written notation for music
1054: formal split between the Western (Latin) and the Eastern church
fourteenth to fifteenth century: late Middle Ages and beginning of the Renaissance
1517: beginning of the Protestant Reformation with Martin Luther's call for renewal
1545–1563: Council of Trent, Catholic defensive response to the Protestant Reformation
early twentieth century: beginning of the liturgical movement calling for Catholic reforms
1962–1965: Second Vatican Council in Rome

or Episcopal parish. An annual calendar had developed with special feast days and seasons of Advent, Christmas, Lent, and Easter; there were set roles of priest, deacon, cantor (singer), lector (reader); and there was a general sequence to Sunday worship consisting of opening prayers and songs, scripture readings assigned to particular days, a rite of holy communion with its Eucharistic Prayer and sharing in the blessed bread and wine, and brief concluding prayers and dismissal. There was much local and regional variety, and structures and customs continued to grow and develop throughout the Middle Ages, but the basic elements which have remained to our day were in place by the early Middle Ages.

THE LITURGICAL CALENDAR

Paschal Cycle of Lent and Easter ("Paschal" means "Passover" and refers to the death and resurrection of Jesus Christ):

Season of Lent: from Ash Wednesday until the beginning of the Triduum; includes five Sundays of Lent and Palm (or Passion) Sunday, which begins Holy Week.
Paschal Triduum or Easter Triduum: Holy Thursday, Good Friday, and Holy Saturday/Easter Sunday. The Easter Vigil is in the night between Holy Saturday and Easter Sunday.
Season of Easter: fifty days from Easter Sunday until Pentecost Sunday, including Ascension Thursday on the fortieth day (sometimes transferred to the closest Sunday).

Incarnational Cycle of Advent and Christmas:

Season of Advent: Four Sundays before Christmas, including the ferial days starting with the First Sunday of Advent
Season of Christmas: From Christmas Day (December 25) until Epiphany (January 6, sometimes transferred to closest Sunday) or Baptism of the Lord (first Sunday after Epiphany).

Time after Epiphany (until Ash Wednesday) and after Pentecost (until Advent): called "Ordinary Time" in some churches.

Important Feast Days (sometimes called "solemnities"):

Trinity Sunday: first Sunday after Pentecost
Corpus Christi or Body of Blood of Christ: Thursday after Trinity, sometimes transferred to the following Sunday.
Christ the King: last Sunday in Ordinary Time before Advent in some churches.
Annunciation (of the Angel to Mary): March 25
Assumption (of the Blessed Virgin Mary into Heaven): August 15
All Souls (Commemoration of the Faithful Departed): October 31
All Saints: November 1
Immaculate Conception (of the Blessed Virgin Mary): December 8

To understand Gregorian chant in the liturgy, historically as well as today, it is important to know about the Second Vatican Council, a meeting of all the Roman Catholic bishops of the world in 1962–1965, for this council introduced far-reaching reforms into the Catholic liturgy. From the early Middle Ages until the mid-1960s, the Catholic liturgy remained exclusively in Latin, a language known (to varying degrees) only by the ordained clergy. From the beginning of the twentieth century, awareness grew that this was a problem, that it was not this way in the earliest centuries of the church, and that reform was needed. Catholics began to admit that the Protestant reformers of the sixteenth century were perhaps right about some things in their response to problems in the late medieval liturgy.

In calling for a general reform of the liturgy, the bishops of Vatican II mostly issued general principles, with only a few specific examples of what would or would not change in the liturgy. The bishops called for the use of vernacular in worship, simplification of ceremonies and rituals, simplification of the calendar, more scripture readings, scripture-based preaching, greater engagement and involvement of laity, and, especially important to our topic, increased congregational singing. The implementation of these principles was left to official committees after the council. The work of structural change and the issuing of reformed books by Rome were carried out for the most part within about ten years of the end of the council.

There is both continuity and innovation in the reform-minded documents of Vatican II. One can find individual statements of continuity, such as that Gregorian chant is to have pride of place in the (reformed) liturgy, but also innovative statements calling for adaptation to local circumstances and affirming great regional variety. None of these individual statements should be interpreted out of context, and the larger context is that the liturgy has undergone a fundamental paradigm shift. The liturgy is no longer to be, as it had become by the eighth century, a sort of clerical, stylized, sacred drama that the laity observe for their edification, perhaps with some knowledge of the liturgy and emotional attachment to it. The liturgy was once again to become, as it had been in the first centuries of the church and the early Middle Ages, an act of the entire body of people.

A great many elements of the liturgy were not changed in the reforms of Vatican II—there are still Scripture readings, the priest still blesses bread and wine in the Eucharistic prayer, the priest still wears vestments, there are still Latin chant pieces in the reformed chant books, and so forth. But in fact, everything has changed. Everything brought forward in continuity now is part of a new context and must be understood from a different point of view.

The complexities of interpreting the Second Vatican Council are not always grasped by those drawn to what they see as the beauty of the old Latin liturgy and the great musical masterpieces brought forth by it across the centuries. Sometimes individual statements of Vatican II, including those about the use of Latin and Gregorian chant, are used as proof texts by those who do not understand the fundamental principles of the liturgical reform. If musicians are to cultivate Latin chant, or any other traditional music, in the reformed Catholic liturgy, it will be important to have a nuanced and well-informed theological understanding of the reformed liturgy. More will be said about this in the next chapter.

And because there have been great scholarly advances in the original nature and the interpretation of Gregorian chant since the middle of the twentieth century, it will be helpful for those singing Gregorian chant in the liturgy or in nonliturgical concert settings to be aware of the changes in chant books issued since the 1960s.

Gregorian chant developed along with this evolution of liturgical structures, and the chant repertoire continued to grow and develop throughout the Middle Ages. There is a whole range of chant books with Latin names, and the repertoire in these books varies widely in its style and level of difficulty. It might be helpful at this point to summarize the main genres or styles of chant. This will help one to know what to expect and what to look for in the various chant books (which are summarized further below).

Recitatives are formulaic, "sing-songy" ways of chanting prayer texts in which the text is primary and there is very little melodic material. Recitatives are used for brief prayers such as the Collect of the Mass (see chart below), for dialogues between priest and people ("The Lord be with you." / "And with your spirit."), and for easy, primitive forms of acclamations such as the *Sanctus* and the *Agnus Dei* of the Mass. Recitative formulas are also used when Scripture readings are proclaimed in song.

Formulas are melodic patterns that can be used for texts of varying length (e.g., for each successive line of a psalm). If I sing the first syllable of a line of psalm text to F, and the second syllable to G, and the

SOME BASIC LITURGY TERMS

Liturgy: the "work of the people"—the prayers and songs and rituals used by a community with its ordained leaders to worship God.

Eucharist: the celebration of the Lord's Supper instituted by Jesus at the Last Supper; also called Mass, Holy Communion, or Divine Liturgy. The term is also used to refer to the blessed bread and wine.

Liturgy of the Word: the first half of the Mass, with Scripture readings, psalms, a Gospel reading (which is the high point), and a homily or sermon.

Liturgy of the Eucharist: the second half of the Mass, with an offertory in which bread and wine are prepared and a Eucharistic prayer in which Jesus Christ's death and resurrection is remembered and made present. The risen Christ is believed to be present in the celebration and through the blessed bread and wine shared by the community.

Liturgy of the Hours, also known as the "office" or "divine office": the daily cycle of liturgies throughout the course of the day, celebrated especially in monasteries. Best known today are the offices of vespers (or evensong) and compline. An office consists primarily of a hymn, psalms, scripture readings, and prayers; note that Eucharist (Holy Communion) is not in any way part of the office.

Psalm: a text of praise, confession of sin, lament, or petition found in the psalter, the books of psalms of the Old Testament. There are 150 psalms. Legend had it that King David wrote all the psalms.

Canticle: a text in the genre of a psalm but from another part of the Bible, either Old Testament or New Testament.

Liturgical Year or Church Year: the annual cycle of seasons (Advent, Christmas, Lent, Easter) and saints' days. The cycle of seasons is called the temporal cycle, and the cycle of saints' days is called the sanctoral cycle. It should be noted that in the Catholic liturgy, medieval or modern, only God (Father, Son, and Holy Spirit) is worshipped. In a Mass or office of Mary or a saint, Mary or the saint is remembered, honored, and perhaps prayed to, but the entire liturgy is still addressed to God.

Feast Day: a day of particular importance, such as Christmas Day or Easter Day. The most important days have to do with events in the life of Christ or his mother, Mary, or the Holy Spirit; less important are the feasts of apostles and of lesser saints. Sometimes the most important feast days are called "solemnities," and sometimes lesser days in the sanctoral cycle are called "memorials."

> **Ferial Day**: a sort of liturgical "weekday" that is not a special feast or saint's day.
> **Missal**: the book used by the priest-presider with all the necessary presidential prayers and chants.
> **Lectionary**: the book with the Scripture readings of the Liturgy of the Word arranged for use on each day of the liturgical year.
> **Acclamation**: a liturgical song originally intended for the entire congregation such as the *Sanctus* or *Agnus Dei*.
> **Antiphon**: the liturgical name for a "refrain" that is typically sung before and after each psalm in the office. There are also some freestanding antiphons in the liturgy of the Mass and office.
> **Schola**: a small choir of adult men (monks) and choir boys. Its name derives from the Latin *schola cantorum*, the "school of singers" or song school.

rest of the text of however many remaining syllables on A, I am using a rudimentary "psalm tone" that can be used for any line of psalm text. Eventually, psalm tones developed that are in simpler or slightly more ornate style.

Metrical formulas (for metrical texts) refer to metrical hymns in which each stanza has the same number of syllables (e.g., four lines of eight syllables) and the same melody is used for each stanza. Metrical hymns are sung at each office of the Liturgy of the Hours but are for the most part absent from the classical medieval liturgy of the Mass.

Simpler through-composed pieces are antiphons sung before and after psalms in the office, which are sometimes quite simple, with mostly just one note on each syllable; some antiphons are less simple because there are note groups (melismas) of greater length on some syllables. Chant is called "melismatic" when there are more melismas of greater length throughout the piece.

More difficult through-composed pieces include the antiphons sung at the entrance, offertory, and communion of the Mass, which are intended for a trained singing group, and the verse of the "gradual" psalm (see below) and the Alleluia of the Mass intended for a skilled soloist or small group.

These genres were fully developed by about the seventh or eighth century, and a rather extensive repertoire of pieces assigned to the liturgy for every day of the year was established. Within this well-developed liturgical culture, each individual liturgy had constant alternation between various genres, with interaction between many players: priest-presider, deacon, cantor or lector, choir (choirs were small by today's standards), and congregation.

It should be noted, though, that by the time the chant repertoire had been developed for the entire liturgical year, the liturgy had become rather dominated by ordained clergy and musical specialists, and it remained in Latin in the West even though the people no longer knew Latin. Only the educated clergy and very few lay people did. The exclusion of the people from direct participation in the Latin liturgy increased throughout the course of the Middle Ages. All this was to change only in the 1960s with the Second Vatican Council, mentioned earlier and discussed in greater detail in chapter 3.

The chant repertoire continued to grow throughout the Middle Ages. Proper antiphons were composed for the Mass and office of new feasts days, which were constantly being added to the calendar of the liturgical year. More ornate melismatic melodies were composed for Mass acclamations such as the *Sanctus* and *Agnus Dei*, as these were no longer sung by congregations but were becoming the preserve of cathedral choirs and monks in monasteries. Beginning in the ninth century, sequences (see below) were composed for more and more feast days. Later reforms removed most sequences from the liturgy.

Latin chant has been composed in every century right up to the present day, as new saints' days are added to the calendar and as liturgical reforms create the need for settings of new texts. Specialists sometimes distinguish between "neo-Gregorian" pieces of recent centuries, which are sometimes of inferior quality compared to those from the so-called Golden Age of, roughly, the eighth to eleventh century. But some neo-Gregorian melodies are well-known and much beloved—for example, the simple *Salve Regina* sung in honor of the Blessed Virgin Mary from the seventeenth century.

By now the reader is aware of the important distinction between the two major types of liturgy: Mass and office. The Mass was originally celebrated every Sunday but came to be celebrated every day of the week by about the eighth century. The office was celebrated several times a day in monasteries from the beginnings of the monastic movement in the fourth century and came to be celebrated eight times a day by the time of St. Benedict in the sixth century. The office was also celebrated in cathedrals and parishes, but with perhaps one or two offices a day, at least on Sundays, being more common than the full monastic daily round.

It will be helpful at this point to understand the structure and main elements of the Mass in its common medieval form, including the particular chants sung at each point in the liturgy. For reference, the chart on pp. 34–35 gives each name in Latin as well as English and includes in the rightmost column the corresponding element from modern-day Eucharistic liturgies in their most common Catholic and mainline Protestant forms.

Note that there is a useful distinction between the "ordinary" and the "proper" of the Mass. The ordinary consists of elements that remain the same in their text whenever they are used, though different musical settings of this text might exist. The proper consists of elements with a text that is used only on a particular day of the year. To understand the distinction, a modern-day worshipper might think of the Lord's Prayer ("Our Father") as part of the ordinary, though perhaps there is more

NAMES OF THE OFFICES

Matins (with one *t*) or Vigils or Nocturns or the Night Office: celebrated when the monks arose in the middle of the night as a lengthy service, lasting over an hour, of readings and responses. Modern-day "Lessons and Carols" is based loosely on this office.

Lauds or Morning Prayer or Morning Praise or, confusingly, Mattins (with two *t*'s): originally celebrated at sunrise as the first of two "hinge" offices at beginning and end of day.

Prime, Terce, Sext, None: the four "little hours" which are brief offices of ten to fifteen minutes originally celebrated at the first, third, sixth, and ninth hour after Lauds.

Vespers or Evensong: the second "hinge" office at the end of the day, originally sometime in late afternoon or later. Lauds and vespers last approximately twenty to twenty-five minutes.

Compline: the brief "little hour" sung before retiring each night. In the eleventh century, antiphons of the Blessed Virgin Mary such as *Salve Regina* began to be sung at the end of compline.

than one musical setting of this unchanging text in use; but "Silent Night" is, roughly, a sort of proper sung only on Christmas Eve.

The terms "ordinary of the Mass" and "proper of the Mass"— *ordinarium Missae* and *proprium Missae* respectively in Latin—are still used today. But it is now more helpful to categorize musical elements in accord with their function within modern, reformed liturgical structures—e.g., whether a chant is freestanding or whether it serves to accompany a ritual. The main musical elements are included in the chart that follows; not every spoken prayer of the priest is included here.

From the word "missa" of the last element (no. 18), the entire Eucharistic liturgy came to be called *Missa* in Latin; from this comes our English word "Mass."

To summarize, the most important elements of the classical ordinary (*ordinarium Missae*) are:

- Kyrie
- Gloria
- Credo
- Sanctus
- Agnus Dei

Down through the centuries, when a composer wrote a Mass for use in the liturgy or concert hall, these have been the five movements of it. A *Missa brevis* is a "brief Mass"—so called because some movement (e.g., the lengthy *Credo*) is not set or because the text of lengthier movements is telescoped by various voices singing successive parts of the text at the same time for brevity.

The most important parts of the classical proper (*proprium Missae*) are:

- Introit
- Gradual
- Alleluia (or Tract)
- Offertorium
- Communio

To this can be added, for some feast days, a sequence after the Alleluia.

Table 2.1. Structure of the Mass

ORDINARY (Ordinarium Missae) Latin Name	PROPER (Proprium Missae) Latin name	English Name	Sung by	Modern-Day Corresponding Element
	1. Introitus	Introit = entrance antiphon	Antiphon by schola, verses by cantor(s)	Entrance Antiphon (or Opening Hymn)
2. Kyrie		Lord, have mercy	Originally cantor and people, then schola	Kyrie or Lord, have mercy
3. Gloria in excelsis Deo (except in Advent and Lent)		Glory to God in the highest	People or more likely schola	Gloria or Hymn of Praise
	4. Collecta	Collect or Opening Prayer	Priest	Collect or Opening Prayer or Prayer of the Day
	5. Epistula	Epistle or New Testament Letter	Subdeacon	Old Testament Reading (Acts of the Apostles from Easter to Pentecost)
	6. Graduale	Gradual	Schola, cantor on single verse	Responsorial Psalm with several verses Epistle or New Testament Letter

7a. Alleluia; 7b. Lent only: replaced with Tractus	Alleluia; Tract	Schola, cantor on single verse; cantor on several verses	Gospel Acclamation, Alleluia
8. Sequentia (on many feast days)	Sequence	Schola, with some vernacular of people by the late Middle Ages	Sequence (perhaps only on Easter and Pentecost, if done)
9. Evangelium	Gospel reading	Deacon	Gospel reading
10. Homilia or Sermo	Homily or Sermon	Priest	Homily or Sermon
11. Credo	Creed	Schola	Creed or Profession of Faith Prayers of the Faithful or Prayers of the Church
12. Offertorium (sung during quiet prayers of priest)	Offertory	Schola	Offertory or Preparation of the Gifts (Offerings)
13. Sanctus (or Sanctus-Benedictus)	Holy, holy, holy	Schola (originally people)	Sanctus or Holy, holy, holy
14. Canon (said silently during Sanctus)	Canon	Priest	Eucharistic Prayer (several versions) with people's acclamations
15. Pater noster	Our Father	Priest silently	Lord's Prayer
16. Agnus Dei	Lamb of God	Schola	Agnus Dei or Lamb of God
17. Communio	Communion antiphon	Schola, verses by cantor that gradually fell away	Communion antiphon or other music
18. Ite, missa est	Go, the Mass is ended	Deacon	Dismissal

Sacred music repertoire to this day makes use of many of the elements in the above chart. For example, the funeral Mass is called a *Requiem* because its introit begins *Requiem aeternam* . . . ("Eternal rest . . ."). *Dies Irae* ("Day of Wrath") is the famous sequence of the *Requiem*, and the famous Gregorian chant melody of this has been used by later composers (e.g., Berlioz in *Symphonie Fantastique*).

The office also has its ordinary of unchanging texts (some of them in varied musical settings) and proper texts for particular days and seasons. The most important elements of each day's office are a hymn, several psalms with antiphons, a reading and short response to it, and a closing collect. Lauds, vespers, and compline each have near their end a New Testament canticle from the Gospel of Luke as follows:

- Lauds: *Benedictus*, the Canticle of Zechariah, "Blessed Be the God of Israel," Luke 1:68–79.
- Vespers: *Magnificat*, the Canticle of Mary, "My Soul Magnifies the Lord," Luke 1:46–55.
- Compline: *Nunc dimittis*, the Canticle of Simeon, "Now Let Your Servant Depart," Luke 2:29–32.

The names of the principal Gregorian chant books will be given further below. At this point it will be helpful to be aware of two chant books, one for the office and one for Mass. A book with everything needed for singing the office is called an *antiphonale*, "antiphonal" in English. Though it has many types of pieces including hymns, psalms, readings, and prayers, its name comes from the fact that every psalm in the office has an *antiphon* (a "refrain") sung before and after it. A book with the propers and the ordinary of the Mass is called a *graduale*, "gradual" in English. This term is used both for the book and for no. 6 in the chart above, the individual chant that gave its name to the entire book.

It was customary beginning in the early Middle Ages for parents to "donate" young boys or girls to a monastery of monks or nuns, where they were taught to read Latin, sing, celebrate the liturgy, and perform charitable works. Similarly, cathedral schools for youth developed. The *schola cantorum* (song school) was the place for the cultivation of Gregorian chant. Even very young children attended all the daily offices including the lengthy night office. At some time in their teens (the minimum age was gradually raised in the course of the Middle Ages), children were allowed to make religious vows for life. All this was no doubt more fathomable in a culture where marriages were also arranged by parents, and some of the "donated" youth probably considered themselves fortunate to be part of the small, elite class of literate people. The presence of boys in a male monastery, with a *schola* consisting of both monks and boys, meant that all the Gregorian chant was sung in octaves rather than in unison in the strict sense.

It was in the *schola cantorum*, probably in modern-day France, that the cycle of Mass propers for the entire year was developed in the second half of the eighth century into the melodic form still used today. Only beginning in the eighth and ninth centuries was liturgical chant called *Gregorian* chant—named after Pope Gregory the Great who reigned 590–604. The legend and artistic theme developed that the Holy Spirit, in the form of a dove, dictated all the chant melodies to Gregory for him or a scribe to record.

Polyphony, literally "many-voice" music sung in harmony by a choir, developed from the desire to enhance unison Gregorian chant. It seems that at least some Gregorian chant was sung in primitive harmony perhaps as early as the eighth century. The earliest harmony is called *organum*. It could take the form of a second voice singing at the interval of a fourth or fifth in relationship to the main voice, or a second voice singing the same pitch repeatedly, such as the first note of the scale, while the main voice sings the composed melody of the chant as it ascends. The second voice could also hold one pitch as a drone while the main voice sings the composed melody.

After the turn of the millennium, florid organum developed in which each note of the original chant melody was held out for a long time while a second voice sang a lengthy melisma (note group). Organum was originally improvised but came to be written out by composers in the second millennium. Eventually more than two voices were used. As compositional techniques evolved, including the use of metrical rhythmic patterns, Western music was well on the road toward the summits of Renaissance polyphony, which would be attained some centuries later. But it is important to remember that even in the late Middle Ages, most of the liturgy was sung in unison, and harmony was reserved for a few high points of the service on a few important days of the year. ♪

Written musical notation began to develop in the West in the ninth century and became widespread only in the beginning of the second millennium. Even then, it was customary for only one copy of the "score" to exist, and this remained in the library for the conductor's reference. In rehearsal and in liturgy, all the music was sung without a score. The reader should stop to ponder what this must have meant for the experience of the singers. With neither conductor nor singers looking down at music but singing by heart, singers must have been very comfortable with their music and able to relate to the conductor and each other with attentiveness, sensitivity, and flexibility.

The earliest chant notation was lineless. Above the Latin text, squiggles were written in the manuscript that reminded the singer of the general shape and the rhythmic nuance of melodies known by heart. After the turn of the second millennium, it became more common to use lines (first one, then two, then up to four or five) so that pitches were indicated, and by the thirteenth century, four-line notation similar to today's chant books was becoming standardized (see figure 2.1). But lineless notation continued to be used throughout the Middle Ages in some places. The revolution in chant interpretation that began in the middle of the twentieth century came from a decoding of the rhythmic nuance and flexibility witnessed in the earliest lineless notation.

Only gradually did the reference book with notation migrate to the rehearsal room and then to the church for use during the liturgy. It is only in the later Middle Ages that large (and oftentimes very beautiful) manuscripts were used, which allowed the entire small group of singers to read from them. But even then, there were important monasteries that were not yet using the innovation of written notation with lines and preferred the earlier practice of singing by heart. For most of church history, liturgical singing has been by heart without written music.

Figure 2.1. Four-line staff along with early lineless notation for Gregorian chant. Courtesy of Anthony Ruff

For our purposes here, it is not necessary to trace all the steps in the gradual evolution in compositional complexity from the earliest primitive organum of the eighth century to the glories of multivoiced choral polyphony by Renaissance masters such as Palestrina, Vittoria, Hassler, or Byrd. It is only necessary to emphasize that the liturgical framework and terminology laid out thus far also applies completely and entirely to the sacred choral repertoire. Although there was certainly secular, nonsacred music composed in the Middle Ages and Renaissance, the locus of creativity was almost exclusively the liturgy. Composers lived in a thoroughly Christian culture—this is known as Christendom—in which life in cities and towns of any size, and even in some smaller villages, was punctuated by the daily round of sung offices and a sung Mass. ♪

It should be noted that chant melodies supplied the melodic material for much of the later polyphonic composition. A chant melody that was originally sung quite quickly in unison was slowed down, sometimes markedly, and used as a melodic excerpt that could then be used in other voices in imitation and melodic development. Much counterpoint of the late Middle Ages and the Renaissance was composed using chant melodies as its melodic building blocks.

We will never know the level of singing quality in parishes and villages in the Middle Ages or even how many liturgies were sung rather than entirely recited without music. We can surmise that the level was considerably lower than in great liturgical centers such as major monasteries and cathedrals, from which most of our written evidence comes. But at the least, many a medieval illiterate laborer who attended church maybe two or three times a week would have heard, from the nearest monastery or church or cathedral, bells rung throughout the course of every day announcing the beginning of yet another liturgical service.

Composers of choral music—they would have been clergy or numbered among the small number of nonordained laity able to read—were thoroughly conversant with the overall structure and individual elements of the Mass and office and how these changed in the course of the church year. By the time of the late Renaissance, much more of the liturgy in important liturgical centers was sung polyphonically, and most any part of the liturgy—Mass or office, ordinary or proper—could be set polyphonically.

Basic knowledge of the framework for the Mass and office over the course of the liturgical year will be helpful in understanding the origin and original purpose of historical sacred choral music, even if it is sung today in a different place in the reformed Catholic liturgy or a Protestant worship service or in a concert setting. Composers of medieval and Renaissance sacred polyphony were not simply composing out of personal piety or respect for favorite biblical texts. They were setting liturgical pieces in the full knowledge of how they would be used in the liturgy.

Perhaps some examples of famous choral literature from more recent centuries will illustrate the value of knowing original liturgical context. The choral piece *Locus Iste*, written in 1869 by Anton Bruckner, is the gradual (i.e., the psalm sung after the first scripture reading) at the annual Mass celebrated on the anniversary of the dedication of a church building. This particular gradual is actually a canticle from Exodus 3:5, "This place (was made by God) . . ." The piece *O Sacrum Convivium*, composed by Olivier Messiaen in 1937, is the antiphon sung before and after the *Magnificat* canticle of vespers on the feast of Corpus Christi, which is called the Body and Blood of Christ since Vatican II: "O sacred banquet (in which Christ is received) . . ."

MUSICAL CHARACTERISTICS

Trained singers today tend to think of music first of all as what is written on the page, with performance being about everything that happens in the movement from the page to the sung rendition. As the discussion above on the liturgical origins of Gregorian chant makes clear, this is to have it backward. For most of church history, notation was not the starting point but something that came into being as the end point of a long process of evolution based originally on vocal improvisation.

To understand the musical characteristics of Gregorian chant, it is necessary to get behind the score and imagine the score's prehistory. One should have in mind the historical evolution from exuberant cantor improvisation to the development of stock melodic bits and pieces to the compositional creation of masterpieces using the improvisatory bits and pieces. By the time *scholas* (choirs) were singing Mass propers in the seventh or eighth century, the melodies had to be stable in order for a group to sing them together. But the melodies bear the characteristics of the uninhibited expressiveness of improvising cantors of earlier centuries. And the earliest lineless notation indicates that singing groups sang stable melodies with the nuance and flexibility of the improvisational framework from which they emerged.

Modality

A mode is a scale pattern. With its combination of whole steps and half steps, it gives the pitches available for use in a piece of music and creates the various intervals made possible by the relationships between the available pitches. The reader is no doubt aware of the difference in sound between a major scale and a minor scale. There is quite a difference in mood between the playing of the white keys on the piano C-D-E-F-G and the alteration of this half-scale by changing the third pitch to E♭. And going down the scale, the final pitch of C has a different character depending on whether one arrives there by way of an E♮ or an E♭.

As Gregorian chant melodies evolved, they eventually fell into eight scale patterns. Or to be more accurate, it was observed that most of the melodies seemed to fit into these eight patterns, and those melodies that didn't fit were adjusted so they would fit. These are the eight modes. In chant books it is customary to give the mode at the beginning of the first line of music via a Roman numeral (e.g., VIII).

Before going into the technical details of the eight modes, such as their range, intervals, most important pitches, and ending notes, it is helpful to grasp what is at stake in the examination of the modality of Gregorian chant. This is not analytical study for its own sake. It is the key to understanding the spirit of the Gregorian melodies. For the chant melodies are not just one pitch after another. Rather, they are the expression of text by means of forward motion from one important pitch to another, with fewer or more passing tone pitches used in between the important pitches and more or less ornamentation of important pitches by neighboring tones.

Though we do not have surviving evidence of the nature and evolution of cantor improvisation in the many early centuries in which written notation did not yet exist, perhaps it is helpful to reconstruct a bit fancifully how improvisation might evolve from simple important pitches into more complex melodies. Even if the historical process was not as linear as this example will suggest, this way of imagining it will help one get behind the melodies in the chant books and see their underlying modal structure.

Suppose one sings the text "O praise the Lord, my soul!" from Psalm 104 on a single pitch E. Then one improvises this text using only the pitches E and F, with the pungent half step between them. One can use one note per syllable, or one can use several. One could alternate rapidly, perhaps six or eight times, between the two pitches, all on one syllable. In any event, one would want to end back home on E. Then, the next step would be to improve using these two pitches plus the lower pitch of D. With these three pitches, now there is the possibility of a half step, a whole step, and a minor third relationship between notes. Again, one could sing on one syllable of text one pitch, or two, or five, or twelve. And this process can be extended—by adding to one's palette in turn the higher pitch G and then A and by adding lower pitches C and B♮ and perhaps lower A. As new important pitches are added, the improviser would naturally move from one important pitch to another, with less important pitches added in between for ornamentation and as passing tones. With a longer text, say of two lines, one might end the first line on F or D to give a sensation of incompleteness and then end the second line on the home pitch of E.

At the end of this imaginary process, one has arrived at what is now called Mode III. But in the journey there, the uppermost thought was not how to sing in Mode III with all its particular characteristics. It was to express the text by using important pitches ornamented with less important pitches.

By way of comparison, consider the melody of "Amazing Grace." It emphasizes F, A, low C, then high C. Low D first appears as a passing tone but then is used later as an important pitch. G is only used as an unimportant passing tone on the way to the home pitch of F. It is the same principle of movement between important pitches with the modality of the chant melodies.

The imaginary exercise above could be done again, but with greatly different effect, by starting on the pitch D. To this would be added the higher pitch E and the lower pitch C. With two whole steps, the feeling would be very different from D-E-F. Then one would add higher pitches of F, then A, then G, and then low A, and then B♮ or B♭ in between. Or

GREGORIAN CHANT AND POLYPHONY

again, the exercise could begin by starting on C, with D and E above and B♭ and A below the home pitch. Clearly, the feel of the piece is greatly changed in each case by the pitches and intervals available in the mode. The modal stakes are higher, and the subtlest melodic differences are more striking, since it is purely unison melody without harmony.

The eight modes can be put into four larger categories, two modes in each category, with the final pitches of D, E, F, and G. That is to say, modes I and II end on D, modes III and IV on E, modes V and VI on F, and modes VII and VIII on G. Any piece of chant always ends on the final note of its mode, whether or not this home pitch is used that much in the piece itself. But more important for the character of a mode is its dominant pitch, the pitch that is used most throughout the piece. This dominant pitch is a perfect fifth higher in the odd-numbered modes and higher at the interval of a third or fourth in the even-numbered modes. While one must start with the final pitch in determining the mode of a piece, it is the dominant pitch that is determinative for the modal character of the piece.

In fact, one widely held theory holds that there were originally three modes centered on C, D, and E, each of which ended on the same pitch as that which dominated the mode. With the discovery that one could move downward from this dominant pitch and it would feel "right" to end on the lower pitch, one of the eight modes was born with its higher dominant and its lower final. According to this theory, the dominant of each of the eight modes was once both the dominant and final of one of the ancient three modes. In modern chant books, pieces that seem to have the same pitch for their dominant and final are assigned to reconstructed modes called C, D, and E.

In the eight modes, the dominant is always higher than the final. For the odd-numbered modes, the range is mostly the octave above the final, with the dominant at the midway point. For the even-numbered modes, the range is mostly the half octaves above and below the final, with the dominant closer to the final.

The following list gives the dominant, final, and range for each of the eight modes:

I ends on D with dominant A. Its range is mostly the octave above D.
II ends on D with dominant F. Its range is mostly the half octaves above and below D.
III ends on E with dominant B. Its range is mostly the octave above E.

IV ends on E with dominant A. Its range is mostly the half octaves above and below E.

V ends on F with dominant C. Its range is mostly the octave above F.

VI ends on F with dominant A. Its range is mostly the half octaves above and below F.

VII ends on G with dominant D. Its range is mostly the half octaves above and below G.

VIII ends on G with dominant C. Its range is mostly the half octaves above and below G.

Psalm tones in each mode follow the rules of the mode exactingly, though a psalm tone need not end on the final because the piece always ends with the antiphon, not a psalm verse. The predominant pitch of the psalm tone (known as the "tenor" or "reciting note") is always the dominant of the mode.

The singer will also find modes such as II* in more recent chant books. Modes with asterisks are modern reconstructions to account for the fact that some antiphons seem not to fit into the eight modes and require a dominant other than the "correct" one according to the eight-mode system.

Of course, medieval singers did not have pianos at their disposal or absolute pitch names in mind. The above note names establish the scale degrees and intervals of each mode, which remain whether a piece in a given mode is transposed higher or lower. The effect of the intervals between pitches is what is important.

To summarize: modality is the study of the relationship between pitches, but it arises as analysis of what evolved naturally in the expressive use of more important and less important pitches. To grasp the character of a piece's modality, one might begin simply by singing the piece as expressively as possible and noticing what pitches might have been primary if such a melody had ever been improvised. Then one might consult the above list to see whether the piece behaves in accordance with its mode. Most chant melodies do, but sometimes the melody was put into the mode that best fit though it has characteristics of a stage of development before the modes were finalized. As one sings more chant, one will also notice how longer melodies "modulate" to other modes internally and use bits of melodies characteristic of other modes before returning to their home mode.

Treatment of Text

Four-line notation with square notes gives the impression of evenness, but we can be sure that chant was sung according to natural speech rhythm for most of its history. Lighter and weaker syllables were sung more quickly than accented syllables. Today, because of hesitation and lack of confidence in singing a foreign language such as Latin, there is sometimes a tendency to sing all syllables evenly. One should begin by reciting the text as naturally as possible, with all the accelerations and decelerations that happen in a vernacular language. Then one might sing the melody on one pitch while striving to retain the text-based rhythms. Finally, the text can be sung with the notated melody, taking care that the melody does not cause one to even out the rhythmic values.

There is a nuanced and creatively varied treatment of text in the chant melodies. Sometimes important accented syllables are highlighted by having a higher pitch. But sometimes accented syllables are given a lower pitch that is modally important. Sometimes, especially in simpler chants, the note groups of two or three notes tend to fall on the accented syllables. But even in simpler melodies, and especially in more melismatic melodies with longer note groups, there is a highly creative placement of note groups on unimportant syllables of a text, such as the syllable before or after the accented syllable. This might seem surprising. We can surmise that the variety is for expressive effect. It is certainly expressive to put note groups and high pitches on accented syllables, and the text is presented clearly in this treatment. But if chant always did this, it would become monotonous. In chants where the note groups are on the "wrong" syllables, if the singer strives to make the text dominant, emphasizes accented syllables (more by length than volume), and moves quickly through longer note groups, the discovery will be made that the melody still serves the text, but it does so with greater artistic creativity.

Finally, it should be noted that note groups express not just individual words but entire phrases and sentences. Oftentimes there are long melismas (note groups) on final syllables or final words of a phrase, not because that final syllable or word is important but because the melisma rounds off the phrase as a whole. Note groupings sometimes bring out important words, but other times they express the grammar and syntax of the text as a whole.

TRAINING REQUIREMENTS

The first requirement in singing chant is reading the four-line notation that has been in use since approximately the thirteenth century and is used in all official chant books.

In principle there should be no objection to transcribing the chant into modern five-line notation (see figure 2.2). As history shows, four-line is not original, and chant was sung without notation for most of history. What is most authentic is what allows the singers to express the text musically. If one transcribes a piece into five-line notation and transposes it to a suitable pitch level, it is advisable to use black note heads without stems suggesting rhythmic values of quarter notes or eighth notes. Music engraving programs might automatically space the notes out evenly; one should respace the notes according to the text rather than the melody. It is also advisable to notate note groups with the note heads close to each other rather than evenly spaced out as engraving programs might automatically do, in order to suggest to the singer that note groups are sung rather quickly and the text is primary.

Four-line notation with square note heads probably appears daunting at first—all the more because the Latin text is in a foreign language. Experience shows this notation can be learned readily and soon becomes easily read even by beginning singers. It is in fact very similar to five-line notation in that the intervals are indicated by the use of lines and spaces. There is either an F clef or a C clef at the beginning of each staff. Mapping out the pitches of each line and space is rather easy by starting from which line has the F clef or C clef. Everything is read from left to right, as in five-line notation. But when one note is directly on top of the other, the *lower* note is sung first, unless the upper note is bigger.

Figure 2.2. Five-line staff for Gregorian chant (modern notation). *Courtesy of Anthony Ruff*

GREGORIAN CHANT AND POLYPHONY

To make use of all the repertoire in official chant books, the conductor will want to learn all the conventions of four-line notation to ensure that the melody is being read correctly. This can be learned from various brief guides given below in the Repertoire and Resources section and is not covered in this book.

Vocal Technique

Gregorian chant has been and still is sung with widely varying vocal techniques, depending upon the beliefs and the skills of the directors and singers. There is no particular vocal technique specific to Gregorian chant—apart from the importance that any technique support good intonation, a pleasing sound, and good balance and blend among singers. As to how to achieve this, there are different schools of thought among leading choral conductors and specialists in vocal pedagogy today. Some believe that a straight sound with no vibrato is more "authentic" (which is a rather problematic concept), but others believe that one should sing freely and not manipulate the voice to achieve any particular effect. Conductors will generally use the vocal technique for Gregorian chant that they consider most suitable for other classical choral music.

Interpretation

Chant has been sung many different ways historically. It seems likely that an originally free and flexible declamation of the text, with flowing exuberance on note groups, was gradually lost in the second millennium as the chant became slower and the rhythmic values became more even. The resonant acoustics of increasingly large churches would have played a role in this. Some have pointed to the first use of the term *cantus planus*, "plainchant," in the thirteenth century as an indication that the chant had started to become "plain" and evened out by then.

At the beginning of the twentieth century, a method of chant interpretation was developed by Andre Mocquereau of the abbey of Solesmes, France, which was very influential throughout the Roman Catholic Church. This method held that all notes are of equal value, but some notes are doubled because an editorial dot is placed after them, and other notes are lengthened by an editorial horizontal line (an "episema") that in practice also resulted in doubling. This method held that the notes of a melody are to be divided into groups of twos and threes, and a vertical line (called in "ictus") marks the beginning of each group. Because the ictus did not necessarily correspond to either the textual accent or the melodically important pitches, the result was a certain lightness that had its own beauty. In all this, it was the melody rather than the text that was primary.

This method, sometimes referred to as the "Solesmes Method" or "Old Solesmes Method," has fallen out of favor ever since another monk of Solesmes, Eugene Cardine, began in the middle of the twentieth century retrieving rhythmic interpretations based on the earliest lineless notation. This notation witnesses to the primacy of text rather than melody. This text-based approach is now dominant in the scholarly world. Official chant books since the 1980s have adjusted the four-line notation so that it gives more of the rhythmic information of the earliest lineless notation, and these more recent editions are intended for text-based rendition.

Pronunciation

In the Catholic Church in the United States, the Latin of Gregorian chant usually has been pronounced according to modern Italian pronunciation rules, also called "Church Latin," "Roman Latin," or "Liturgical Latin." This is as good a solution as any, though it surely was not the universal practice throughout history. Texts of liturgical chant and polyphony were pronounced with much regional variety historically, with influence from local vernacular languages. If one is performing a chant from an eighteenth-century Austrian or German manuscript or book, one might want to use the German pronunciation mostly likely used then, as one might in singing the choral music of Mozart. Whether it is Mozart or Gregorian chant, in liturgy or in concert, a decision is to be made about whether to use only Italian pronunciation of Latin or to use various pronunciations in accord with the original practice.

Translation

As the above descriptions of modality and text treatment will have made clear, it is important to know the meaning of the Latin text as a whole and, as much as possible, each word, in order to sing the text expressively. In the Repertoire and Resources section below, the reader is directed to sources for translation.

When a vocal ensemble sings Latin chant in worship or concert, it is advisable to give translations to the congregation or audience in the worship leaflet or concert program. This is true of Gregorian chant as well as Latin polyphony. No translation is perfect and every translation involves editorial decisions. One should not hesitate to put a published translation into more idiomatic or poetic English or to draw from a well-known translation of a scriptural text. One need not be limited by the translation given in some books and octavos, especially when these are given in archaic or overly literal English that one might not otherwise want.

Tempo, Note Lengthening, and Breathing

One should not hesitate to sing chant at a rapid and flowing tempo, and note groups in particular should be moved through quickly. There is generally greater danger of going too slowly than going too quickly. That is not to say that chant should sound rushed, however. It should sound naturally expressive, driven by the primacy of the text.

In some editions, there are horizontal lines over some notes indicating that they be lengthened. The amount of lengthening is always contextual—more for an accented syllable or melodically important pitch and less for a syllable that is before or after an accented syllable or important pitch. Lengthening before an accented syllable should serve to highlight the accent by moving toward it with anticipation; lengthening after an accented syllable should serve to round off a word or slightly extend an inner syllable of a word. In no case should lengthening throw off the proper accent of a word, and one should not hesitate to lengthen accented syllables whether or not this is indicated.

Official chant editions give gradated levels of bar lines, from double bar to full bar to half bar to quarter bar (tick on the top line) to breath mark (comma on the top line). All these are modern editorial editions not found in medieval manuscripts, but they are generally helpful indications for understanding the syntax of the piece and the varying levels of pauses needed to convey the meaning of the text. If the ensemble is able to sing at a quicker and flowing tempo, however, it will oftentimes be possible to disregard quarter bars and connect textual phrases, and one should not hesitate to do this. Where a breath is needed—and it is possible to add breathing points oneself if it will help the ensemble convey the piece convincingly—the length of the breath should be shorter where the text calls for connection, longer where the text allows for more of a break.

Men and Women Singing Together

Since monasteries that cultivated Gregorian chant in the Middle Ages had choir schools, and boys and monks sang together in chant *scholas*, there is precedent for singing in octaves rather than strict unison. In a way, it is historically more authentic to use men's and women's voices together. On the other hand, it is challenging to preserve good intonation in unaccompanied, unison music, and for this reason the conductor might choose to use men alone or women alone or the two registers in alternation.

Conducting

Practices of conducting chant have varied widely historically. According to one widely held theory, the earliest lineless notation traced onto the manuscript the hand patterns used by conductors. For those very familiar with early lineless notation, which is to be found in some modern editions, it is possible to conduct chant according to this theory by reproducing the shapes of the lineless notation in the air. But this involves trying to make an indication for every note. Those who set out with this method oftentimes end up moving toward smoother, broader motions that indicate the main goal points at which the group must arrive together, without conducting every individual note.

Ultimately, conductors must develop their own style so as to hold the group together and achieve the desired expressive effect. Both clarity and smoothness of line should mark the conductor's gestures. It seems most advisable to indicate an ictus in the air, a sort of gentle bounce, at important points such as primary accented syllables, beginnings of note groups, and notes following a longer-held note.

GREGORIAN CHANT AND POLYPHONY

REPERTOIRE AND RESOURCES

The following is a list of essential books of chant repertory for the practicing church musician:

Iubilate Deo (note the spelling with I), given to all the world's bishops by Pope Paul VI in 1974 and then expanded in 1987, as a core repertoire for all congregations to learn.

Graduale Romanum ("Roman gradual"), the 1974 book from Solesmes with the melodies of the 1908 pre–Vatican II graduale rearranged for the reformed liturgy, containing all the Mass propers and the ordinaries now in use for the entire liturgical year.

Graduale Novum ("new gradual") (ConBrio, 2011), a private edition of the *Graduale Romanum* with melodies corrected by scholars, which the Second Vatican Council called for but which has not yet been issued in an official edition.

Graduale Triplex (Solesmes, 1979), the 1974 graduale with the "squiggles" of medieval lineless notation written above and below the four-line notation—for the specialist who can read early notation and derive rhythmic interpretation from it.

Gregorian Missal (2014), a useful excerpt from the *Graduale Romanum* of all the Sundays and the main feast days, in each case with an English translation of the Latin text.

Graduale Simplex (1975), created after the Second Vatican Council from easier chants of the Divine Office, which are borrowed and arranged for use at Mass.

Anthony Ruff, *Canticum Novum: Gregorian Chant for Today's Choirs* (Chicago: GIA Publications, 2012), with each chant in both four-line and five-line notation on facing pages and psalm verses for singing in either Latin or English.

Liber Hymnarius (Solesmes, 1983), all the strophic Office hymns of the entire year, for both Roman and monastic reformed Liturgy of the Hours.

Antiphonale Monasticum (Solesmes, 2005–2007), for the monastic Liturgy of the Hours, which changed very little after Vatican II. The preconciliar book was issued in 1934.

Antiphonale Romanum II (Solesmes, 2007), with Vespers for Sundays and feast days. Apart from this and the *Liber Hymnarius*, the Liturgy of the Hours of the Roman rite as reformed after Vatican II has not been issued yet by Rome in an official edition; there is only the 1912 *Antiphonale Romanum*.

Introductory and Scholarly Books about Gregorian Chant

Luigi Agustoni and Johannes Berchmans Göschl, trans. Columba Kelly, *An Introduction to the Interpretation of Gregorian Chant*. Vol. 1: Foundations (Lewiston: The Edwin Mellen Press, 2006). A foundational introduction for the interpretation of early lineless notation according to the school known as "semiology."

David Hiley, *Western Plainchant: A Handbook* (Oxford: Clarendon Press/Oxford, 1992). A massive scholarly overview of the repertoire in its historical development.

David Hiley, *Gregorian Chant* (Cambridge: Cambridge University Press, 2009). A smaller, but still quite comprehensive, overview in the Cambridge Introductions to Music series with treatment of recent musicological scholarship but not of the liturgical changes since Vatican II affecting chant in the liturgy.

Alberto Turco, trans. Stefano Concordia, *Gregorian Chant: Tones and Modes* (Rome: Edizioni Torre D'Orfeo, 2002). A textbook giving a thorough introduction to the repertoire.

Guide to the Graduale Romanum: Preface, Rubrics and Titles in English to Assist in Using the Graduale Romanum (Oakmont, PA: CanticaNOVA Publications, 2004) and *Guide to the Graduale Simplex: Preface, Rubrics and Titles in English to Assist in Using the Graduale Simplex* (Oakmont, PA: CanticaNOVA Publications, 2004). Helpful translation to help find one's way in these two Latin books.

Daniel Saulnier, *Gregorian Chant: A Guide* (Solesmes: La Froidfontaine, 2003). A brief introduction.

Mary Berry, *A Collection of Gregorian Chants* (Cambridge: Cambridge University Press, 1979). A delightful presentation of a few simple chants, with explanation of where they came from and how they were used.

Noel Jones, *A Beginner's Guide to Reading Gregorian Chant Notation* (Englewood, TN: Frog Music Press, 2008). As the title says, an explanation of how to read four-line notation.

The Correct Pronunciation of Latin According to Roman Usage (Chicago: GIA, 1973). Gives the Italian pronunciation most used in the United States.

FINAL THOUGHTS

At the end of the fourth century, St. Augustine wrote of "beauty, ever ancient, ever new." The same could be said of Gregorian chant: it is ever ancient and ever new. It takes us back to the ancient roots of Christian singing in its purity and simplicity. It has been found to be new by every generation that has discovered (or rediscovered) it. Over time the repertoire has evolved and expanded, and singers have found their own particular way of making chant their own. The beauty of chant has always been that it exemplifies so well the *vocal* quality of worship music. As the U.S. Catholic bishops once wrote in their 2007 publication *Sing to the Lord: Music in Divine Worship*, "Of all the sounds of which human beings . . . are capable, voice is the most privileged and fundamental. . . . The primary liturgical instrument . . . is the human voice." Gregorian chant invites us to rediscover the beauty of the human voice.

❸

CONTEMPORARY CATHOLIC DIRECTIONS

Anthony Ruff

Catholic music has a long and complex history, and the variety in its music is great. The previous chapter dealt with the early history of liturgical music, from Gregorian chant to early polyphony. This chapter will pick up where the previous one left off, beginning with the Council of Trent and chronicling Catholic music to the present day.

LITURGICAL ORIGINS

From Trent to Vatican II

The single most important event for understanding the Catholic Church from the sixteenth to the twentieth century is the Council of Trent, a meeting of Catholic bishops that took place in northern Italy from 1545 to 1563. It was the Catholic Church's defensive response to the Protestant Reformation that broke out earlier in the sixteenth century. The efforts of reformers eventually led to the formation of great traditions—the Anglican Church in England, the Lutheran church in northern Germany and Scandinavia, the Reformed churches inspired by Calvin in various European lands, and so forth. The official Catholic response to all this was to define Catholic teaching more clearly, defend

Catholic practices, and condemn Protestant and Anglican deviations from Catholicism. All this is called the Counter Reformation.

The adjective form of "Trent" is "Tridentine." This is important for musicians to know because one speaks of the "Tridentine" liturgy to refer to the rite of Mass issued in 1580 after the Council of Trent. As the council specified, the 1580 Missal (book for Mass) is exclusively in Latin, for the council rejected Protestant calls for vernacular worship.

The Council of Trent had great influence on Catholic Liturgy and music right up until the reformist Second Vatican Council (1962–1965). Because of the significant developments of Vatican II, it will be important for the reader to keep in mind that the historical information treated below does not necessarily apply to Catholic worship today.

The Catholic Reformation and the Birth of the Baroque

The term "Counter Reformation" remains in use, but that one-sided term does not tell the whole story. There was also, in the wake of the Council of Trent, a Catholic Reformation. This was not simply a defensive reaction to Protestantism but a positive movement aiming for the renewal of Catholic life. New religious orders (such as the Jesuits) were founded, catechisms were written and religious instruction improved, preaching was newly emphasized, and efforts were made to help laity appreciate the clergy-dominated Latin liturgy.

And most important for our purposes, though it could not have been foreseen at the time of the Council of Trent, the great artistic and musical impulses of the baroque era were about to rise, and this left a huge imprint upon the way the Tridentine liturgy came to be celebrated.

The baroque era tended toward exuberance—highly ornamented décor with colorful paintings and statues, increasingly complex musical counterpoint, extensive musical forces in various combinations, greater emphasis upon artistically developed solo voices, and increased attention to the "affect" or emotional impact of music. This exuberant artistic style aligned well with the triumphalist attitude of the Council of Trent, with its emphasis on the superiority of Catholic doctrine and practice over other proposals. It encouraged a style of liturgy and music that was self-confident (some might say arrogant), majestic, colorful, creative, supportive of artistic excellence, and highly engaging. It is not a coincidence that opera was born during the baroque era, and there are at least some similarities between the ethos of opera and of the Tridentine liturgy in its most elaborate celebration.

Two Streams of Catholic Sacred Choral Music

To understand Catholic choral repertoire created since the Council of Trent, it is important to know that there are two streams: one compositional style more bound to tradition and one compositional style more open to innovation. Leading composers typically wrote in both styles.

At the beginning of the seventeenth century, a distinction was made between the two styles. The first is sometimes called *prima prattica* (Italian for "first practice" or *stile antico* (Italian for "ancient style") or "Roman School Polyphony." The second is sometimes called *seconda prattica* (Italian for "second practice") or *Le nuove musiche* (Italian for "the new music"). The first style is written in conscious imitation of Palestrina and Renaissance composers, with counterpoint between several voices of equal importance. The second is written in the contemporary compositional style of the era—i.e., in the early baroque style of the seventeenth century with its emphasis on a predominant solo voice.

As the reader perhaps knows, it is customary to divide Western art music into six major eras: medieval, Renaissance, baroque, classical, romantic, and modern. Catholic choral music has tracked the compositional developments of succeeding eras, as composers wrote "new music" or "second practice" sacred music in the style of contemporary art music as it continued to develop and innovate. And so it is that Mozart and Haydn, for example, wrote Masses for choir and orchestra in the eighteenth century with all the musical innovation and harmonic technique of the same period found in their symphonies for the concert hall and operas for the opera house.

For much of the history of these eras succeeding one another, the most important developments in compositional innovation took place precisely within the liturgy. As the centuries wore on, the locus of innovation shifted gradually from the liturgy to elsewhere. In the Renaissance era, most polyphony by far is sacred and intended for liturgical use, but there are also secular madrigals that were composed during this time. In the baroque and classical eras, important composers such as Pergolesi and Mozart wrote innovative compositions both for liturgical use and for other venues such as the opera house. As the classical era developed into romanticism, the emphasis for composers such as Beethoven increasingly became the concert hall, although leading composers typically also wrote for the liturgy. By the end of the nineteenth century, the shift was nearly complete, as the main locus of musical innovation had now moved outside the church and its liturgy. In the twentieth century, there are certainly important composers of sacred music such as Messiaen and Duruflé, but the compositions most noteworthy for inclusion in textbooks of Western music history are written for the most part for secular use.

As the locus of innovation shifted from the liturgy to elsewhere, the character of music composers wrote for performance in the liturgy also shifted. Leading composers wrote sacred music with more attention to the criteria of extra-liturgical venues than the needs of the liturgy. The concert hall or the opera house set the standard for sacred music performed in the liturgy. This shift in emphasis is seen, for example, in Mass settings for choir and orchestra of the romantic era, which are artistically excellent but whose movements are far too long for proper proportionality within the liturgy. In some ways, the liturgy had become a concert venue.

Parallel to all this ongoing evolution, composers also wrote in the older style, in conscious imitation of Palestrina and other Renaissance masters. "Roman School" polyphony is inspired especially by the music of Giovanni Pierluigi da Palestrina (ca. 1525–1594), the great Italian Renaissance composer who became known as the "Savior of Catholic Church Music." It was once thought that Palestrina wrote a polyphonic Latin Mass setting for use at the Council of Trent that, because it allowed for the Latin text to be understood clearly, convinced the bishops not to ban polyphonic music from the liturgy. This is now known to be a legend that does not accurately reflect the concerns of the bishops at Trent. Be that as it may, Palestrina's choral music very quickly achieved status as a quasi-official, approved style. His repertoire remained in continuous use in the Sistine chapel after his death. He is the first composer of Western art music whose music remained in continuous use. (More typical is J. S. Bach, whose music was used only in his lifetime and then passed into disuse, until it was revived in the nineteenth century.)

Beginning in the seventeenth century, composers such as Anerio, Soriano, and Allegri wrote in the style of Palestrina, which differed from contemporary emergent baroque music. In the eighteenth century, Johann Fux codified Palestrina's compositional technique in the music textbook *Gradus ad Parnassus*. It became customary for composers to write in the "Roman style" especially for the penitential seasons of Advent and Lent, when instruments were not allowed in the liturgy. But for most composers, though it was considered important to be able to write in the older style, the interest in contemporary art music was much greater.

A Catholic Ethos of Sacred Music?

This coexistence of two compositional styles running through Catholic liturgical history, one more traditional and one more innovative, raises an interesting aesthetic and theological question: is there an identifiable Catholic ethos of music?

Many people have been and continue to be interested in the promotion of sacred music that is authentically "Catholic" or "sacred," in contrast to styles that are thought inappropriate for liturgical use because they are "secular." These efforts are generally tied to a defense of "high-quality" masterpieces of the Western-European tradition of sacred music. Behind such efforts are genuine spiritual longings and laudable concerns for dignified worship. But such attempts to set boundaries run the danger of narrowness and of exalting the music of one's own (or one's preferred) culture above other musical styles and repertoires. In our age of globalization and ever greater exchange between cultures, one can readily see why many, including those who deeply appreciate traditional Western choral music, are critical of a "Eurocentric" bias.

The nature of the historic repertoire itself presents another difficulty. This repertoire is so diverse—from Palestrina to Monteverdi to Mozart to Bruckner to Messiaen—that it is exceedingly difficult to identify the characteristics common to all of it that would constitute a Catholic ethos. The Catholic Church has shown great openness to high art music in its ever-changing contemporary manifestations, and all of this music, so differing in style, all of it at one time contemporary, has been admitted into Catholic worship.

Efforts to promote a Catholic ethos typically begin with Gregorian chant as a stylistic ideal and then attempt to associate other repertoires to chant because of their affinity to and compatibility with it. This seems to work well with Gregorian chant and Renaissance (or Roman School) polyphony, and many reformers have upheld these two categories as the ideal styles of sacred music. But the venture to define a Catholic ethos becomes more difficult with each succeeding era of Catholic sacred music in the "second style," as the stylistic distance between the contemporary music (of the baroque or classical or romantic era) and Gregorian chant grows ever wider.

This stylistic diversity in Western sacred music is one of its most notable features. It stands in contrast to Eastern Orthodoxy, where the liturgy has exercised much greater disciplinary limitation upon musical development and art music has been admitted into worship with much greater reserve. A key Western development is the admission of instruments—the pipe organ and then brass and strings and percussion instruments such as timpani. This contrasts with Eastern Orthodox music, which is exclusively choral and unaccompanied and consequently tends to be in a somewhat more restrained choral style as a rule.

For those who deeply appreciate the cultural achievements of the Western church and wish to promote traditional choral music in the liturgy today, it is important to grasp that the question of suitability for worship is at root a *theological* and not simply a *musical* question. That is to say, good music is not its own argument, and one cannot advocate music on the basis of its artistic quality exclusively. One must start from the nature of the liturgy in all its aspects, including its structure, the purpose of each of its individual parts, and its manner of engaging the entire congregation. And in attempting to define what is "Catholic" or "sacred" in music, and to exclude what is not, one should be aware that one is making theological claims about which music is most acceptable to God and best reveals God to people. The diversity of the existing repertoire, and the complexity of the theological questions involved, suggest a good degree of humility and an openness to God, who speaks to people in often unexpected ways and who remains an elusive mystery not contained by human categories or judgments.

MUSICAL CHARACTERISTICS AND REPERTOIRE

Navigating the Choral Repertoire

The result of all the developments discussed here is that there is a very broad body of Latin sacred choral repertoire available to us from the past five or six centuries, in a wide variety of musical styles, mostly connected to the liturgical celebration but sometimes independent from it and more suited to nonliturgical use.

Knowing something of this history is useful, whether historic choral repertoire is sung today in the liturgy or in a concert setting. In the case of the liturgy, one will need to be aware of the reforms of the Second Vatican Council and the nature of the postconciliar liturgy (see below) in order to know how to transplant music originally written for one liturgical setting so that it fits well in a rather different liturgical setting. In the case of nonliturgical settings such as concerts, one can appreciate the music more greatly when one knows its original context and the setting for which a composer wrote it. And as will be seen below, there are various performance settings and venues, both historically and today, falling somewhere between a liturgy and a concert—including various "devotions" close to but alongside the liturgy.

The reader should refer to the preceding chapter on Gregorian chant for foundational information on the liturgical year and the explanation of the most important musical elements of the Mass and the Liturgy of the Hours (Office). All of what was said there remains true of the Tridentine liturgy down through the centuries until the Second Vatican Council (1962–1965).

Musical Performance within the Liturgy

The reader should be aware of one surprising aspect of the performance of sacred music in the traditional Latin liturgy: a disjunction between the action of the liturgy as celebrated by the priest and the timing of the music performed by choir (and orchestra). Each operated on their own plan and at their own pace, in the same sequence but not at the same time.

In the high Middle Ages, the practice developed of the presiding priest reading every word of the liturgy for himself, including texts read or sung by others (such as deacons, cantors, and choirs). While a scripture passage was read or a psalm or acclamation sung by others, the priest simultaneously mouthed the words to himself. This highlighted the presiding priest's role as the one who "said" Mass. It could not but make it seem as if only the priest's words counted, as if only he spoke with God. The music sung by others, though based on the actual texts of the liturgy sung to make the liturgy more expressive, could not but seem secondary and not integral to the liturgy.

As musical settings became more elaborate and took more time, priests were able to read quickly the texts being sung by the choir and then move on to their next spoken text—a different text—while the choir continued singing the previous text. It became standard practice for the priest to recite the *Sanctus* ("Holy, Holy, Holy") and then go on to the Eucharistic Prayer while the choir continued singing the polyphonic *Sanctus*. The priest waited for the choir to complete the first half of this acclamation and then in silence prayed the Institution Narrative over the bread and wine. Then, while the priest silently recited the second half of the Eucharistic Prayer, the choir continued with the second half of the *Sanctus*, the *Benedictus*, as a sort of motet in honor of the Blessed Sacrament.

As unfortunate as this separation between altar and choir loft was, it should not be overstated. Even within this lack of coordination, there was certainly a commonality in purpose and common faith, and composers certainly sought to provide music worthy of accompanying the sacred action at the altar, even if it wasn't quite integral to it. Still, it is understandable why reformers in the twentieth century sought to realign things.

The Mass

As stated in the previous chapter on Gregorian chant, the Mass consists of the ordinary (with unchanging texts) and the proper (with texts that change for each liturgy). When we speak of a *Missa* or *Mass* as a musical form today, we generally mean a setting of the five movements of the ordinary for choir or for choir and orchestra. There are hundreds upon hundreds of such settings, from every era and every region, since most every Catholic composer in history has contributed to the repertoire of this musical genre. Historically, up until the Second Vatican Council, the choir (and orchestra) performed the successive movements of the Ordinary—*Kyrie, Gloria* (except in Advent and Lent), *Credo, Sanctus-Benedictus*, and *Agnus Dei*—as a sort of musical atmosphere surrounding the parallel action of the priest at the altar. With the reforms of the Second Vatican Council (discussed below), some parts of this repertoire are more readily usable in the reformed liturgy than others, and even these parts will have a different purpose and a different relationship to the rest of the music in the liturgy than they did historically.

Composers also set elements of the propers of the Mass polyphonically historically—in fact, interest in the propers was as great as interest in the ordinary from the Middle Ages well into modern times. For all Sundays of the year, and especially for more important feast days, there are settings of the Introit, Graduale, Alleluia, Offertorium, and Communio for choir (and orchestra).

With the revival of Gregorian chant in the mid-nineteenth century and into the early twentieth century, interest in polyphonic propers receded. Mass propers were more typically sung in Gregorian chant, with polyphony (including orchestra) employed for the Mass ordinary.

By sometime around the middle or end of the nineteenth century, "Mass" had become a musical genre no longer necessarily intended for use in the liturgy but for performance in the concert hall. Because of the long and venerable tradition of the art form, composers wished to make their contribution to the genre, without intending that their work be used in worship. Up until the Second Vatican Council, then, there were two distinct emphases in the composition of a polyphonic Mass ordinary: a setting could be written with the structural and formal constraints that made it suitable for liturgical use, or it could be written with no such constraints and complete artistic freedom.

The Requiem

One particularly important type of Mass setting is the Requiem, which is the funeral Mass. Its name comes from the first word of the propers, the introit *Requiem Aeternam*. A musical Requiem typically consists of settings of both the Mass ordinary and the propers of the funeral liturgy.

Since the Second Vatican Council, alongside all the other reforms affecting the use of choral settings of the ordinary and proper in the liturgy, it is noteworthy that the famous sequence *Dies Irae*, with its depiction of the terrors of judgment day, is no longer part of the funeral liturgy.

Liturgy of the Hours (Office)

The preceding chapter on Gregorian chant described some of the important musical elements of the Liturgy of the Hours. As increasingly elaborate music for choir and orchestra evolved after the Council of Trent, some particular parts of the office developed into important musical genres. Among these are Vespers, the *Te Deum*, and Tenebrae.

Vespers is the last major office of the day, traditionally celebrated in late afternoon. We see this developed into a musical form in, for example, Monteverdi's *Vespers of the Blessed Virgin Mary*, written for large choir and instruments. The psalms, hymn, and Magnificat are set as major musical works. The antiphons of the psalms are not set, but there are choral motets in between the psalms that perhaps were intended to replace the proper antiphons. (Such less than strict attention to liturgical propriety for the sake of musical elaboration is not entirely untypical in the Tridentine liturgy.) Many composers wrote settings of Sunday Vespers, whose five psalms are the following: *Dixit Dominus, Confitebor, Beatus Vir, Laudate Pueri,* and *Laudate Dominum*.

The *Te Deum* is the canticle sung at the end of the lengthy office of matins (the night office) on Sundays and feast days. It also became used as a general hymn of praise on festive occasions such as the visit of a bishop or civic leader, a royal coronation, the publication of a peace treaty, the canonization of a saint, and the like. It is understandable that so many composers wrote festive settings of the *Te Deum*.

Tenebrae is the name given to the offices of matins and lauds celebrated together after midnight on Holy Thursday, Good Friday, and Holy Saturday, but later moved up by way of anticipation to the preceding evening of each day. The name Tenebrae, meaning "darkness," derives from the custom of gradually extinguishing candles after individual psalms and readings, until the service ends in complete darkness. The service no longer exists in the reformed Catholic liturgy; there is only a rather simple "Office of Readings" on the morning of Good Friday and

Holy Saturday with no provision for extinguishing of candles. But various Tenebrae services, modeled closely or loosely on the historic model, continue to be celebrated in some Catholic and Protestant services during Holy Week.

Sacred Choral Music alongside the Liturgy

Alongside the principal elements of the liturgy, which are Mass and Office, there were other services closely connected to the liturgy or to the devotional life of the people that took on important musical forms. Among these are the oratorio, devotions to the Blessed Sacrament, and devotions to the Blessed Virgin Mary.

The oratorio developed in the oratory of St. Filippo Neri in Rome in the sixteenth century. It began as a devotional service with scripture, prayer, and preaching, followed by vernacular songs. Gradually, the scripture texts and narrator texts set in recitative were interspersed with choral pieces, and this form became known as an oratorio. The form is rather loose, with texts freely chosen to reflect biblical and religious themes. Oratorios were composed both in vernacular (Italian at first) and Latin in succeeding eras. Ultimately, the most famous examples of the genre were English works on Old Testament themes by George Frideric Handel, all of which were composed in the first half of the eighteenth century.

As much as the Mass, the celebration of the Eucharist, is the center of Catholic liturgy, laypeople oftentimes received Communion infrequently when they attended Mass. Their piety was centered rather on looking at and adoring the Host (the consecrated bread) put on display for worship at devotional services of adoration. The popularity of such services, though much subordinated in importance to the Mass, no doubt owed much to the fact that some of the prayers at them could be recited in vernacular.

In Benediction of the Blessed Sacrament, after a period of exposition and adoration, the priest blesses the people by making the Sign of the Cross over them with the Host. Benediction was celebrated frequently, sometimes at the end of Mass on every Sunday and at the end of other devotional prayer services during the week. Latin pieces sung at Benediction include "O Salutaris Hostia," "Tantum Ergo," "Laudate

Dominum" (Psalm 117) and "Ave Verum Corpus." The frequency of Benediction in the centuries of the Tridentine liturgy explains why some composers wrote so many settings of these texts.

Catholic cultures have generally developed a strong devotion to the Blessed Virgin Mary, seen in the number of churches named for Our Lady ("Notre Dame" in French). Catholic teaching has always stated that only God is worshipped, whereas Mary and the saints are rather venerated, and that only God is the source of grace, whereas one may pray to Mary or the saints so that their intercession would win God's grace, and that only Jesus Christ is the mediator between God and humanity. But at the popular level, there is no denying that Mary became an overly prominent focus in the lives of many Catholics, perhaps because they were distanced from the texts of the God-centered Latin liturgy. This is reflected in the extensive choral music written in Mary's honor. Composers set the Marian antiphons sung at the end of the office of Compline in various seasons—*Salve Regina* in Ordinary Time, *Alma Redemptoris Mater* in Advent, *Ave Regina Coelorum* in Lent, and *Regina Coeli* in Easter season. The sequence for the feast of Our Lady of Sorrows on September 15, *Stabat Mater*, has been oftentimes set. Hymns from the office of Marian feasts such as *Ave Maris Stella* were also popular.

High Mass, Low Mass, and Vernacular Hymnody

In the Tridentine liturgy, an important distinction was made between an entirely sung and an entirely spoken Mass. The former, when celebrated with assisting ministers, was called a High Mass, and the latter was called a Low Mass or *missa lecta* ("read Mass"). A High Mass was also called a *missa solemnis* ("solemn Mass"); a sung Mass without assisting ministers was called a *missa cantata* ("sung Mass"). Although everything in the ordinary and the proper was supposed to be sung in a *missa solemnis*, sometimes musical movements were omitted or shortened, which brought about disciplinary decrees at various times.

A Low Mass was defined by the fact that the priest did not sing any of the parts belonging to him. He recited all his parts, which including reciting all the texts of the ordinary and the proper. Since it was not required to sing the proper or the ordinary at Low Mass, and in fact no official text of the liturgy was sung, the practice of singing vernacular music, by congregation or choir, developed. This was parallel to and simultaneous with the Latin recitation of the priest. Because this music was not officially part of the liturgy—only the Latin recitation of the priest was—there was held to be no prohibition on it being vernacular.

The effect of this was that much vernacular hymnody was sung by choirs or congregations at Tridentine Low Mass. This could have been at daily Mass or at Mass on Sunday that was not a solemn or sung Mass. Vernacular hymnody was most developed in German-speaking lands, Slavic regions, and Hungary and was less developed in Romance-language countries such as Italy and Spain.

And to complicate matters, the popularity of congregational vernacular hymnody meant that it sometimes crept into the celebration of High Mass, either in addition to or in replacement of Latin elements, though this was not officially permitted. In 1943, in acknowledgment of long-standing illegal custom, at a time when there was much reformist discussion about increasing congregational participation, Rome officially permitted the practice in Germany (which then included Austria). This is known as *Deutsches Hochamt* ("German High Mass").

Sacred Music in Concert

To conclude this review of sacred music from the Council of Trent until the Second Vatican Council, it will be helpful to comment upon the use of sacred music outside the liturgy in concert settings. This might be in a church setting, in a "sacred concert" that perhaps has elements of prayer and Scripture reading, or in a concert series sponsored by a church. Or it might be in a concert outside of a church setting.

In nonsectarian or secular settings, such as public schools in the United States where sacred music can be sung for its artistic and cultural value but its underlying religious beliefs may not be promoted, one will be careful to speak to students only about the historical context of the piece. One does this with both accurate information about the origins of the piece and neutrality about the meaning of the piece today. It is important to show utmost respect for the convictions (religious or nonreligious) of students. One's own belief, or nonbelief, can be kept to oneself. But all of this should not prevent one from giving accurate historical information about the piece, which can be very helpful for understanding and appreciating it.

In selecting sacred choral literature, one might think about the season of the year when it is sung and, depending on the setting, whether it is appropriate to select or avoid particular pieces. Of course, in some secular settings, there will be no reason to take this seasonal aspect into consideration. But even in secular settings, some listeners with a Christian background might relate better to a piece if it matches their daily experience of prayer and worship—e.g., that a concert piece has a Lenten theme if the concert is during Lent, for example. In making these connections, it will be important to have an accurate understanding of the church year and the character of each season and feast day and celebration. There is nothing "Lenten" about a Requiem, to name one possible misunderstanding, though Lent and funerals might seem to have in common a restrained mood. Lent is about conversion and renewing one's baptismal commitment in preparation for Easter. A Requiem Mass is a prayer for a deceased Christian, which could take place during any season of the year and has a character of both sorrow and hopeful confidence in God's mercy in the light of the resurrection of Jesus Christ.

In listing the piece in a concert program, several decisions have to be made. It is important to give what is most helpful to the listener. This means, for example, providing titles not only in Latin but also in translation. The listener will appreciate having a translation of the entire sung text, if possible. One might even wish to provide the entire Latin text and its translation side by side—taking care that the vernacular lines up with the parallel Latin line. One should not hesitate to adjust the translation, provided the meaning is not changed, so that its style and register is in the idiom one wants. Depending on one's judgment, for example, it is possible to change "thou" and "thine" to "you" and "your." Depending on the audience and one's estimation of their background, it can be appropriate to provide a brief statement of what the piece is and where it is located—e.g., "Antiphon of Vespers" or "Hymn for Epiphany." If the text is from the Bible, the reference can be given—some listeners who are familiar with the Bible might appreciate making a connection they might not otherwise have made.

Program notes should be accurate, of course. As much as possible, one should avoid mischaracterizing Catholic beliefs or making inaccurate claims about how a piece was used. For example, one would not write of a piece being used to "worship" Mary since Catholics only worship God. (Mary and the saints are honored and venerated.) One should be clear about what was done in the liturgy before Vatican II and what is done now, so that statements confusing the two are not made.

Depending on their background and their familiarity with liturgical history, some readers might find it rather daunting to navigate all the issues identified here. One will probably want to find a trusted advisor or two, people with knowledge of liturgical history as well as modern-day reforms and people with knowledge of Latin, to double-check that one is giving accurate and helpful information.

THE SECOND VATICAN COUNCIL (1962–1965)

The Second Vatican Council is a pivotal event in the history of the Roman Catholic Church. It is held to be the twenty-first ecumenical (here meaning "universal" or "worldwide") council of the Catholic Church. More than any of the preceding councils, it is reformist in a thoroughgoing way and sets forth a comprehensive vision of the Christian life. To understand the role of music in the reformed Catholic liturgy, it is necessary to understand the nature of the Second Vatican Council, and so it is worthwhile to pause a bit and examine this topic.

By way of introduction, it should be noted that the Second Vatican Council did not arise suddenly out of nowhere. It was the culmination of discussion and research and desire for reform that stretches back into the nineteenth century and had reached a high point by the 1940s and 1950s.

The history of the pre–Vatican II "Liturgical Movement," with its call for reform of the Latin liturgy to make it more accessible to laypeople and allow for their active participation, need not be reviewed here. It will suffice to note two important liturgical reforms that took place before the Second Vatican Council. First, Pope Pius X changed entirely the order and distribution of the psalms at all the offices of the Liturgy of the Hours in 1911. Second, Pope Pius XII moved the liturgies of Holy Thursday, Good Friday, and the Easter Vigil from the morning to their original times—evening, afternoon, and night respectively—and greatly changed and simplified their ritual structure in the 1950s. The Old Testament readings of the Easter Vigil, for example, were reduced from twelve to four. (After the Second Vatican Council they were increased to seven, a tacit acknowledgment that the reforms in the 1950s had gone too far.)

These two examples show that there was an awareness, long before the Second Vatican Council, of the need for liturgical reform and a willingness to implement reforms in particular areas that represented a rupture with previous practices. Such examples are helpful in understanding the backdrop of the Second Vatican Council. They suggest that there was something expected and even inevitable about the massive reforms adopted by Vatican II, once the decision was taken to examine comprehensively the entire life of the church.

There is both continuity and innovation in the reform-minded documents of Vatican II. There is both affirmation of past liturgical practices and musical repertoires and also a mandate for deep changes in the structure of the liturgy, with far-reaching implications for the role of music in the liturgy.

There is a creative tension between the traditionalist and the reformist streams found in the documents of the Second Vatican Council, and it is not always easy to know how to balance the seemingly contradictory statements of the Council. There is a whole body of official documents from Rome since Vatican II that offer helpful and necessary guidance. There is also a large body of literature from theologians and liturgists advising how to implement the reforms. But the reader should be aware that there is a great variety of viewpoints and much disagreement about how the Second Vatican Council should be interpreted. This has implications for how music is seen to function in the reformed Catholic liturgy today.

One can name three important reformist impulses associated with the Second Vatican Council:

- There is a *communal* understanding of liturgy as an act of the entire congregation under the leadership of the clergy, rather than a *clericalist* (i.e., clergy-dominated) understanding of liturgy as something that clergy do *for* worshippers. Similarly, while there is certainly still much room for musical performance by specialized ensembles such as choirs, there is greater emphasis on the communal aspect—i.e., *congregational* singing. The admission of vernacular, rather than the exclusive use of Latin, is a key aspect of this communal dimension.

- There is greater local and regional *variety* in the liturgy, rather than a centrally prescribed uniformity throughout the entire world. For *pastoral* reasons (i.e., out of sensitivity for what will help a given congregation enter into the liturgical celebration), there are more options open to local planners.

- There is greater openness to *dialogue* with others—other Christians, other believers, and all people of good will—rather than a *defensiveness* that emphasizes Catholic identity and the superiority of Catholicism over other worldviews. This suggests openness to musical styles and practices and repertoires from Protestantism, for example, and perhaps even openness to "secular" musical styles, although this last is a point of contention.

The implication of all this for musicians, it must be admitted, is that the balance has shifted from a more elitist to a more egalitarian attitude. It is not as self-evident as previously that great masterpieces of choral music merit performance in the liturgy simply because of their intrinsic artistic or spiritual value. The rationale must now be found within the communal, pastoral, and dialogical matrix of the reformed liturgy.

One need not overstate the distinctions being made here. It is not a matter of black-and-white opposition between "before" and "after" Vatican II. It is a matter of shifting emphasis. To be sure, there were aspects of Catholic worship before the Second Vatican Council that were communal, pastoral, and influenced by forces in surrounding culture, even as the emphasis was on the hierarchical, uniform, and traditional. And since the Second Vatican Council, these traditional aspects are by no means eliminated, but now they are balanced by reformist impulses. That is to say, the Second Vatican Council proposed, without always defining precisely, some sort of new balance between the role of clergy and musical leaders and that of the entire congregation; between centralized supervision from Rome and planning at the national, regional, and local level; and between Catholic identity and openness to goodness, truth, and beauty, wherever they can be found.

The Second Vatican Council issued sixteen documents. The first, *Sacrosanctum Concilium*, is the constitution on the sacred liturgy. Other documents treat the interpretation of scripture and its relationship to tradition, the nature of the church, the office of bishops, the training and ministry of priests, the role of laity, the renewal of religious life, Catholic education, the means of communication, ecumenical relations with other Christians and interfaith relations with other believers, religious freedom, and dialogue with the modern world. Running through all these reformist documents is a notable shift from earlier position of Catholic superiority to a stance of dialogue with others in which the church is open to learning as it searches for greater truth. ♪

While it might seem that only the first document of the Council, the liturgy constitution, is relevant to our topic, in fact the reform of the liturgy is closely connected to the reformist attitude of all the Council's documents. It is important to examine what *Sacrosanctum Concilium* says, for example, about the preservation of Latin chant and traditional choral polyphony and the development of new music; but it is also important for liturgical and musical practice to look at what is said in other documents of the Council about dialogue with contemporary culture and positive relations with other Christian traditions. Such important material from other documents shows that there is a concern for preservation of Catholic identity, including the fostering of traditional repertoire, but this is not the only concern. It must be complemented by a discerning openness to musical practices from other Christian traditions and from contemporary culture.

The Liturgy Constitution: *Sacrosanctum Concilium*

Our examination of Chapter VI of the liturgy constitution on sacred music begins by placing it in context by describing the most important features of the liturgy constitution as a whole. By way of summary, the following pastoral principles can be listed:

- Liturgy is an act of Christ above all. Then it is an act of the church—the entire church, including laypeople and clergy. The liturgy is communal by nature.
- Liturgy expresses the nature of the church. The liturgy should be communal and participative because the church is to be (or become) that.

- Active participation of the people is paramount. This concern is stated repeatedly and emphatically.
- Vernacular is admitted into the liturgy for the sake of people's comprehension. Though it is stated that Latin is preserved, bishops are given full permission to determine liturgical language, and soon after the Council bishops approved, with the Vatican's approval, an entirely vernacular liturgy.
- The rites are to be simplified and made easier to understand and follow. Ceremonial is to be reduced.
- There is to be greater use of scripture in the liturgy.
- Liturgy is to be adapted to local cultures so that people can relate to it better and bring their cultural gifts to it. The liturgy need not be rigidly uniform throughout the world.

Alongside these reformist pastoral principles, one can also name some principles in *Sacrosanctum Concilium* that are more preservationist in nature:

- Gregorian chant is to have pride of place.
- The Latin language is preserved (but see above).
- The pipe organ is to be held in high esteem.
- New liturgical forms should grow organically from previous forms, and innovations are not to be introduced unless necessary.

It is appropriate to list these two sets of principles, with their differing sets of concerns, next to each other, for this shows that there are tensions and even contradictions found within the liturgy constitution. Depending on one's convictions, one can highlight one or the other set of principles and find individual statements to support one's position. Statements of both sorts—calling for preservation and calling for innovation—are found throughout *Sacrosanctum Concilium*, oftentimes next to each other in the same article.

Further comment is needed on the fourth preservationist principle above concerning organic growth, for it stands in tension with the overall character of the liturgy constitution. Though it is not stated explicitly, it is clearly implicit throughout the liturgy constitution that a fundamental paradigm shift is proposed in the understanding of liturgy. It is a shift from the Carolingian (eighth-century) view of liturgy as a sort of clerical (clergy-dominated) sacred drama to the earlier, more communal view of liturgy as the action of the entire body of people. With a paradigm shift this monumental, one sees why the implementation of the liturgy constitution's vision necessarily involved ruptures and breaks with past practices and customs. Furthermore, the call of Vatican II for a return to a vision of liturgy more like that in the earliest centuries of the church makes clear that not all organic development is necessarily for the better. The liturgy slowly and organically developed, already in the first millennium, in ways that the Council saw as unfortunate and needing to be undone and corrected.

From this brief summary, the musician wanting to understand liturgical reform perhaps finds it rather challenging to make sense of the Second Vatican Council and know how to interpret it. This response is entirely understandable. Ever since Vatican II, there has been a wide variety of views about how to interpret Vatican II, and the church as a whole has not come to agreement about what it means and how it should be implemented. There are various schools of thought and widely varying approaches for how the liturgy should be celebrated and what sort of music should be used in it. Further below we will look at what some of these main streams of interpretation are and what they mean for the practice of sacred music. For now, as we turn to the statements on sacred music in the liturgy constitution, it is good for the reader to be aware of the complexity of interpreting any individual statements and the need to understand each statement in its wider context and in conjunction with other statements offering complementary viewpoints.

Chapter VI of the Liturgy Constitution

As is generally the case in the documents of ecumenical councils, the statements of Vatican II on sacred music are rather brief. The ten articles (nos. 112–121 of *Sacrosanctum Concilium*) for the most part give general principles, or when they call for specific reforms, they leave the details of their implementation to other official bodies after the Council. One notes that Chapter VI on sacred music places greater emphasis on preservation, rather than innovation, than does the rest of the liturgy constitution, though both impulses are found throughout the chapter.

Chapter VI affirms the musical tradition of the church and the "treasury of sacred music" and calls for choirs to be promoted. It affirms that music is to be closely tied to the liturgy—i.e., it is a part of the liturgy and not something independent performed for its own sake. The sung form of liturgy is strongly affirmed. The teaching of music in seminaries, religious houses, and Catholic schools is strongly emphasized. Gregorian chant is given pride of place, but polyphony is also affirmed. There is a call for a reissuance of all the official Gregorian chant books to make their melodies more accurate and a call for a new book with easier melodies (which was issued in 1967 as the *Graduale Simplex*). Active participation and religious singing of the people is to be fostered. Music of local cultures, especially in mission lands, is to be considered for bringing into the liturgy. The pipe organ is to be esteemed, but other suitable instruments are also admitted. Composers are called to write genuinely sacred music for larger choirs, for smaller choirs, and especially so as to provide for the active participation of all the people.

The Liturgy of the Second Vatican Council

After the close of the Second Vatican Council, the reformed liturgical books were gradually issued in Latin and translated into various vernacular languages. We can treat the two major categories of liturgies and give their main liturgical books, their explanatory documentation, and the relevant revised official Latin chant books.

- Mass: the reformed order of Mass was issued in 1969 (English in 1974 and 2011). This is sometimes called the "Mass of Paul VI," named for the Pope in 1969; or sometimes it is called the "Novus Ordo" ("new order"). (See the section on *Summorum Pontificum* below for why this is also called, since 2007, the "Ordinary Form.") In the front of the missal, and also reprinted elsewhere, is the "General Instruction of the Roman Missal," which describes the liturgy of the Mass and explains how it is to be celebrated. The reformed *Graduale Romanum* with the ordinary and proper in Latin chant was issued by the Abbey of Solesmes in 1974—but not yet with the melodies corrected as called for at Vatican II. The new *Graduale Simplex*, with simpler melodies taken from the office and arranged for use at Mass, was issued in 1967 and then revised in 1975 to match the 1969 missal.

- Liturgy of the Hours: the reformed Roman Rite Liturgy of the Hours was issued in Latin in 1970 (various English editions). Note that the office book is no longer called a "breviary." In the front of the office books is the "General Instruction of the Liturgy of the Hours," which describes the office and explains how it is to be celebrated. The reformed *Antiphonale Romanum* for the Roman office has not yet appeared. The *Liber Hymnarius* was issued in 1983, with all the office hymns for the Roman and the monastic rite. A partial book, the *Antiphonale Romanum II* with just vespers for Sundays and feast days, appeared in 2010. For the monastic office, the *Antiphonale Monasticum* appeared in three volumes from Solesmes Abbey 2005–2007.

A first official attempt to provide guidance in musical matters, in greater detail than the brief statements of Vatican II, was the 1967 Roman document *Musicam Sacram*. Though it was issued before the reformed rites were in place, it was written in anticipation of the reformed rites and provides foundational principles for the role of music in the liturgy of the Second Vatican Council.

For musicians, there are two important principles in *Musicam Sacram* that should be kept in mind:

- Structure: Music in the liturgy should relate integrally to the reformed liturgical structure. It is not helpful, for example, to speak of the "ordinary" and the "proper" of the Mass, though these terms are still sometimes used. It is more helpful to speak of chants that accompany other ritual actions and chants that are themselves freestanding rites. Examples of the former are the entrance chant or the communion chant. Examples of the latter are the *Gloria* or the Responsorial Psalm.

- Function: Each piece of music in the liturgy should serve the function of that element of the rite, in relationship to the liturgy as a whole. The various elements of the entrance rites (before the Liturgy of the Word), for example, including the entrance chant or song, the *Kyrie*, and the *Gloria*, should not only fit the structure of the entrance rites; they should also provide for the proper interplay between ministers, musicians, and congregation and serve as a spiritual introduction that does not overshadow the more important Liturgy of the Word and Liturgy of the Eucharist that follow.

In addition to the general instructions for Mass and office referred to above and *Musicam Sacram*, there have been many official documents issued from Rome or national bishops' conferences since Vatican II that describe various aspects of the reformed liturgy such as the lectionary, the liturgical year, art and architecture, inculturation and multicultural liturgy, Sunday worship in the absence of a priest, and so forth. Anyone working in Catholic music ministry should have a reference collection with all the major documents of liturgical reform (see the Resources section below).

Sing to the Lord: Basic Orientation

For the musician who is not able to be a specialist in all aspects of the reformed liturgy, it is advised to seek one's orientation in the 2007 document of the U.S. Catholic Bishops titled *Sing to the Lord: Music in Divine Worship*. This document helpfully synthesizes and summarizes the most essential information from the numerous postconciliar documents and presents it as a comprehensive explanation of the role of music in the liturgy. The section on "Music and the Structure of the Mass," for example, in its sixty-three articles, runs fifteen pages in the official edition and describes every part of the Mass and the role of music within it. This is essential information for any musician serving in a Catholic church. ♪

Sacred Music, Liturgical Music, or Pastoral Music?

These terms are sometimes used interchangeably, and their meanings overlap (and vary for different users), but the ways these terms are used sometimes signal differences in understanding of the role of music in the liturgy or elsewhere.

"Sacred music" is sometimes used with traditionalist undertones, indicating preference for traditional Western art music. There is a traditionalist school of thought that favors this term and advocates traditional "Catholic" rather than "secular" music in the liturgy. But as we have seen above, the Western art music tradition gradually distanced itself from the liturgy over the course of the centuries, and sacred music began to be written intentionally for use in the concert hall rather than the liturgy. So the term does not necessarily indicate connection to the liturgy. As the term is used in official church documents, however, it refers to music for the liturgy and implies an integral connection to it.

"Liturgical music" is sometimes used to make more explicit the connection of music to the liturgy. It is sometimes favored by those who wish to emphasize their acceptance of the reformed liturgy of the Second Vatican Council as their starting point for the role of worship music.

"Pastoral music" is sometimes used by those who emphasize sensitivity to the needs and preferences of members of the congregation and sensitivity to cultural context. Therefore, it sometimes has connotations of egalitarian leveling, which is, depending on your bias, either laudably anti-elitist or artistically mediocre. The term is widespread especially because of the name of a large American organization and its journal: the National Association of Pastoral Musicians and *Pastoral Music*.

Congregation versus Choir?

Starting with the nature of the church and the nature of the liturgy, one can list the singing forces involved in the liturgy of the Mass as follows:

- the entire congregation,
- the ordained ministers (priests or deacons),
- the cantor,
- and the choir.

It is appropriate to start with the entire congregation, and fostering congregational singing should be the uppermost concern of every music director and choir conductor. The cantor is listed before the choir because most liturgies probably do not have a choir, but every liturgy, including liturgies with a choir, should have a cantor to sing solo elements of the liturgy (such as Responsorial Psalm verses) if they are not sung by the choir and also to facilitate congregational singing.

The choir is listed last. This is not because it is unimportant but because its important role can only be understood in relationship to the other singing forces. Quite a large role can be given to the choir, and there is room in the liturgy for the singing of great choral masterpieces. But extensive choral offerings will be better received, and will take on their full spiritual depth for worship participants, if choral repertoire is programmed with a view toward the whole in which each piece is appropriate to its place in the reformed liturgy.

One can enumerate parts of the liturgy that are more congregational in nature and parts of the liturgy that are more suited to choral singing. There are not hard and fast rules, however, for there is flexibility inherent to the reformed liturgy (in some points more than others), there is place for adaptation to local circumstances and customs, and there is some creativity called for in balancing the musical forces of the liturgy as a whole.

Pieces most strongly congregational in nature include:

- entrance song or chant (though this can be sung by choir alone);
- *Kyrie* (if it is sung);
- Responsorial Psalm refrain;
- Gospel Acclamation (Alleluia except in Lent);
- Creed, which is typically recited;
- the acclamations of the Eucharistic Prayer: *Sanctus*, Memorial Acclamation, and Amen (although some argue for a choral *Sanctus* by way of exception);
- a Communion refrain or antiphon—which is strongly recommended;
- a closing hymn if there is one.

Elements of the liturgy or points in the liturgy most open to choral singing include:

- prelude;
- *Gloria*, though this generally incorporates congregational singing;
- freely chosen piece at Preparation of the Offerings;
- *Agnus Dei*, though this is generally congregational;

- piece during Communion, though ideally the congregation should sing;
- piece after Communion, though this might also be congregational;
- postlude.

Within the wide range of interpretations given to the Second Vatican Council, as discussed above, there are schools of thought that allow for a greater role for the choir. Maximally, it is possible that the choir sing the entire so-called ordinary and proper in chant or polyphony, and one can find in the official documents enough provisions and loopholes to make this seem possible. This practice is open to critique in the case of the Gregorian chant gradual after the first reading, for the documents strongly prefer the Responsorial Psalm of the reformed three-year lectionary of scripture readings. It is also highly questionable to have the choir alone sing the *Credo*, for this is intended to be a statement of affirmation of faith of the entire congregation.

On a deeper level, one might question the starting point—whether striving to have the choir sing "as much as possible" is in the spirit of the congregation-based reforms of Vatican II. On the other hand, it could be argued that diversity and sensitivity to varying local situations legitimize such exceptional approaches. But for most choral directors by far, the issue as posed does not arise, for there is more than enough to do in preparing choral pieces for the parts of the liturgy that most clearly allow and call for it.

Schools of Thought in Catholic Liturgical Music

Reference has been made several times to the range of interpretation given to the meaning of the Second Vatican Council and its liturgical reforms. In the area of liturgical music, there are several schools of thought that have differing priorities in their understanding of the role of music in the liturgy. The following listing is meant to indicate broad tendencies. Within each school of thought, there is a range of opinion, and the boundaries between schools are necessarily flexible. One's position might draw on elements of more than one school of thought.

- Traditionalist: This paradigm emphasizes continuity with pre–Vatican II practice and the use of traditional repertoire as much as possible, with theological and liturgical understandings influenced as little as possible by the reforms of the Second Vatican Council. The emphasis is on traditional Catholic identity, Latin, Gregorian chant and traditional polyphony, and attention to church law. Less attention is given to dialogue with contemporary culture, ecumenical use of repertoire from other Christian traditions, and active participation of the congregation. There is oftentimes skepticism toward congregational hymnody and preference for Mass propers in Latin or English chant. This school of thought is often tied to liturgical practices such as the priest facing eastward (in effect away from the people), Communion under only the form of bread, Communion distributed only by clergy, use of only male lay ministers, and selecting the preconciliar variant when several options are given in the reformed liturgy—for example, the first Eucharistic prayer, the Roman canon.

- Modern Classical: This paradigm is more informed by the reforms of the Second Vatican Council than the traditionalist paradigm is. It seeks a new synthesis between the reformed liturgy, which is the starting point for the understanding of the role of music, and classical music, which is understood as a developing tradition. Active participation of the congregation is fully endorsed, and there is oftentimes openness to the use of the classical Protestant hymnody. Traditional repertoire such as Gregorian chant and polyphony is affirmed, but there is emphasis also on the development of new artistic music for choir and congregation in vernacular. There is ready acceptance of the entire scope of the liturgical reforms with all the various options and permissions. Emphasis is upon aesthetically high-quality music but, perhaps a bit narrowly, as understood by the canons of Western art music. This paradigm has been most represented in cathedrals, although more recently there has been a shift in some cases to a more traditionalist ethos.

- Multicultural: This paradigm refers to the music of various cultural and ethnic groups other than classical European/Western, which has increasingly been accepted in Catholic worship in recent decades. Depending on the customs and traditions of various ethnic groups, their traditional or newly composed music sometimes relates loosely with liturgical structures. It is customary in many Hispanic traditions, for example, to sing texts that are loose paraphrases rather than officially approved texts of Mass acclamations. Ethnic paradigms are increasing in importance as the Catholic Church in the United States becomes less white and is enriched by the presence of increasing numbers of people from various ethnic cultures.

- Contemporary: The label for this paradigm is imprecise, but it is the label that has most typically been used since Vatican II to describe various styles of folks and popular music. It has been inspired by secular styles of popular music—folk music of the 1960s protest movements at first and then other styles of soft rock, ballads, and easy listening music. This paradigm, which has been predominant among English-speaking Catholics of European descent, has been represented by the "contemporary ensemble," which uses guitar and (electric) piano rather than organ. This paradigm is associated with progressive and liberal theological positions and an informal style of liturgy with adaptations (not always permitted, strictly speaking) for the sake of perceived needs of contemporary people.

- Evangelical: This paradigm could be considered a subset of the contemporary paradigm or perhaps its most recent manifestation. It seems to merit listing as a separate paradigm, however, because of its growing influence, especially among young people. More than the contemporary paradigm, it draws on Protestant evangelical and megachurch styles of music, including "contemporary Christian music" and "praise and worship." And where the contemporary paradigm has been informed by contemporary Catholic theology, and hence has sought to create new repertoire informed by the structure of the reformed liturgy, the evangelical paradigm seems more open to Protestant evangelical music because of its appeal to worshippers, even when its texts might not be entirely consonant with Catholic liturgy.

In doing musical work for a Catholic community, it will be important to be aware of what paradigm(s) dominate for it and what expectations are present because of local traditions and customs. It is important to note also that in Catholic church law, the pastor (priest) has ultimate say in all matters, more so than in other Christian traditions. Parish councils and lay liturgical committees have an important role in offering advice and guidance, and church documents admonish priests to work collaboratively with others. But church law still assigns exclusive decision-making authority to the priest-pastor and understands all opinions from lay committees as advisory. This means that the pastor's understanding of what music is desired weighs heavily upon the work of musicians. It also means that a change of pastor can bring about a rather sudden change in the direction of the music program.

A Step into the Past: *Summorum Pontificum* and the "Extraordinary Form"

Ever since the Second Vatican Council, there have been small groups who have not accepted the Council's teachings or the reformed liturgy that resulted from it. They have existed in uneasy relationship with church authorities, sometimes remaining (barely) with the church, sometimes separating from it and celebrating the preconciliar Latin liturgy without authorization. Under Pope John Paul II in the 1980s and 1990s, it was made possible for these groups to celebrate the unreformed liturgy with special permission from the local bishop, in order to facilitate their remaining within the Catholic Church.

In 2007, this permission was extended greatly by Pope Benedict XVI with the document *Summorum Pontificum*. Special permission of the bishop is no longer required, and every priest is now permitted to celebrate at any time the liturgy according to the 1962 missal that was in use before the Second Vatican Council. The reformed liturgy is now called the "Ordinary Form," and the 1962 liturgy is called the "Extraordinary Form."

Though the groups making use of this provision are very small in number, the issuing of *Summorum Pontificum* is emblematic of an important trend in the church. There is a difference of opinion within the church not only about *how* to interpret Vatican II, but *whether* to accept Vatican II. During the papacy of Benedict XVI (2005–2013), the reformed liturgy was increasingly criticized, and the charge was increasingly made that the liturgical reforms after Vatican II were carried out in too radical a manner. A movement known as the "reform of the reform" has sought to alter or undo the postconciliar liturgical reforms and return to some or much of the preconciliar practice. The 2007 document seems to give encouragement to these traditionalist tendencies, and in effect it calls into question at least some aspects of the conciliar reform.

For a musician in the Catholic church, then, it is possible that he or she has to be able to provide music for the "Extraordinary Form," in addition to the "Ordinary Form" that has been the emphasis of this entire chapter.

PERFORMANCE SKILLS FOR MUSIC IN THE LITURGY

In general, the musical skills needed for performing music in the liturgy are the same as the musical skills needed anywhere else. Whatever approach one favors regarding breathing, vocal production, diction, pronunciation, choral blend, and the like is used also for singing sacred music in the liturgy. But there are some unique aspects to liturgical performance that cause particular challenges and require particular solutions.

In the liturgy, there is a back-and-forth between spoken elements and sung elements. This means that singers have to be ready to sing at a given point in the liturgy, without a warm-up, after longer or shorter periods of not singing—e.g., during a homily or sermon. One should prepare singers for this and point out to them the importance of thinking ahead and being mentally "on" when the time comes. It is important that singers know where their music is and not be searching around in their folders or struggling to find the right page when the liturgy demands that a piece of music begin.

Musical pieces sometimes come in rapid succession during the liturgy. There are also cues for movement at certain times—e.g., when a singer goes to the stand to sing a Responsorial psalm, when musicians go to receive communion, or when a microphone needs to be moved. There is not always sufficient time to think about what happens next, and the conductor will want to think through the sequence and timing of everything before the liturgy begins. The conductor will also have to be the one who remembers the entire sequence for others, since individual musicians do not always remember everything. It will oftentimes be helpful to make notes to oneself at the end of one piece so that one is ready immediately to do the next necessary thing—e.g., "Give pitches to priest," or "Signal soloist to move toward microphone," or "Remind men to move to the front row for a TTB piece."

There is typically a rehearsal or warm-up of musicians immediately before the liturgy. With experience, one learns how to drill with appropriate repetition the things that are most challenging for singers to recall when they come up in the liturgy. Sometimes proper texts are sung (e.g., verses of a Responsorial psalm or a Gospel acclamation) that change with the day but are set to musical formulas that repeat. Because the music is not that difficult or is well-known, it is not necessary to spend a great deal of time on such pieces. But the conductor should learn to anticipate where text underlay or textual variants (is it "Here I am" or "Here am I"?) are likely to cause stumbling or hesitation, so that such problem spots can be isolated and drilled. Singers need to be reminded to mark in their scores things that they will otherwise not remember by the time they come up in the liturgy.

In the case of unaccompanied chant or polyphony, or any choral music that begins without an instrumental or keyboard introduction, it is important that singers not only have their pitches but also the modality of the piece. This can be difficult in the liturgy if a piece immediately preceding is in another key or mode. If a previous piece ended in D major, for example, it will not be sufficient to give singers the pitch A if their piece is in F major. One will have to give enough notes to indicate the new key, with F natural rather than F sharp. Sometimes a priest or deacons sings his solo part such as to wander into unexpected keys and registers, and the conductor must be ready to hum or convey the correct pitches to singers in short order.

In music that involves alternation between congregation and soloist or singing ensemble, which is very common in the reformed Catholic liturgy, there is a whole set of skills involved in making the transitions so as to enable clear entrances and encourage congregational participation. First, the keyboard or instrumental accompaniment should vary noticeably in volume between the congregational and the solo part. A louder volume for the congregation signals clearly when the people are meant to sing. A softer volume for the singing ensemble (for example, on verses of a Responsorial psalm) ensures that the text is heard and not drowned out by the accompaniment. Rhythmically, there is a "feel" one needs to cultivate in the lead-up to and at the point of the congregational entrance. Without losing the overall rhythmic beat, there is sometimes, depending on the context, a slight rubato that retards in the lead-up and then an emphatic downbeat as the regular tempo is reestablished at the entrance. To do this convincingly, in a way that elicits participation, it is important that one knows the music very well and is able to look up from the score and move together as an ensemble. If one is gesturing the congregation—which should be done only if needed, and always as minimally and unobtrusively as possible—it is crucial that one maintains eye contact with the congregation.

One oftentimes works with volunteer singers and musicians in music ministry. It is important to be considerate and encouraging to such people and to do everything possible to make the experience a pleasant and rewarding one for them. It is also important to show gratitude by thanking people often who give generously of their time.

STRUCTURES AND ORGANIZATIONS

At the universal level, the Congregation for Divine Worship and Discipline of the Sacraments (CDWDS or CDW) is the "liturgy office" of the Vatican. It issues reformed books and decrees that apply to the entire Roman Catholic Church, with varying degrees of authority and importance.

At the national level, the national conference of bishops typically has a liturgy office (also known as a "secretariat") with a staff with responsibilities in the area of music and liturgy. The United States Conference of Catholic Bishops (USCCB) has the Bishops' Committee on Divine Worship (BCDW), which issues a BCDW Newsletter each month. National conferences issue documents applicable in their country, such as *Sing to the Lord: Music in Divine Worship*.

In each diocese, the bishop is the chief liturgist with responsibility for oversight of worship in his diocese. Bishops sometimes issue decrees or teaching documents on liturgy and music. Some dioceses staff a liturgy and/or music office, and many dioceses have an advisory diocesan committee for liturgy and/or music.

There are two major organizations in the United States for the music of the Catholic Church: the National Association of Pastoral Musicians (NPM) and the Church Music Association of America (CMAA). Both have an active website with many helpful musical resources. NPM, which is larger, is officially connected to the USCCB and has a bishop who is appointed to serve as liaison to the organization. NPM strives to represent all paradigms described above, but has been associated most strongly with the contemporary paradigm, with some presence also of the modern classical and, to a lesser extent, the ethnic paradigms. More recently, the contemporary paradigm has expanded into the evangelical in a few cases. Many of NPM's members have been skeptical of the traditionalist paradigm. CMAA is generally associated with the traditionalist paradigm. It publishes the journal *Sacred Music*. ♪

An important ecumenical organization, which is predominantly Protestant but includes many Catholic members, is The Hymn Society in the United States and Canada. It publishes the journal *The Hymn*.

The three major publishers of Catholic liturgical music in the United States are GIA Publications, Oregon Catholic Press (OCP), and World Library Publications (WLP). They all publish music for the various paradigms and schools of thought described above, to varying extents. Other publishers of liturgical music for Catholic worship include Liturgical Press, Morning Star, Ignatius Press, and International Liturgy Publications. In more recent times, many smaller publishing enterprises and online resources have arisen, such as Illuminare Publications, Corpus Christi Watershed, and St. Boniface Parish in Lafayette, Indiana, which issued the somewhat widely used *St. Michael's Hymnal*.

REPERTOIRE AND RESOURCES

Official Church Documents and Studies of Them

Robert Hayburn, *Papal Legislation on Sacred Music: 95 A.D. to 1977 A.D.* (Liturgical Press, 1979), mostly a catalog of documents major and minor, with some commentary.

Sing to the Lord: Music in Divine Worship (United States Conference of Catholic Bishops, 2007), an excellent condensed summary of much other material; a basic resource.

The Liturgy Documents (Liturgy Training Publications, 2012 and after) appears in several volumes. The first volume has the most important foundational documents.

Gerald Dennis Gill, *Music in Catholic Liturgy: A Pastoral and Theological Companion to Sing to the Lord* (Liturgy Training Publications, 2009), a somewhat conservative interpretation of the U.S. bishops' document.

Edward Foley, *A Lyrical Vision: The Music Documents of the U.S. Bishops* (Liturgical Press, 2009), treating *Sing to the Lord* and also the important American predecessor documents on music.

History and Theory of Worship Music

New Catholic Encyclopedia, 2nd ed. "Liturgical Music, History of." A useful twenty-three-page summary of the two-thousand-year history.

Edward Schaefer, *Catholic Music through the Ages: Balancing the Needs of a Worshipping Church* (Liturgy Training Publications, 2008) is written from a quite conservative perspective; it does not incorporate the then-recent 2007 U.S. document *Sing to the Lord*.

Ken Canedo, *Keep the Fire Burning: The Folk Mass Revolution* (Pastoral Press, 2009) is an interesting history of "folk/contemporary" music in the United States from a passionate advocate of it.

Claude Duchesneau and Michel Veuthey, trans. Paul Inwood, *Music and Liturgy: The Universa Laus Document and Commentary* (Pastoral Press, 1992) is an important document on the role of music in worship from a "progressive" standpoint.

Bernard Huijbers, *The Performing Audience: Six and a Half Essays on Music and Song in Liturgy* (North American Liturgy Resources, 1980) is a manifesto written by this Dutch author shortly after Vatican II from a radically progressive viewpoint.

Kathleen Harmon, *The Mystery We Celebrate, the Song We Sing: A Theology of Liturgical Music* (Liturgical Press, 2008), a theology of music based on the paschal mystery.

Anthony Ruff, *Sacred Music and Liturgical Reform: Treasures and Transformations* (Liturgy Training Publications, 2007) is a lengthy and comprehensive study of the history and theory of Catholic sacred music, with special emphasis on the Second Vatican Council and its implications for traditional repertoire.

Practical Guides

David Haas, *Music and the Mass: A Practical Guide for Ministers of Music*, 2nd ed. (Liturgy Training Publications, 2013) is a textbook and workbook, focusing only on Mass.

Kathleen Harmon, *The Ministry of Music*, rev. ed. (Liturgical Press, 2016) covers primarily the Mass, with treatment of theology and spirituality of music.

Jennifer Kerr Breedlove and Paul Turner, *Guide for Music Ministers*, 2nd ed. (Liturgy Training Publications, 2010) covers history, theology, and spirituality, with some practice advice also.

M. Francis Mannion, "Paradigms in American Catholic Church Music," *Worship* 70 (1996): 101–128, gives an overview from the 1990s that continues to hold true in many respects.

FINAL THOUGHTS

The Second Vatican Council stated, "Sacred music is to be considered the more holy in proportion as it is more closely connected with the liturgical action, whether it adds delight to prayer, fosters unity of minds, or confers greater solemnity upon the sacred rites" (*Sacrosanctum Concilium*, no. 113). There is a rich diversity in Catholic musical traditions, from the historic treasury of sacred music to the creative output of contemporary composers and the contributions of various ethnic groups. May our music-making, whether in liturgy or concert, truly add delight to our lives and foster unity among the whole human family.

4

SACRED CHORAL TRADITIONS

Matthew Hoch

When one thinks of traditional church music, particularly in England and the United States, the church choir—usually accompanied by the organ—comes to mind. Throughout much of the church's modern history, the church choir has been a fixture of worship, and this is true across numerous Christian denominations. Many singers have their first singing experiences as members of church choirs, and many others continue to sing in church choirs throughout their adult lives.

There are many kinds of church choirs, from all-volunteer groups in both small and large parishes to elite professional ensembles in large cities. This chapter is intended to give an overview of these choral experiences with an emphasis on technique necessary to sing in these ensembles. Whether one is a paid professional or an excellent amateur, the skills required to sing well in a choral ensemble are the same. Choir conductors work on the same aspects of singing with choirs of all levels.

While there are many resources that address choral technique from a conductor's perspective, this chapter is intended for the singer. It is also written from a personal perspective after many years of singing as a professional singer in churches across several denominations. Like many students with a background in vocal performance, I learned during my graduate school years that taking on a "church job" (as singers call them) was a fulfilling way to supplement my income while simultaneously nurturing my spiritual life. Many singers—particularly strong sight readers who genuinely love sacred choral music—likewise find that church choir positions are a great fit for their personality and skill set. While there is essentially no full-time work for choral musicians in churches, many singers and singing teachers supplement their incomes through church jobs. A number of my singing colleagues maintain a thriving musical career that combines teaching and performing while also singing in churches.

After a brief survey of the sacred choral repertoire, this chapter lays out a technical approach to working as a professional chorister in churches while also providing a roadmap for securing and keeping church jobs. While choral experiences continue to be a part of one's formal schooling in music, there is less discussion in voice studios about the technical aspects of good choral singing. Stylistic differences between solo and choral singing will also be addressed, as well as nonmusical attributes that are essential to working in the industry.

I am writing this chapter from my own experiences as a professional chorister who later became a full-time singing teacher and part-time choral conductor. As an Episcopal choirmaster, I now employ my own singers for church work, and the experience I have gained from seeing the profession from both sides has been valuable. Much of the content of this chapter will be written from a personal perspective after many years of working in the Episcopal Church, but much of this material will apply equally well to churches of other denominations that maintain traditional choral programs. Likewise, while an intended target audience is for classical singers seeking church jobs as professional choristers, the technical and practical advice given will also be useful to volunteer amateur singers. It is my hope that all church choir singers will benefit from the content and wisdom collected into this chapter. This is the resource I wish I had had at the beginning of my journey twenty years ago.

LITURGICAL ORIGINS, MUSICAL CHARACTERISTICS, AND REPERTOIRE

Historical Overview

Any history of sacred choral music in the Christian tradition begins with the Catholic Church, particularly the Gregorian chant repertory, which marks the recorded beginning of Western music. This repertoire was discussed in detail by Anthony Ruff in chapter 2 of this book. Most undergraduate students who study music take a standard music history sequence, which chronicles Western music through its six epochs:[1]

Medieval Era: c. 850–1400
Renaissance Era: 1400–1600
Baroque Era: 1600–1750
Classical Era: 1750–1825
Romantic Era: 1825–1900
Modern Era: 1900–present

Examining choral music through the lens of broad historical epochs reveals an interesting musicological point, as instrumental music did not become a seminal force in compositional practice until around 1600, the dawn of the baroque era. In fact, the use of instrumental accompanying forces alongside a newer, bass-oriented method of composing (called *seconda prattica* to distinguish it from the polyphonic *prima prattica* of the Renaissance era) is a stylistic advent that heralds the beginning of the baroque. ♪

Thus, the study of medieval and Renaissance music—usually the contents of the first semester of a music history sequence—is essentially a study of the early history of choral music. In addition, the vast majority of the choral repertoire composed during this era was sacred choral music written for the Catholic Church.[2] These genres, including Gregorian chant, Mass settings, canticles, antiphons, psalms, and motets, were musical settings of sacred Latin texts that were composed for a specific purpose within the liturgy.

All sacred Christian music was Catholic music until the year 1517, which marked the beginning of the Protestant Reformation. In this year, Martin Luther issued his 95 Theses, a list of grievances against the Catholic Church that resulted in the establishment of the Lutheran Church several years later. In 1534, King Henry VIII likewise broke away from the Catholic Church via the Act of Supremacy, effectively establishing the Church of England. Within a span of less than twenty years, new denominations were born, and along with them new liturgies, musical genres, and performance practices.

The history of Christianity is an encyclopedic topic, and there are many parts of this rich story that must be skimmed over here.[3] The

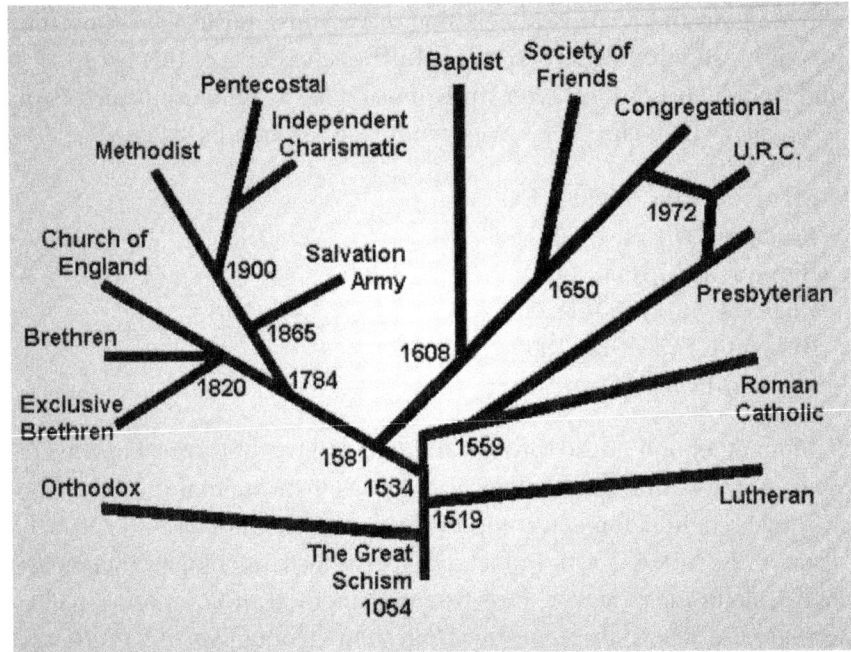

Figure 4.1. **Denominational branches of Christianity.** *Creative Commons (CC BY-SA 3.0)*

most significant impact that Protestantism had on sacred choral music was primarily within two areas: the introduction of new genres and the introduction of sacred choral music in the vernacular; in other words, non-Latin sacred texts began being set to music.

Protestant Choral Genres

The most significant contribution that Lutherans made to sacred music was in the area of hymnody. To be fair, the Bohemian Brethren compiled the first recorded hymnbook in 1505, but the Lutherans took this genre to new heights with their own homophonic compositions, which they called chorales. The Lutheran chorale—a four-part setting of a German poetic text (Johann Sebastian Bach composed some of the genre's most famous examples)—is the most important ancestor of modern-day hymnody. Hymns have since become a standard part of the musical liturgy across many denominations. In addition, hymns were an important addition to worship because they emphasized congregational participation. Music was no longer confined to the choir stalls or the altar—with hymns, everyone was invited to sing.

The Church of England began contributing English-language settings of Catholic genres, including canticles, psalms, and motets, but Anglicanism's most important contribution to church music was a brand new genre: the anthem. The anthem—officially introduced to the liturgy in the 1662 revision of the Book of Common Prayer—was an additional poetic English text, often biblical, that was set to music and inserted to complement the scripture of the day and liturgy of the season. This genre offered wide creative latitude and inspired many composers, who prolifically began churning out anthems. Perhaps most important, the anthem was soon borrowed by other denominations. Although it was originally an English invention, virtually all denominations with traditional programs have now incorporated the anthem as part of their liturgy, and it is viewed as the most significant "choral moment" of a church service. The anthem is often performed during the offertory or communion.

As denominations continued to proliferate, many developed their own unique liturgies, retaining some liturgical elements of their ancestors while inventing new musical traditions. Whether these choral moments are performed by the choir or the congregation is invited to participate depends on the denomination as well as the tradition and size of the church in question. Large cathedrals, for instance, are more likely to have a professional choir and more music in their services than small parishes. Examples of these choral genres include psalms, which rotate according to the church's lectionary, as well as a broader category known simply as "service music." In the Episcopal Church, for instance, the service music category would include any portion of the Book of Common Prayer that is set to music, such as the Sanctus, Fraction Anthem (which is sung immediately after the breaking of the bread during communion), or the Lord's Prayer. Whether these texts are sung or spoken also depends on the denomination and how "high church" the style of the service is. Among church musicians, the term "high church" is often used to refer to how much singing there is in a given service. If the priest is intoning the Eucharistic Prayer, this is considered to be "high church." (Smelling incense can always be another giveaway.)

Liturgical Considerations

Most churches with traditional choral programs also follow a lectionary, a sequence of scripture readings that are organized according to the calendar and seasons of the church year. The lectionary also considers high holy days as well as the feast days of major and minor saints. The major seasons of the church year include the following:

Advent: begins four Sundays before Christmas (December 25)
Christmas: lasts for twelve days (until Epiphany on January 6)
Epiphany: length of season varies depending on when Easter Sunday falls
Lent: begins on Ash Wednesday, forty days before Easter Sunday
Easter: lasts for fifty days (until Pentecost Sunday)
Pentecost: also known as Ordinary Time (from Pentecost Sunday until Advent 1)

Choral music programmed for use in the liturgy must be appropriate for the season in which it is programmed as well as complement the appointed scripture readings. Choirmasters and soloists must select their texts carefully and accordingly. Changes of liturgical season also coincide with musical traditions. For example, most churches will not incorporate treble descants or brass instruments during Lent, and the word "alleluia" is not permitted to be sung (or spoken, for that matter). Churches observe the seasons and feasts in nonmusical ways as well, through colors (purple for Lent, white for Easter, red for Pentecost), pageantry (a Palm Sunday processional), and other rites (the Great Litany on Lent 1 and beginning the service in darkness at Easter Vigil). The church musician who does not come from a liturgical background learns and adapts to these traditions.

The Organ

In the Protestant tradition, the organ is inextricably linked with the history of sacred choral music. Although a cappella music continued to be written long after the Renaissance era, the majority of canticles, service music, and anthems written in the late baroque and beyond were composed with organ accompaniment. Organs were also a fixture

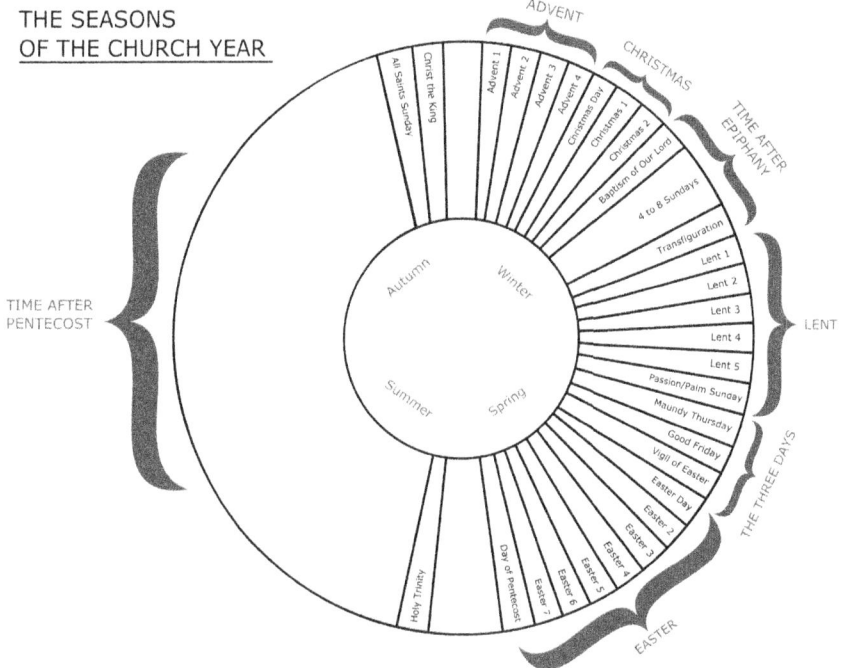

Figure 4.2. Seasons of the church year. *Creative Commons (CC BY-SA 3.0)*

in both small parishes and large cathedrals and were designed and built to complement the church's architecture. As the importance of hymn singing increased (early in the Lutheran tradition and during the nineteenth century in the Anglican tradition), the organ further solidified its place in worship due to its important role in supporting congregational singing.

Singers seeking employment as church musicians can benefit from familiarizing themselves with the organ and its important role in church music for several reasons. First, churches with great organs also tend to have great music programs; where there is an excellent organ, employment and performance opportunities are likely to exist as well. Second, in many cases the principal musician of the church—and the one who hires professional singers—is an organist. Being able to engage competently in discussions involving the organ can be advantageous. Last, singing with organ accompaniment is a different animal than singing a cappella or with piano. The skilled professional chorister will quickly adapt.

TRAINING REQUIREMENTS AND CHORAL TECHNIQUE

Training to Be a Professional Chorister

Most singers who find work as professional choristers begin their training in undergraduate music programs, where art song, opera, and choral singing are firmly established as part of the curriculum, as well as subjects like music theory, ear training, and sight singing. Through voice lessons, repertoire assignments, ensembles, and coursework, singers who are trained in these traditional classical programs secure the basic vocal technique and musicianship needed to pursue success as a choral musician. In other words, since choral music is a classical genre, the same technical foundation—including breath management, posture, and a healthy approach to the singing voice—applies. For the aspiring professional chorister, an undergraduate degree in vocal performance is an excellent foundational degree to obtain.

While choral music is an important part of the undergraduate experience, graduate school curricula tend to be different. If one pursues a master's degree in vocal performance, there is usually a focus on solo classical singing with a post-baroque emphasis. These genres include opera, art song, oratorio, concert music, and chamber music. Most Master of Music (MM) programs do not require graduate students to enroll in choral ensembles. The emphasis is on solo singing as opposed to ensemble singing, and the repertoire draws primarily from the classical, romantic, and twentieth-century repertoires.

Throughout much of the twentieth century, young singers who had a strong interest in choral singing were encouraged to pursue the MM in choral conducting for their master's degree as opposed to an MM in vocal performance, since graduate programs in vocal performance tend to ignore choral genres altogether. Over the past thirty years, however, a new graduate degree has emerged that has gained considerable traction in the voice performance world: the MM (or MSM) degree in early music. These programs emphasize a different repertoire than the traditional degree in vocal performance, instead focusing primarily on baroque repertoire as well as one-on-a-part Renaissance polyphony. While solo singing is still emphasized—such as the arias within the cantatas of Bach and Buxtehude—small ensemble choral singing is also an integral part of the early music specialist's training. Singers in these training programs also gain experience in singing with period instruments and at baroque pitch (often A=415), and they study ornamentation, period diction, and other performance practice issues. Established and reputable early music graduate programs in the United States and Canada include those at Boston University, Indiana University, McGill University, Peabody Conservatory, University of North Texas, University of Southern California, and Yale University, and new programs continue to emerge each year. ♪

Graduates of these early music programs have had enormous impact on the professional choral world over the past two decades. Twenty years ago, a professional choir was likely to have had its roster filled with graduates of choral conducting programs. Now professional choirs are far more likely to be composed of singers with vocal performance degrees. In the contemporary market, almost all professional choral singers are also proficient soloists, usually specializing in the early music repertoire. It is no longer enough just to be a good choral musician; one has to be a well-trained soloist as well.

It should be noted that the choral standards espoused by these programs and the professional choral world (largely through an ever increasing number of professional recordings) have begun to trickle down to the undergraduate level as well. In recent years, there has been ever-increasing pressure for undergraduate choirs to sound like professional choirs, and many of these choirs have risen to the occasion thanks to competitive showcase venues such as the American Choral Directors Association (ACDA) biennial convention. While choral singing at the undergraduate level has in most ways never been better, this "raising of the bar" has challenged singers technically and at a younger age than ever before. Emphasis on straight-tone singing and ever-increasing rehearsal and touring hours has been somewhat controversial and has strained relationships between some choral directors and teachers of singing. Good communication, collegiality, and mutual understanding of one's values and priorities have never been more important in the diverse world of vocal music.

The choral experiences and training offered by these academic programs provide a solid technical foundation for singers entering the world of sacred choral music. Although the repertoire narrows considerably when one enters into an employment contract with a church, the skills valued in elite college and professional choral ensembles are the same ones valued by church musicians. One of the biggest shifts that the singer will encounter during the transition from an educational environment to a professional environment is an emphasis on product as opposed to process, but the well-trained singer will be prepared for the challenge.

Technical and Stylistic Differences between Choral and Solo Singing

As stated above, the basic technique of choral singing is foundationally the same as solo classical singing. Good technique is good technique, and the performer's fundamental approach to the voice should be the same. There are, however, many stylistic differences between elite choral singing and classical solo singing (in the traditional *bel canto* sense). The following chart articulates some of these distinctions:

SOLO SINGING	CHORAL SINGING
Emphasis on Legato	Non-Legato Is Often Desirable
Vibrato	Significantly Less Vibrato (or Minimized Extent)
Vowels Tuned for Optimal Resonance	Vowels Matched to Blend with Others
Emphasis on Individual "Ring" (Singer's Formant)	Emphasis on "One Voice" within Section
Solo "Fach" Based on Operatic Repertoire	Choral "Fach" Is Sometimes Not the Same
Emphasis on Size of Voice/ Acting Ability	Emphasis on Sight Reading/ Musicianship

The strong relationship between solo singing in early music and professional choral singing was mentioned earlier in this chapter, and it should be pointed out that many of the attributes in the "choral singing" column above would be highly valued in the early music community. It is obvious to say that baroque music is sung in a different style than romantic Italian opera, which brings us to an important point: great choral singers understand that choral music must be sung *in a different style* than much of their solo repertoire. Singers, especially younger singers, tend to confuse technique and style. I think it is productive to think of technique as something fundamental and unchanging that allows one to sing effectively in any style.

Imagine a great opera soprano singing Violetta or the solos in the Verdi *Requiem*. There would almost certainly be an emphasis on legato and *portamento*, and there would be a perceived vibrato, perhaps with a wide extent, present at all times in the sound. These works would probably be sung in an opera house or other large venue, and she would need to tune her vowels accordingly so that her voice has ring and projects in a resonant way. All of these descriptive qualities are positive in this context; the soprano is singing appropriately and in style.

Now imagine a Violetta who deliberately pares back her voice, choosing to sing with a narrower vibrato extent and less resonance. She de-emphasizes legato and *portamento* in order to sing with more rhythmic clarity, slightly detaching each note. When singing with Alfredo, she is more interested in blending seamlessly into his sound than in the projection of her own voice. This is of course absurd—it is hard to imagine such a thing! And yet singing most choral genres in the style of Verdi should be equally absurd to us. Choral directors should not have to remind singers to blend with others or to prioritize the ensemble over their own resonance—singers should *want* to sing in the proper style to make the best music possible.

Educating singers on appropriate choral style is the province of choral directors during a singer's formative years, and applied singing teachers should also play an active role in discussing the differences between solo and choral singing with their voice students. Historically, too many singers and singing teachers have been so immersed in their own operatic world that they forget that singing in a choral ensemble requires a different style altogether. It should also be mentioned that a baby dramatic soprano or budding *Heldentenor* will probably not be happy constraining her or his voice in attempting to blend into the soprano or tenor section in choir. Perhaps singing alto or baritone (bass 1) would be more pedagogically appropriate and a huge relief to the singer; solo and choral *Fachs* are not necessarily the same. In academic environments, the voice teacher and the choral director should not shy away from frank and open minded discussions with each other to foster the best possible learning environment for students.

It goes without saying that not all singers have equal aptitude for all types of singing. Comparing musicians to athletes can be fruitful: a champion pole-vaulter might be a poor javelin thrower or weak long-distance runner. By the same token, some singers might find that they are more at home singing Puccini than Handel. While the undergraduate choral experience is good for everyone, not all singers will be equally well-suited to pursue choral music at a professional level, just as not all singers will end up singing at a prestigious opera apprenticeship. While a pianist may have the luxury of playing different repertoire on a different instrument, the singer has to sing within the limitations of his or her own God-given voice.

In recent decades, the voice pedagogy community has come together on the notion that singers can sing in a variety of styles in a healthy way. This is most evident in the explosion of pedagogical resources that now exist for music theater and contemporary commercial music styles. The near-universal embrace of these styles as legitimate pedagogies was unthinkable thirty years ago. As the profession continues to evolve and minds continue to open, an ever-increasing number of voice teachers will embrace the stylistic differences between choral singing and solo singing.

Last, it must be mentioned that just as there are stylistic differences between romantic opera and baroque oratorio, there are also certain choral styles that do not fit neatly into the paradigm articulated above. In large symphonic works like Beethoven's Ninth Symphony or genres like the African American spiritual, some of the attributes from the left-hand column might be welcome and valued. The attributes listed in the right-

> "Clearly, a Palestrina motet must be approached with a different vocalism than a Verdi opera aria. However, the physical characteristics of the singer whose voice is suited to Palestrina are likely as different from a Wagnerian as a virginal is from a modern Steinway, yet we do not expect these two instruments to play all repertoire written for the keyboard. Perhaps we should think about singing the same way."
>
> —Scott McCoy, DMA, Ohio State University[4]

hand column, however, will ring true for most choral situations, including the majority of sacred repertoire sung in church music programs.

Some Thoughts on Vibrato

It is the elephant in the room that everyone is afraid to talk about. In the Harry Potter series, the evil Voldemort is known as "He-Who-Must-Not-Be Named." In Scotland, superstitious Shakespeare lovers refer to the "Scottish Play" to avoid saying *Macbeth*. And among singers and singing teachers, there is a certain, ubiquitous term that is so thoroughly offensive in some circles that you find pedagogues doing somersaults in an effort to avoid saying it. The term is "straight tone"—to some, the most dreadful thing that a singer can possibly hear or say.

Regardless of how one feels about this term, and regardless of the decades of pedagogical literature and practice that have encouraged choral directors and organists to move away from using it, the term is still widely used and probably always will be. Teachers of singing should actively and directly engage in discussion about vibrato with their students. There is no question that control of vibrato (for lack of a better phrase) is an essential aspect of choral style and something that choral singers of all levels must discuss and confront.

Choral artists should think of vibrato the same way that early music singers do: as a device used for ornamental purposes as opposed to something that is omnipresent in one's tone quality. This concept provokes some controversy. Many pedagogues and voice scientists will argue that there is in actuality no such thing as a straight tone and that vibrato is always present on some level. Technically, these critics are correct. What we hear as straight tone is actually a minimized extent (pitch variation) of one's vibrato. Extent is the aspect of vibrato that one can adjust with good vocal technique, whereas the other variable—rate (the number of pulses per second)—is something that is more individually hardwired and not as easily controlled.

Before proceeding further, let's summarize some basic facts about vibrato:

1. Vibrato is a variation of pitch.
2. Vibrato is a muscular resistance to the flow of air.

3. Since muscles and airflow can be controlled, so can vibrato. (Think of popular music styles.)
4. There are two components of vibrato: *extent* and *rate*. Extent can be malleable with practice and training. Rate is more fixed.
5. The classical singing world has cultivated an aesthetic regarding what constitutes a pleasing vibrato rate. The average is 5.5–7.0 cycles per second (cps).
6. Extent, on the other hand, can vary from singer to singer. Larger voices singing bigger repertoires at louder volumes tend to have greater vibrato extents. Narrower extents are more desirable in most choral genres. Technically advanced singers can become deft in controlling their vibrato extent.
7. One can convincingly argue that there is no such thing as a pure straight tone. What we perceive as straight tone is actually minimized extent.
8. Vibrato extent should never become so wide that it obscures the written pitch. This is advisable in solo singing as well.

The notion that vibrato must always be audibly present in singing is actually a nineteenth-century *bel canto* concept. The baroque monodists viewed vibrato as an ornament, and a more nuanced, twenty-first-century view of vibrato marks a return to its original ornamental purpose. Thanks in large part to our contemporary commercial music colleagues, pedagogies on teaching healthy control of vibrato are emerging. And, as stated earlier, graduate schools are also offering degrees in early music performance as well. These curricula offer solid training for aspiring professional choral singers.

It should also be mentioned that conductors sometimes become overly obsessed with vibrato in choral situations when the problem is actually something else altogether. Other common variables include volume, intonation, vowel matching, too much ring/singer's formant, or too much *portamento*/legato. Delineating these issues from one another is extremely important if one is to home in on the real technical problem of a given passage. Often, a problem with blend or intonation can be solved without mentioning vibrato at all.

I have to admit that after many years of singing and teaching, the term "straight tone" doesn't bother me anymore. And—honestly—I find it to be effective, regardless of whether it is fact-based or politically correct. When I try to nudge my church choir into blending better on final cadences with other phrases or terms, it somehow doesn't work as well as when I say "straight on the final chord" or "write *non-vibrato* in this *pianissimo* section." Those are instructions that singers of all levels seem to understand, and the result is palpable and immediate. That's probably why the term "straight tone" is never going to go away, and that's why I insist on actively talking about this important topic with my students. At some point in their career, they are going to hear this instruction from a conductor.

Control over one's vibrato extent will of course be easier for some singers than others. As a lyric baritone, I confess that I have never had any trouble blending my voice in professional choral situations, but many of my colleagues (particularly sopranos) have expressed that it can be a great challenge to give the conductor what he or she wants, especially in extreme tessituras. In the end, however, the ability to control one's vibrato extent is an absolute must for continued employment as a professional chorister. The singer who is not willing or able do this will quickly find himself or herself out of work in sacred choral music circles.

Sight Reading and Musicianship

To succeed as a professional chorister on the church music circuit, you have to be an outstanding sight reader. Period. Sight singing and perhaps some ear training (such as the ability to recall a series of intervals) are likely to be part of the audition for a church position. During my audition at Trinity Church Boston years ago, I recall being given a twelve-tone row to read and only about ten seconds to look at it!

There is a reason for this kind of grilling, and a good one. In church music positions, you are not just being hired for your voice. You are also being hired as a principal musician of your section. Many church choirs will have a blend of professionals and amateurs, and the paid singers are expected to be leaders within their group of volunteers. It is paramount that the professional's sight-reading abilities are better than his or her unpaid colleagues' skills. In addition, church choirs sing a lot of music—perhaps fifty to seventy anthems a year plus music for special services and other events. No matter how dedicated one is to personal practice, there simply would not be enough time to learn all of the music you are expected to sing unless you are a strong sight reader in the first place. The most successful professional choral singers can read anything well the first time they lay their eyes upon it.

Diction and Language

Students of classical singing tend to steep themselves in the "big four" languages of opera and art song: Italian, German, French, and English. While the Lutheran tradition has brought us much sacred music in German, this repertoire is only occasionally used in worship in English-speaking countries (though excellent programs do enjoy the occasional Bach and Brahms motet). The two primary languages of sacred choral music used regularly in workshop are English and—less frequently—Latin. The pronunciation rules of Latin are straightforward. Church Latin only contains five vowels, and while the occasional work by Bach, Mozart, or Schubert might require Germanic Latin (which contains thirteen vowel sounds, including the four mixed vowels), most professional choral singers will have significant experience and excellent facility in both varieties of Latin.

Interestingly, English is the language that ends up being the more challenging one in professional church music situations. The reasons for this are manifold. First, English is a complex language with numerous diphthongs and irregular pronunciations; singers who do not speak English as their first language can face significant challenges when trying to match vowels in choral situations. Second, most singers in American choirs speak English as their first language but bring their own idiosyncratic regionalisms into the ensemble; special attention must be paid to these inconsistencies so that they can be ironed out and unified. Third, since the anthem repertoire is an English genre, most of the repertoire from the anthem canon must be sung with British pronunciation for historically informed authenticity. Many singers will need to be educated on the nuances of Anglican pronunciation, including rolled and flipped *r*'s, elimination of the American vowel [ʌ], a "dropping" of the second half of diphthongs, and a higher placement of the schwa [ə], to name only a few hallmarks of the style.

Good Anglican choral diction requires the singer to pronounce words in a way that may sound artificial as a soloist or speaker. But what a difference this can make in the choral sound! Singers inexperienced with the British style and repertoire are encouraged to steep themselves in British choral music. A selected discography will be listed at the conclusion of this chapter.

Coping with Vocal Fatigue

One of the greatest challenges for professional choral singers is preserving one's voice through many hours of rehearsals and services. Two or three services on a Sunday can be very tiring, especially when congregational hymns and service music are part of the mix. The fact that careers as church musicians are usually combined with other work—such as teaching and solo singing—adds to the daily wear and tear on the voice. Excellent vocal technique, adequate hydration, and sleep are an absolute must. Professional singers must become adept at pacing themselves as well as knowing when to be quiet. In addition, church choirs tend to be very social organizations. The temptation to go across the street to the bar as a group after rehearsal is tempting but must be avoided if one is experiencing vocal fatigue. The singer who listens to her body and remains aware of his boundaries will attain longevity in a career that can place great demands on the voice.

CHURCH JOBS: SECURING WORK AS A PROFESSIONAL CHORISTER

Auditioning

Having a successful audition for a church job requires a certain understanding of the culture of church music and professional choral singing. An audition for a graduate school or an opera company bears little resemblance to a professional choral audition. The format is completely different, and the person for whom you are auditioning is looking for a completely different skill set than an opera director. Knowing what to expect is very important.

First, positions in church choirs are rarely advertised. As of 2016, there is no YAP Tracker for church jobs. How, then, does one find this kind of choral work? Upon moving to a new city, the first thing you should do is get the lay of the land by identifying all of the churches in town that hire professional singers. Generally, but not always, these are the large corporate and program-sized churches, but sometimes well-endowed smaller parishes will hire singers as well. If you have friends and colleagues who are already living in the area, they will likely be able to provide you with an initial list.

After identifying five to ten churches that hire singers, your next step will be to contact the principal musician of the church, almost always the organist or choirmaster. (Often the same person has both jobs.) The title of this person can vary, he or she may be called the "director of music," "minister of music," "canon of music," or simply (and commonly) "organist." This information is easily found on the church's website. Send a brief and professional e-mail and résumé to this person expressing an interest in auditioning for him or her to be considered for future openings. After sending an e-mail, singers should also consider attending a service and speaking to the organist or choirmaster afterward. Following up an e-mail with a personal introduction makes a good impression and solidifies your name in the director's memory.

Note that I said *future* openings. In most cases, there will not be an immediate opening at the program for which you are auditioning. However, I have found that in most cases directors are eager to hear singers anyway. When an opening does occur (or a substitute singer is needed), they will want to have a list of names to call. Church job positions often open unexpectedly, and when they do, a director will be interested in filling those positions as soon as possible. He or she will probably not take the time to advertise or hear several singers for a position—the first qualified singer who fits his or her current needs will be hired.

For the audition, I recommend bringing in two contrasting selections from either the oratorio or sacred concert repertory. Good examples could include a selection from Mendelssohn's *Elijah*, Bach's *St. Matthew Passion*, or Mozart's *C Minor Mass*. Singing an Italian opera aria or French art song is probably not a good choice because these genres and languages are not relevant to the job you are seeking. The director will probably also "get to know your voice" by vocalizing you throughout your range and assess your dynamic range through *messa di voce* exercises. Once I remember being asked to sing a simple melody three times—in the style of Palestrina, Mozart, and Brahms, respectively!

Sight reading is also guaranteed to be a part of the audition. This will often be your line of a choral octavo that you have never seen before. Don't be surprised if you are asked to sing in a straight-tone style—the ability to blend is very important to most church choir directors. And, perhaps most important of all, the director will spend some time chatting with you and getting to know you. It's not just about your skill set—he or she also needs to trust that you are dependable and feel comfortable with your personality.

Practical Skills—It's Not Just about How Well You Sing!

By far the most important attribute to a long-lived and successful career as a professional chorister is to be reliable. Never miss a call for a rehearsal or service. It is very important to most choirmasters and organists that they feel that your church job is your first priority, not your last priority. Whether it truly is or not, it is essential for you to give them this impression. While illness and academic conflicts may seem like good excuses to miss rehearsal (at least to the chorister), excessive absences will wear thin on any choir director, regardless of the reason. There is a joke among professional choristers that you shouldn't miss a rehearsal or service unless you are dying, and even if you are dying, you should try your best to get there anyway. This is an entirely different culture and mindset than you may have experienced in academia, when your teacher or opera director probably told you to "stay home if you're sick so that others don't get your germs!" While you may question the logic of the "show up even if you're sick" culture inherent in many church jobs, this attitude seems to permeate the industry. The professional chorister who never misses a call will find himself or herself in very good stead with the director. Reliable and stalwart singers are the ones who are retained and rehired.

In the unfortunate instance of a legitimate conflict with a rehearsal or service (and in elite church positions, there are very few such excuses, save hospitalization or the funeral of a close family member), the professional chorister should do his or her best to secure an appropriate substitute singer for the dates in question. While the principal musician (or chorus manager) will ultimately have to approve the substitute, offering a solution to the problem up front will show responsibility and commitment to the position.

Committing yourself on holidays, particularly Christmas and Easter, is also a big part of having a church job. Contracts for church jobs will often stipulate the "high holy days" on which absences and substitute singers are not permitted. In other words, don't bother asking the director if you can have off on Christmas Eve—you can probably guess what his or her answer will be. All throughout graduate and doctoral school, I remember getting in my car after the 11:00 Christmas Eve service and driving six hours home, through the night, in order to be with my family on Christmas morning. Black coffee and Red Bull were my good friends during the all-night drive. Was I tired the next day? Of course, but I had the best of both worlds: a church job and a family, both of which I loved. It was always worth it to me. When you have a church job, you sing on Christmas Eve. Like the GEICO commercial says, "It's what you do."

In short, be reliable! Nothing will annoy a director more than if he begins a rehearsal to find that you are not in your seat and ready to go. Always be early to every call. A professional choral singer who oversleeps for a Sunday call will probably be fired, and even if you are given a second chance, you will never under any circumstance be given a third. Also, the church music community is a very small world—all of the music ministers in town are friends, or at least acquaintances, with one another. A singer who burns bridges at one church is unlikely to be hired at another. Loyalty to a position is also highly valued—don't develop a reputation for auditioning at a different church every year simply to "climb the ladder" for higher pay and different opportunities. Five years of consistent work at one church looks much better on a résumé than having three or four jobs during the same time frame.

In addition to being dependable, also be affable and easy to work with. Make sure that you are compliant and easygoing when the director makes requests. Most professional singers also work directly with volunteers on a weekly basis. For this reason, being a likable person with good people skills is also essential. It is important to the director that his paid professions "fit in" on a social level in addition to a musical one. Church choirs tend to be very close-knit communities, and one of the real joys of having a singing position at a church is the opportunity to become a part of that community.

Diversify Your Skill Set

Choristers who develop skill sets beyond choral singing often find themselves in positions to earn additional money beyond their seat in the soprano or bass section. Here is a brief list of additional opportunities and responsibilities that may present themselves through one's position as a paid singer—or even as an experienced volunteer—in a church choir.

Solo Opportunities Most church programs that hire singers will also host special music events, including major works (a Mozart or Fauré *Requiem*, for instance), oratorios (a Bach *St. John Passion* during Holy Week), or a recital series that features organists, instrumentalists, and singers. Choral artists with strong solo chops are likely to be engaged for these opportunities. Singers are also requested on a regular basis for weddings and funerals, and expressing an interest in these opportunities to the organist playing the service will often yield additional income for the singer.

Sectionals (Section Leader Responsibilities) Often during church choir rehearsals, the director will ask for "sectional work," a time where the sections (soprano, alto, tenor, and bass) move into separate rooms to go over their parts. The professional singer then steps into a role as section leader, working with his or her section from the piano. Adequate piano skills are a must in order to assist in this capacity. These sectionals may provide an opportunity to work with the volunteer singers on a technical level as well. A paid singer who is also a fine instructor is a great asset to any music program.

Conducting As mentioned previously, there is a strong historical relationship between professional choral singing and choral conducting, primarily because the two professions are united by the same repertoire. Singers who are also competent choral directors may find themselves asked by the choirmaster or organist to facilitate a rehearsal with a *schola cantorum* (literally "singing school," but a term often used to refer to a smaller, one-on-a-part chamber ensemble) or even conduct an occasional anthem. Singers seriously interested in careers as professional choristers should pay close attention in their undergraduate conducting classes and also enroll in elective graduate conducting courses if at all possible.

Administrative Duties This category is self-explanatory. There are many important nonmusical tasks in church music programs, such as library duties, attendance taking, robe managing, and payroll. If choirs go on tour, paid soloists often step into important roles in trip planning. Or perhaps a director needs help planning meals or breakout sessions for the annual choir retreat. In sum, the singer with a diverse skill set opens himself or herself up for employable opportunities that extend beyond singing.

Do I Have to Be Religious?

This is a million-dollar question because there are no firm answers. When I was in my twenties, my answer to this would have probably been "no" based mostly on my experiences as a professional chorister at churches in Hartford and Boston. Those particular directors never asked me about my faith when I auditioned for their positions. Since I am a person of the Christian faith, it wasn't something I thought about very much. On the other hand, an atheist, Jew, or Muslim auditioning for a job at a Christian church will likely ponder whether he or she will "fit in." When being hired for the kind of church positions described in this chapter, I think it would be unusual for someone to be grilled about their faith, and that is probably a good thing. One's religious beliefs are a very personal matter.

Even if one is not religious or has personal beliefs that conflict with the doctrines of the denomination for which he or she is employed, it is quintessentially important for the church musician to understand that he or she is facilitating worship for a clergy and congregation of believers. One is reminded of a famous quotation by Johann Sebastian Bach: "Where there is devotional music, God is always at hand with his gracious presence." Singing in a sacred music situation requires deep empathy and respect for the people who are participating in worship. For many people of faith, music unquestionably heightens religious experiences. This intimate connection to a congregant's spiritual experience is an enormous responsibility for any church musician.

From personal experience, I can unequivocally say that my personal belief in God and my comfort with the core beliefs and doctrines of the Episcopal Church is a big part of why I find so much joy in being a church musician. Being a part of a religious community and the opportunity to serve a parish that shares my beliefs is deeply fulfilling. For me, a church job has never been just a job.

Summer Work—Where to Sing (and Make Money) When Choirs Aren't in Session

Most church choirs, even ones at large, established music programs, go into a "summer mode" where professional choristers are not hired (or far fewer are hired). While this can create a financial conundrum for church musicians, it also opens up one's summer schedule to pursue other singing opportunities. Most of the major metropolitan areas in the United States host summer music festivals, many of which have opportunities for singers. The Boston Early Music Festival, for instance, is one of the world's most prominent early music festivals.

For professional choral singers in churches, there are three fully paid summer festival choirs, all of which select their singers by competitive audition:

> The Carmel Bach Festival is a three-week summer festival in Carmel-by-the-Sea, California. The festival's repertoire emphasizes baroque choral and orchestral music, and the festival generally hires twenty-four to twenty-eight singers for their all-professional chorale. The Virginia Best Adams Masterclass program also accepts four emerging professional soloists per year, and these singers are given both solo and choral opportunities throughout the festival. ♪

> The Oregon Bach Festival is a three-week summer festival in Eugene, Oregon. Founded by Helmuth Rilling and Royce Saltzman in 1970, the festival is now under the artistic directorship of British conductor Matthew Halls. The festival hires up to fifty-four paid singers for large major works, although many concerts engage smaller ensembles. Choristers can also audition for solo opportunities. Singers are provided with housing and all meals at the University of Oregon, which is a magnificent perk to the contract. ♪

> The Santa Fe Desert Chorale is a six-week summer festival in Santa Fe, New Mexico. Unlike the Carmel and Oregon Bach Festivals, the emphasis in on small-group a cappella singing as opposed to major works with instrumental accompaniment. The repertoire spans all eras, from the Renaissance to new music, and the Desert Chorale regularly adds recordings to its growing discography. Twenty-four singers are generally hired for the summer season. ♪

While it is extremely competitive to be selected for these opportunities, the skills valued by church choir directors—sight singing, musicianship, dependability, and the ability to blend within a choral section—are the same attributes valued in these ensembles. Many church musicians find this kind of festival singing to be a welcome "paid vacation" from the weekly commitments offered by church employment. Singers accepted into these prestigious rosters often return by invitation for successive seasons, so prospective singers may have to wait for an opening regardless of their singing ability or the quality of their audition.

ADDITIONAL RESOURCES

Listening to Church Music[5]

There is a famous phrase—sometimes attributed to actor Martin Mull—that states that "writing about music is like dancing about architecture." The point is well-taken. The music described in this book ultimately has to be experienced by the reader.

To experience the anthems, psalms, and hymns of the traditional Anglican canon, I highly recommend a series of CDs produced by Sir John Scott and the St. Paul's Cathedral Choir, all released by Hyperion Records in London: *The English Anthem* (eight volumes), *The English Hymn* (five volumes), and *The Psalms of David* (twelve volumes). The latter volume is a particularly impressive collection, gathering together recordings of all 150 Psalms sung to Anglican chant. *The English Anthem Collection: 1540–1988* (4 CDs, Alto Records) by John Harper and the Magdalen College Choir, Oxford, also offers a generous sampling of anthems. *The Treasury of English Church Music: 1100–1965* (five CDs, EMI records) offers a historical survey of English music from the medieval era to the twentieth century. Extensive liner notes are included. ♪

Priory Records (UK) is also devoted exclusively to recording and releasing church music. Notable collections released under this label include *Great Cathedral Anthems* (twelve volumes), *Magnificat and Nunc Dimittis* (twenty-one volumes), *The New English Hymnal* (twenty-three volumes), *The Psalms of David* (ten volumes), and *Te Deum and Jubilate* (four volumes). The Choir of Guilford Cathedral conducted by Barry Rose has released recordings of Stainer's *Crucifixion* and Maunder's *Olivet to Calvary*. Both works have been released as a two-CD set on the EMI label. In addition, King's College, Cambridge, has released several famous recordings of its annual Festival of Nine Lessons and Carols. All are recommended. ♪

Where to Experience Sacred Choral Music

The next time you travel to a large city, seek out the great "flagship" church music programs and attend a service. Most of the major churches and cathedrals have detailed websites that list service times, repertoire, concert series, and recitals. For the lover of English choral music, a tour of the English cathedrals is a pilgrimage that many musicians make during their lifetime. Lessons and Carols at King's College, Cambridge, is perhaps the most famous sacred choral service on the planet, and it is broadcast worldwide each year on Christmas Eve. Many smaller cities and communities also have hidden treasures. Seek out the finest music programs in your area and attend worship services or special music events offered by these churches.

Professional Organizations

The American Guild of Organists (AGO) is the large ecumenical professional organization for church musicians. The AGO publishes the *American Organist* monthly and hosts a biennial national convention (with regional conventions held during odd years). The Hymn Society of the United States and Canada is another ecumenical organization devoted to both the scholarship of hymns and the advocacy of hymn singing and composition. Their annual convention is almost always hosted at a university with "dorm-style" room and board accommodations, which makes for a particularly close-knit community over the course of the four-day event. ♪

In addition, most denominations also have their own denominational professional organizations. Many Episcopal Church musicians, for example, are members of the Association of Anglican Musicians (AAM), which hosts an annual convention and publishes the *Journal of the Association of Anglican Musicians*. While all of these organizations tend to be dominated by organists and choral conductors, singers can also benefit from many of the resources the conferences and publications provide. Professional choral singers can also benefit from membership in the American Choral Directors Association (ACDA), which publishes the *Choral Journal*, as well as Early Music America (EMA). Links to these organizations' websites and other resources are available on the companion webpage located on the NATS website. ♪

Further Reading

For a survey of the sacred choral repertoire, Dennis Shrock's *Choral Repertoire* (Oxford, 2009) is a great place to start. Chester L. Alwes's two-volume *A History of Western Choral Music* (Oxford, 2015 and 2016) also provides a detailed and exhaustive summary of the genre's history. Andrew Gant's *O Sing unto the Lord: A History of English Church Music* (Profile Books, 2015) is a highly readable account of the history of English church music with an emphasis on the anthem and canticle repertory. John Walter Hill's *Baroque Music: Music in Western Europe, 1580–1750* (Norton, 2005) provides illuminating insight into many performance practice issues germane to early music singing, including style and rhetoric.

FINAL THOUGHTS

Of all of the options available to the classical singer, choral music opportunities are perhaps the most ubiquitous. Most singers will sing in a choir at some point in their training or career, so understanding the stylistic differences between choral and solo singing is extremely important. Understanding what choral conductors and organists want is important for approaching the genre in a healthy and stylistically correct way. Choral opportunities offered by churches can not only supplement one's income but can also be deeply fulfilling experiences for many singers.

NOTES

1. The dates for all of these eras are approximate and oversimplified for the sake of categorical convenience. Certainly newer styles emerged before the boundary dates while older styles persisted into subsequent eras.

2. Secular choral genres during the medieval and Renaissance eras included secular motets, madrigals, and polyphonic secular songs (such as the French *chanson*), genres that are beyond the scope of this book.

3. An excellent one-volume resource for those interested in exploring this topic in more depth is Diarmaid MacCulloch's *Christianity: The First Three Thousand Years* (New York: Penguin, 2009).

4. Sharon Hansen et al., "Choral Directors Are from Mars and Voice Teachers Are from Venus: 'Sing from the Diaphragm' and Other Mistructions," *Choral Journal* 54, no. 11 (June/July 2014): 47.

5. This particular passage was previously published in the author's book *Welcome to Church Music & The Hymnal 1982* (New York: Morehouse Publishing, 2015).

5

CONTEMPORARY CHRISTIAN MUSIC

Sharon L. Radionoff

> Each generation of the church in each setting has the responsibility of communicating the gospel in understandable terms, considering the language and thought-forms of that setting.
>
> —Frances Schaeffer (1912–1984)

In the late 1960s a revolution was emerging in church music. Through Ralph Carmichael, noted composer and arranger for artists such as Ella Fitzgerald, Nat King Cole, Peggy Lee, and Rosemary Clooney, a new type of church music called contemporary Christian music was growing. It is noteworthy that while there were record labels such as Motown and Stax that were specifically geared toward African Americans, Light Records and Lexicon Music—founded by a Caucasian—became the label for an important early contemporary Christian music pioneer, African American gospel artist Andraé Crouch.

If music is viewed in retrospect, the word "contemporary" may seem to be somewhat of a misnomer. However, contemporary Christian music began as a current or popular style of music of the day. If a song stands the test of time, it then becomes a "classic" within the genre. As Bill Gaither once told a group of young gospel artists (as he was working on establishing a trust fund for them), "You are contemporary only today; you're going to be old, or at least traditional, in a few years, so this fund may be important to you as well."[1]

Today there is much debate about the role of contemporary Christian music in churches regarding who sings (and does not sing along) in the service. That discussion, however—which has been discussed at length in social media—is for another time.[2] Certainly music must function to facilitate a particular congregational/denominational demographic. This must be taken into account by ministers of music and worship leaders when preparing worship music for service. In a letter to Ralph Carmichael, Billy Graham once stated: "A communication medium is chosen on how well it reaches an audience. In sharing Christ and the Gospel, it is natural that the contemporary sound, with its freshness and spontaneity, has become a popular medium, reaching beyond the influence of traditional methods. Christian composers have proven that you can be musically relevant to contemporary society and yet have Gospel content with which the Holy Spirit can comply."[3]

Another excellent quotation comes from Dr. Lloyd Ogilvie, pastor of First Presbyterian Church of Hollywood. He writes:

> I believe that we need to run with our Lord on a two-legged Gospel. Musically, this means that we must have one foot in the great tradition of creative church music and the other foot squarely planted in the best of the contemporary expressions which touch all dimensions of human experience. The truly great church is one that can blend these together and not fall into the devastating tyranny of the either/or. When we can have the best of Bach, Beethoven, and Mendelssohn and couple it with the viable contemporary expression, then the richness of the total music program enables the growth of persons. Any time that a person comes to a service, he should have all dimensions of his existence touched profoundly. He should be stretched intellectually, healed emotionally, liberated volitionally, and strengthened physically. Music which is pleasing to a few esoteric musicologists may not touch the deep needs of people who have come to worship.[4]

When churches are contemplating adding a contemporary worship service or changing their current service, the issue of change—or "new" versus "old"—has the potential to be a cantankerous one among congregations, and conflicts may arise. Usually these conflicts are based on prejudices and misconceptions. In his 1993 book *I Don't Like That Music*, author Robert Mitchell discusses both sides of the aisle in regard to "new" versus "old" music. For the sake of discussion, he categorizes genres into three categories: *pop*, *ethnic* (i.e., non-Western music), and *classical*. Mitchell states that the problem occurs when we insist that we can only worship through music of our liking. Furthermore, all music has the potential to be an expression of emotion, and those in music ministry must seek to balance personal taste with the variety of music available. He states that when people say "I know what I like," perhaps they actually mean "I like what I know." He goes on to state that experiences may create a feeling of right versus wrong that may limit our perceptions of how God can work through music.[5]

Mitchell also states that change and growth are linked together and that change is painful, inevitable, valuable, and biblical. It seems that behaviors and objections toward change often include stances that—when viewed in retrospect—may be perceived as silly or unbelievable. Examples of drastic change could include events such as the Protestant Reformation, eighteenth-century music reading being taught in churches (which resulted in the formation of choir or singing schools), and the 1970s Catholic community, which was by and large upset that the Mass was no longer being delivered in Latin.

When looking at the inevitability of change, John Calvin and John Knox protested at the price of the expensive robes and clothing clergy wore. Therefore, they wore their "work clothes" when they preached, which were black robes with white collars. Martin Luther used a love song text and set it to music, which became a much-loved hymn: "O Sacred Head, Now Wounded." I would venture to say that black robes, white collars, and the hymn mentioned above do not hold their original meanings. Mitchell here illustrates that meaning can change with the passing of time. It is also interesting to note a tract written in 1712 by Rev. Thomas Symmes of Bradford, Massachusetts, which included ten points on why the "new" way of teaching music was unfavorable. My favorites were objection numbers 6 and 7:

> (6) The names given to the notes [*do, re, mi*, etc.] are bawdy, yea blasphemous; and
> (7) It is a needless way since our fathers got to heaven without.[6]

"New" may be disparaged and rejected at the outset but over time may become part of the musical experience in the church. Mitchell states that the church exists in a changing society, and therefore to change nothing is to change indeed. Also, change may be useful in bringing our spirits out of a rote behavior and lead us back to meaningful worship. Eugene Nida of the American Bible Society discusses the potential pitfalls of familiarity and predictability in his book *Message and Mission*. He states that "if we can predict the occurrence of a particular word or expression, then that word carries very little information or impact."[7]

Mitchell attributes change being biblical to many scriptures that declare "sing a new song," such as Psalms 33, 90, 98, 144, and 149. He further states that while God remains the same, we are to sing in new ways, which we can find not only in the Old Testament scripture but in the New Testament as well (Matthew 13:52). Mitchell does caution that there may be possible unfavorable aspects of change and that to change simply for the sake of change may not lead toward improvement. Consideration must be given toward the useful function of a particular musical genre or expression for a given congregation. There also needs to be a deliberate blending of old and new.[8]

LITURGICAL ORIGINS

Historical Context

Contemporary Christian music has its origins in the gospel tradition. The history of gospel music is rich, varied, and diverse and includes Southern gospel, traditional black gospel, and contemporary gospel. In its earliest days, Southern gospel music was strongly influenced by early nineteenth-century hymn singing (especially the hymns of Sir Isaac Watts from England), and there were regular camp meetings during which hymns were sung. After the Civil War, there was separation of white people and African Americans in worship, and this had an effect on congregational service music.

In 1899, we see the birth of Thomas A. Dorsey and the beginning of the blues and over the next two decades came the birth of jazz. Prior to what many consider to be the "golden age" of gospel music, Viv Broughton—in her book *Too Close to Heaven*—discusses that gospel music boomed as society collapsed. She notes that during the Great Depression, "the church movement focused on being a refuge for the dispossessed."[9] This was a time period that marked a liturgical phenomenon as well as a musical one. There were many greats during this time, including Dorsey and his most well-known protégé, Mahalia Jackson.

At this time, the blues were thought of as songs of despair, while gospel music offered songs of hope. Gospel singers and songwriters were "quite literally ministers of the Christian gospel, communicators of good news through a new medium of song."[10] There is a song, written by Dorsey, that was called a "gospel anthem"; part spiritual uplift and part blues, it was entitled "Precious Lord." Today it remains a standard and appears in hymnals across many denominations. ♪

Lee Poquette, veteran minister of music, composer, arranger, and producer, outlines the origin and growth of contemporary Christian music into three main historical groups: Group 1 encompasses 1940–1960, Group 2 spans 1961–1989, and Group 3 takes us from 1990 to the present.[11] The next section of this chapter will provide a brief overview of each group along with an enumeration of a person or trend of importance during the time period discussed.

Group 1: 1940–1960

The "golden era," or Group 1, encompasses the period from 1940 to 1960. The years during—and especially after—World War II were a blossoming time for churches to grow due to the work and spiritual ethic of the era. Also, the dissemination of music became much more accessible as a result of the emergence of television in American households. It is during this time that Billy Graham became the first of what we now call "televangelists," and there were noted musicians such as pianist Dino Kartsonakis who were introduced to the masses via television. Also there are notable songs such as "How Great Thou Art" (Stuart K. Hine's translation) that were hits during this time. On the East Coast, there was the music of Fred Bock; in the Midwest, John W. Peterson; on the West Coast, Ralph Carmichael; and in the South there was Kurt Kaiser. Please refer to Ralph Carmichael's biographical inlay to examine the life and lasting influence of this golden era veteran on the church music world. ♪

Featured Artist from Group 1: RALPH CARMICHAEL

Ralph Carmichael can rightly be called the grandfather of contemporary Christian music. He came from a family of preachers and missionaries, and his own father was an Assembly of God preacher who held positions in Quincy, Illinois, and Fargo, North Dakota. The family moved to San Jose, California, when Ralph was twelve years old. Carmichael had a variety of musical influences from a very young age. He studied the violin and his father took him to many concerts, at which he heard a wide variety of musical genres. The more he experienced musically, the more he began to think that the typical music he was hearing in churches was weak. He left home in 1944 at the age of seventeen to attend Southern California Bible College, following in the family footsteps of becoming a minister. At that time, he did not realize that "minister of music" was a career option, so he felt that his choices were limited to being a pastor, evangelist, or missionary. From the very beginning of his college experience, he was often asked to provide music for various student gatherings, and he never said no.

In his 1986 book, *He's Everything to Me*, Carmichael recounts that during this time he made "crude attempts" at arranging. He would write embellishments for hymns and gospel songs that he felt amplified the message or created a mood. He also experimented with a mixed quintet of two girls and three guys, which he called the Modernaires. Already at that time his "new" music was considered "too worldly," and it was often not well received in the church. During his college years, he would often stay up late working on music and would not attend classes, which led to a period of time when he was put on probation at school.

In 1946, Carmichael became the choirmaster of Calvary Assembly in Inglewood, California, even though he had very little experience directing choirs at the time. One of his duties was to write a new choir arrangement each week. He also played violin on a weekly radio program called *The Family Bible Hour*. Carmichael credits the previous choirmaster at Calvary, Bob Bowman, as an important mentor during this time.

In the years that followed, Carmichael simultaneously wrote music for Hollywood, church, and television shows (*What's the Name of the Song*, 1964). He also wrote music for film scores for the Billy Graham World Wide Pictures team, which included Billy Graham, George Beverly Shea, Cliff Barrows, Ted Smith, Dick Ross, and Jim Collier. Carmichael was commissioned to write the music for Billy Graham's first movie, *The Restless Ones* (1965); he wrote three songs: "The Restless Ones," "The Number Song," and "He's Everything to Me." Carmichael realized that changes were needed for the music to be relevant, so he went into the studio with a Fender bass, a set of drums, two guitars, and a keyboard. This did not sit well with executives at first, but the song "He's Everything to Me" was soon picked up and sung by kids across the nation. It has since become a classic of contemporary Christian music. ♪

After these successes, Bufe Karraker, director of the organization Youth for Christ, asked Carmichael to create a title song for an upcoming movie. The title song, "Love Is Surrender," was not accepted by producers, so he wrote another title song for the movie entitled "The Searching Generation" in 1968. Interestingly, the song "Love Is Surrender" was released by the famous brother/sister duo The Carpenters with some lyric modification on their 1970 album *Close to You*. ♪

Ralph Carmichael wrote his first children's musical with Kurt Kaiser, director at Word, Inc. *Tell It Like It Is* was recorded in Fort Worth, Texas, in early 1969, and albums and books were shipped to retail stores across the United States and Canada. The musical took off like wildfire and was branded as a "folk musical." (This label would eventually cause problems.) Ralph began to give workshops about this new "folk music" form of contemporary Christian music. This music was called "a tool of the devil" by some, and he was accused of bringing rock 'n' roll music into the church with the ulterior motive of "desecrating God's house and corrupting the young people." Jarrell McCracken told Ralph that Word did not want to produce and release contemporary children's music, so Ralph created a new label to release all of the experimental music called Light Records, a division of Lexicon Music, Inc. ♪

In the late 1960s, Carmichael was introduced to Andraé Crouch, and in 1968 the first Andraé Crouch album on the Light Records label was recorded. This was the first recording artist to be distributed by Word, and to Ralph Carmichael's knowledge the first black gospel record released by a white gospel label. This label went on the record such luminaries as the Continental Singers (*Share*), Jimmy Owens (*Tell the World*), Dino (*He Touched Me*), The Good News Circle (*Growing Together*), The Winans (*Yesterday, Today and Tomorrow*), The Archers (*Stand Up*), Bryan Duncan (*Holy Rollin'*), Resurrection Band (*Colors*), Sweet Comfort Band (*Cutting Edge*), Shirley Caesar (*After 40 Years: Still Sweeping Through the City*), Jessica Reedy (*From the Heart*), and many recordings from Andraé Crouch and the Disciples. ♪

In 1971, Carmichael was asked to speak before the general assembly of the National Religious Broadcasters (NRB). The topic was "New Trends in Gospel Music." It was not well received, and naysayers and audience attendees on either side of the discussion were yelling constantly during the presentation. It is noteworthy that in 1984 an outspoken naysayer who attended the 1971 presentation recanted and gave a positive, proactive statement in regard to new music, much to the credit of both Ralph Carmichael and the naysayer.

At the beginning of this "new" music dissemination, Ralph Carmichael assumed that radio broadcasters would be on his side and was surprised to learn that this was not the case. As he mulled over how to get broadcasters interested in contemporary Christian music, he conceived of a new radio format and created the Light Radio Division of Lexicon Music. A half-hour show entitled *Check the Record* would play cuts and interview contemporary recording artists from Light Records. It is interesting to note that it actually took five years for this idea to catch on and become popular. Years later he was invited back to the NRB to present music for the opening night, where he presented the contemporary musical released by Light recording artists Jimmy and Carol Owens entitled *If My People*. This had a much more positive response than his first experience at the NRB in 1971.

Carmichael states that he had both the pleasure and the pain of introducing musical expressions from outside the church (such as jazz) into worship at the beginning of the gospel revolution. He further states that intrinsic to the process was the combining of sacred words—God's unchanging message—and truly secular music, that is to say, music of the people or pop music. An important part of the dynamic in operation was the fact that the church was speaking with a kind of music that was generally thought of as "non-sacred."

Finally, it is noteworthy that the "Great Gospel Concert" at the Hollywood Bowl—a mega-concert put together by Carmichael on September 4, 1976—overlaps with the new happenings of the "Group 2" era outlined in this chapter.

Much of the content is drawn from Carmichael's book, *He's Everything to Me* (Waco, TX: Word Books Publisher, 1986).

Group 2: 1961–1989

Across the United States, there were many things happening during this second era of contemporary Christian music. There was a paradigm shift during 1965 and 1966 due to the Vietnam War, and television wanted to capture a broader audience. The teams of Bill and Linda Cates and Ted and Betsy Overman in Nashville wrote the first "folk" youth musical in 1968. Also in 1969 there began to be a movement by Chuck Smith that reached the surfer/hippie population in Costa Mesa called Chapel by the Sea. ♪

Most notably there was the rise of Bill Gaither and Gaither Music, the Jesus movement (beginning in 1969–1970), the praise music movement (during the 1970s and early 1980s), and—in the mid-1980s—crossover music. The Jesus movement in Nashville grew out of a discontent with "status quo" evangelical Christianity. Some of the leaders of this movement were Keith Green ("To Obey Is Better Than Sacrifice"), Honeytree ("The Way I Feel"), Barry McGuire ("Pay the Piper"), and the group the Imperials, started by Jake Hess in 1964. The Imperials have had a variety of singers over the years and are still together as a group (famous albums include *He Touched Me*, *No Shortage*, *Big God*, *Back to the Roots*, and *Still Standing*). Also, on the "rock 'n' roll" side, there were leaders such as Larry Norman (some refer to him as the beginning of the Jesus movement with his famous saying, "We need a lot more of Jesus and a lot less rock 'n' roll," as well as his album, *Upon This Rock*), Randy Stonehill (*Born Twice*), and the group Petra ("The Coloring Song"). Other important groups were 2nd Chapter of Acts ("Easter Song") and Truth (numerous albums). Another important solo artist who has written for ensembles as well as solo works is Ken Medema ("Come Let Us Reason" and "Moses"). There was also a youth movement in Waco under the leadership of Louis Giglio at Baylor University. This youth movement, currently based at Texas A&M, is called Impact and currently has more than five thousand students participate every Tuesday evening. ♪

The "praise music" movement was an important outcropping of Group 2. One corridor was that of Hillsong ("Shout to the Lord") with Maranatha as a precursor ("Glorify Thy Name"). While Maranatha was of British influence, Hillsong began in Australia, and there was also the Assembly of God/Pentecostal movement, such as the Integrity Music Group. Songs that came out of this movement include "Awesome God," "El Shaddai,"

"We Will Glorify," "He's Everything to Me," "The New 23rd," "Bless His Holy Name," "Soon and Very Soon," "My Tribute," "Easter Song," "There Is a Redeemer," "Thy Word," "How Majestic Is Your Name," "How Beautiful," "The Final Word," "People Need the Lord," "The Majesty and Glory of Your Name," "Sing Your Praise to the Lord," "Children of the Living God," and "Above All." This list is certainly not comprehensive but is meant to give examples of this movement. ♪

One of the main artists associated with the "crossover music" of the mid-1980s is Amy Grant. This type of music did not start out as music between genres but rather consisted of songs that talked about "love" as a universal concept; lyrically these songs do not mention God or Jesus, such as in Grant's song "Find a Way." She eventually transitioned to mainstream popular music and had her first big hit, "Baby, Baby," in 1991. ♪

Other influential artists from this era included David Meece, Glad, Larnelle Harris, Wayne Watson, Steve Camp, Sandi Patty, Steve Green, Twyla Paris, Michael Card, Michael W. Smith, Russ Taff, Rich Mullens, Ray Bolz, Steven Curtis Chapman, Margaret Becker, Crystal Lewis, Kim Hill, The Newsboys, DC Talk, and Michelle Wagner. However, there was a seismic shift during the late 1980s toward an artist-driven culture. This was due to youth festivals, the crisscrossing of Bible teachers across the nations (and the artists that traveled with them), and airplay on Christian radio. ♪

Group 3: 1990–present

Group 3 includes the most recent decades and represents an artist-driven era in the church. During this era, there are both large venues and house concerts for worship, and we see the rise of the megachurch, a significant development that will be discussed in the following section of this chapter. Along with the megachurch, there is also the houseplant church as well as the modern-day influence of Christianity into mainstream rock.

Groups and solo artists who contributed to this artist-driven era included the following: 4HIM, Susan Hill, Ron Kenoly, Nicole C. Mullen, Michael English, Cindy Morgan, Point of Grace, Wes King, East to West, Sixpence None the Richer, Bob Carlisle, Cheri Keaggy, Greg Long, Aaron Jeoffrey, Sierra, Carolyn Arends, Jars of Clay, Paul Wilbur, Pam Thum, Scott Krippayne, Big Tent Revival, Avalon, Jaci Valásquez, Michelle Tumes, Third Day, Sara Paulson, Delirious?, Fernando Ortega,

Featured Artist from Group 2: BILL GAITHER

Bill Gaither was born in 1936 and grew up in a farming family of Irish and German heritage in Alexandria, Indiana, a rural community with approximately six thousand residents. He began piano lessons at the age of six, and while working on the farm growing up, he listened to gospel singers on the radio. He had a variety of early musical influences including the Dixie Four Quartet, Stamps Quartet, WSM country radio station (Nashville), and Jake Hess, the lead singer of the Statesman Quartet. With the Dixie Four, Gaither loved the rhythmic boogie-woogie style. He was also intrigued by the opportunity to subscribe to receive the music of the Stamps Quartet, and in 1953, he attended the Stamps School. He decided that he wanted to begin a career in gospel music, and he and three others formed a quartet called The Pathfinder. Ultimately, this venture was not successful. He decided to get a job and go to college to major in English literature. While there, he created the Gaither Trio with his siblings. When he graduated from college, he taught English in a junior high school before going back to get his graduate degree in guidance counseling.

Gaither wrote his first song entitled "I've Been to Calvary," which the Golden Keys Quartet sang in concert. This was the beginning of his song publishing career. Ben Speer (of The Speers) published Gaither's first song, and he was soon on his way to a successful publishing career. Gaither soon decided to create his own publishing company called the Gaither Music Publishing Company. During this time, he took a new English teaching job at Alexandria High School and met and married his wife Gloria, who taught French there. ♪

Gloria Gaither was to become an integral part of the Gaither ministry in songwriting and publishing. She even became a reluctant performer and recording artist with the Gaither Trio. The first song that Bill and Gloria wrote together was "Have You Had a Gethsemane," which was recorded by Doug Oldham. Doug Oldham sang many of their songs, but one of the most well-known is "He Touched Me," which is now considered to be a classic of the genre. This song was later sung by The Imperials (founded by Jake Hess), and it is interesting to note that this group was often the opening act for Elvis Presley, who listened to and loved the song. ♪

Bill and Gloria Gaither soon met Bob Benson (of the Benson Music Company in Nashville) and the producer of their first album, Bob MacKenzie. They soon had another hit song called "There's Something about That Name." In 1970, Bill Gaither and Bob MacKenzie formed the Paragon

Association, which brought to light new singer-songwriters such as Gary S. Paxton, Michael W. Smith, Scott Wesley Brown, and DeGarmo and Key. After several years, the association dissolved, but the friendship, musical creativity, and productivity between the Gaithers and MacKenzie continued. MacKenzie continued to be instrumental in connecting Bill and Gloria with other musicians in the industry. Other memorable songs at this time included "Let's Just Praise the Lord"—which became an anthem-like song at the Jesus festivals of the 1970s—and the musical *Alleluia*, written with Ronn Huff. This work became a national and international success and has been performed in many countries, including China. ♪

The Gaither Trio continued to tour and had many notable backup singers, including Sandi Patty and Steve Green. While on tour in 1981, the Gaither Vocal Band was created. Gaither states that this band is difficult to categorize as it does not fit neatly into only one genre or style. The original group included Bill Gaither, Gary McSpadden, Steve Green, and Lee Young, but since has fluctuated in membership to include artists such as Larnelle Harris, Michael English, Mark Lowry, Guy Penrod, David Phelps, and Russ Taff. ♪

During the 1980s, there was a rift among Christian music artists as there seemed to be a "dividing line" between contemporary pop/rock and Southern gospel. In 1991, fifty-five-year-old Bill Gaither could sense this shift. He had always wanted to have the Gaither Vocal Band record a Southern gospel album. He decided to call upon several Southern gospel musicians, including Hovie Lister (The Statesman), Glenn Payne and George Younce (The Cathedrals), J. D. Sumner, and other well-known and experienced gospel artists. He decided to call the album *Homecoming*, and it was recorded in Nashville. They also decided to shoot a video as well, and this became the genesis for the television reunion show called *Gaither Homecoming* and its sequels.

Much of the content is drawn from the book *It's More Than the Music: Life Lessons on Friends, Faith, and What Matters Most* by Bill Gaither with Ken Abraham (London: Hodder & Stoughton, 2003).

Chris Rice, Caedmon's Call, Jennifer Knapp, and Phillips, Craig and Dean. Other artists that were influences in the late 1990s included Nichole Nordeman, Selah, the Martins, FFH, Matt Redman, Paul Baloche, Natalie Grant, Ginny Owens, The Katinas, SonicFlood, Philip and Natalie LaRue, Jill Phillips, and Lenny LeBlanc. During the first decade of the twenty-first century, new groups and artists emerged, including Plus One, Rachel Lampa, Mark Schultz, Wayne Kirkpatrick, Michael Card, Sara Groves, MercyMe, Joy Williams, Shaun Groves, Jonathan Lippman, Jump5, Ten Shekel Shirt, Superchick, David Phelps, Alethia, Casting Crowns, and the Paul Colman Trio. The hip-hop artist Lecrae has also been an enormous influence in recent years and has been the recipient of Dove, Stellar, and Grammy awards. These large-venue artists lead worship not only at conferences and festivals but are also featured on the megachurch circuit. ♪

Megachurches

Christianity Today defines a megachurch as any church with an average weekly attendance of two thousand or greater. The United States currently has more than one thousand such churches, and these places of worship nurture a large segment of the evangelical Christian community. The Hartford Institute for Religion Research has created a database that includes some 1,668 churches defined as megachurches. Although megachurches are something of an American invention, they can now be found all over the world.

Some of today's largest and most well-known American megachurches are the following:

Table 5.1. American Megachurches

Church	City	Pastor	Weekly Attendance
Lakewood Church	Houston, TX	Joel Osteen	43,500
North Point Community Church	Alpharetta, GA	Andy Stanley	30,629
Life.Church	Edmond, OK	Craig Goeschel	30,000
Gateway Church	Southlake, TX	Robert Morris	28,000
Willow Creek Community Church	South Barrington, IL	Bill Hybels	25,743
Fellowship Church	Grapevine, TX	Ed Young	24,162
Christ's Church of the Valley	Peoria, AZ	Don Wilson	23,395
NewSpring Church	Anderson, SC	Perry Noble	23,055

Note: Pastors and weekly attendance figures are from 2015 and were taken from the Hartford Institute for Religion Research.

Many contemporary Christian artists have emerged from this megachurch culture. Some of the most well-known names include Cindy Cruse Ratcliff, Steve Crawford, Da'dra Crawford Greathouse, and Job Gonzalez (Lakewood), Kari Jobe (Gateway), and Jim and Carol Cymbala (Brooklyn Tabernacle).[12] ♪

In Houston, one finds examples of the megachurch as well as its two variations: bilingual megachurches (English/Spanish) and multisite churches—a church that is made up of several campuses. Lakewood Church is an example of a single-site megachurch. It is currently the largest megachurch in America with a sanctuary seating sixteen thousand, and it televises and livestreams services all over the world through Sirius radio. There are three weekend English services—one on Saturday and two on Sunday—as well as one Wednesday service. There is also one Sunday Spanish service and one Thursday evening service.

Champion Forest Baptist Church in Houston is an example of a multisite megachurch with a main campus (whose sanctuary holds approximately 4,300 people) and several smaller campuses. Their pastoral staff includes Caucasian, African American, and Hispanic pastors, and their choirs and worship teams perform in both English and Spanish. Worship pastor Brent Dyer states that the English and Spanish services are highly integrated, and that they are "multicultural, multiethnic, and have a modern blended approach leaning toward contemporary music." He further states that they "have made a strategic choice to be multicultural, inclusive and diverse because we live in one of the most diverse populations in the nation. Our philosophy regarding the broad spectrum of music is to be in the 'big middle.'"[13]

West University Baptist church in Houston warrants a bit of discussion. It is not a megachurch, but it is an example of a multisite/multilingual church. While smaller (main West University main sanctuary seats 500 and CrossPoint holds 498), it is an interesting example of two campuses that provide a multilingual experience. There are ethnically diverse pastoral staffs and congregations. Both campuses offer a contemporary worship experience, while West University also offers a traditional worship experience as well.

Houseplant Churches

Vineyard Fellowship is an example of a "houseplant" church, and their mission is "church planting," or the establishment of churches. Vineyard is an international organization with various national headquarters. In South Africa, their vision is "to establish a church planting and renewal movement in Southern and Central Africa . . . in pursuit of

Figure 5.1. Lakewood Church sanctuary. *Courtesy of Sharon L. Radionoff*

Figure 5.2. Lakewood Church: A view from the soundboard. *Courtesy of Sharon L. Radionoff*

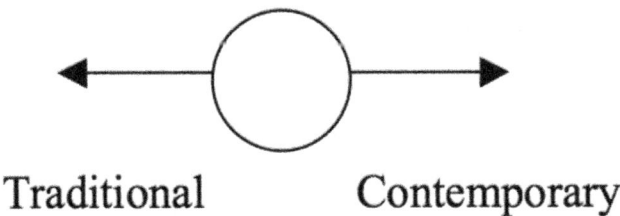

Figure 5.3. "The Big Middle." *Courtesy of Sharon L. Radionoff*

the mission given in Luke 4:16–18, Matthew 28:19–20, and Acts 1:8."[14] The mission of Vineyard in the United States is to "exist as an organic extension of the Vineyard church movement in the USA. We are, in a phrase, from the church, for the church."[15] They go on to state that they are not a music company first and foremost but rather a nonprofit worship ministry. ♪

Mainstream Rock

Finally, it is of interest that in Group 3 there are some very famous mainstream rock bands and individuals who have deliberate Christian themes in their lyrics even though they are not under a Christian label. These artists include Lenny Kravitz, U2, Switchfoot, Kings of Leon, POD, Evanescence, and Lifehouse.

MUSICAL CHARACTERISTICS

So how do we define contemporary Christian music? Some consider the genre to be anything other than traditional choral music and organ-accompanied hymns, while others consider only current music contemporary, excluding classic songs that were written in gospel, rock, or some other style. We therefore have a large umbrella that covers a multitude of genres. As Ralph Carmichael stated, he had both "the pleasure and the pain of introducing musical genres outside of the church into the church."[16]

Current contemporary Christian music ranges from rock to pop, R&B, gospel, Motown, Latin, and hip-hop. Communities representative of this eclectic mix range from houseplant churches (Vineyard Fellowship) to arena-style megachurches that seat approximately sixteen thousand each service (Lakewood). Two churches that have brought contemporary music to the forefront are Brooklyn Tabernacle and Houston's Lakewood Church, the latter of which has a choir roster of approximately 650 members. Cindy Cruse Ratcliff, Lakewood's senior worship leader, defines their style of contemporary music as "diverse and eclectic."[17] She notes that the music often changes style within a song. A good example of a mixed style would be the song "Gloria" from Lakewood's album *We Speak to Nations*. This song has a Latin salsa feel but also incorporates the traditional choral "Gloria" from the Christmas hymn "Angels We Have Heard on High." ♪

Examples of different genres may be examined in the following: Hillsong represents a pop style ("Shout to the Lord"); Vineyard Fellowship, a rock style ("Surrender"); the Pamela York Trio ("I Know That My Redeemer Lives—Glory, Hallelujah!") and Take 6 ("David & Goliath"), jazz; Al Green, R&B ("The Lord Will Make a Way"); Israel and New Breed, contemporary gospel ("You Are Good"); and Ricky Skaggs, country ("Somebody's Prayin'"). Also unique to Houston and its surrounding areas is the "cowboy church" (Lonestar Cowboy Church), with traditional country styles. Finally, Babbie Mason ("Carry On, Trust His Heart") and Anointed ("The Call," "Revive Us") are representative of crossover artists that move across genre boundaries of gospel and contemporary Christian music. Currently crossover is often thought of within the context of English and Spanish lyrics as well as the fusion of Latin influences into contemporary musical styles. ♪

TRAINING REQUIREMENTS

Training and preparation for the field of contemporary Christian music is wide and varied. One can learn by "doing it" and participating in the industry (Bill Gaither, Steve Crawford, and Da'dra Crawford Greathouse) or through life experience or growing up as part of a touring family (Cindy Cruse Ratcliff), college and university programs (Belmont, Liberty, and Baylor), online college programs (Mid-America Christian

University), and institutes (Cruise Institute of the Arts, Catharsis Worship School, and the CanZion Institute) dedicated to the preparation of worship leaders and music ministers. These programs range greatly in terms of content and preparation. Some programs include music history, ministerial training, choral music, ear training, praise team leadership, and technology. Often, however, there is no curriculum for voice pedagogy and most often no courses dedicated to better understanding the voice or vocal health. The aspiring worship leader often must acquire these skills elsewhere.

The contemporary Christian singer must wear many hats to be successful. He or she may be a worship leader, singer-songwriter, or recording artist. The worship leader often leads praise and worship at multiple services onsite as well as at offsite events, from small venues to ones as large as Madison Square Garden or Hillsong Australia. As singer-songwriter, the worship leader may write for church or solo projects. Touring for personal ministry-related events also occurs.

Here is a brief "laundry list" schedule of what a contemporary worship leader may do during a typical week (Tuesday through Sunday): organizational meetings, song list creation, rehearsal with the band or worship team, choir rehearsal, lyric sheet creation, CD creation (with a program like GarageBand for singers to pick up and rehearse with), midweek service leadership, out-of-town events, sound checks, multiple weekend services (including meeting and greeting between services), and Sirius radio livestreams after the services are done. This list does not even mention songwriting, recording, or family responsibilities. This wide variety and amount of activities necessitates keeping the vocal system balanced and aligned.

VOCAL TECHNIQUE AND CONTEMPORARY CHRISTIAN MUSIC[18]

Because contemporary Christian music is a subset of commercial music at large, different vocal outcomes are desired for "commercial" versus "classical" genres. Let's examine some comparisons of the things that create differences between classical and commercial genres. In classical singing, it is desirable to elongate the vowel or rather "sing" on the vowel, while much commercial music is based on speech pattern so elongation of a vowel would sound awkward and unnatural. In classical singing, it is desirable to maximize the resonance tract to achieve the "singer's formant"—the "ring" in the voice that allows a singer to sing over an orchestra without the aid of a microphone—for acoustic purposes on stage, while in commercial music, a microphone is often used and the singer's formant is not the main acoustic goal. In classical singing, vibrato is considered a desired and omnipresent element of the "classical sound," while in commercial singing, vibrato is often employed as a stylistic tool to be used at the end of a phrase.

In singing, there must be a beginning point in order to gain a level of excellence. There are many labels for this beginning set of skills, including "fundamentals," "basic mechanics," or "groundwork." All of these terms refer to baseline skills necessary to create an efficient and beneficial foundation upon which one can build. Prior to examining the basic mechanics, it is essential to understand the systems used to create "sound production." These basic systems are the same no matter what style of music a singer is performing.

Here is an analogy that may be helpful: in the book *Baking with the Cake Boss* by Buddy Valastro, basic cake recipes are found that all consist of common, main ingredients such as flour, sugar, eggs, and some type of butter, oil, or shortening.[19] Likewise, when we examine the human voice, there are basic ingredients or systems, as well as basic mechanics.

Let us briefly review the basic systems and physiology of sound production. The creation of basic sound incorporates three main systems: the respiratory system, the phonatory system, and the supraglottic vocal tract (or resonance tract). Along with this is also the articulatory system. The impulse for making sound begins in the cerebral cortex of the brain, and then information is sent through two branches of the tenth cranial nerve to the appropriate laryngeal muscles. During phonation, the ear picks up sound produced by the vocal system and regulates the shaping of the vocal tract to sculpt the sound. This feedback system is used by the brain to try to match the *actual* sound of the voice with the sound *intended* by the communication centers of the brain that generate the voice.

In regard to vocal styles and stylistic tools, there are many vocal sounds that can be made and some sounds have the potential to be

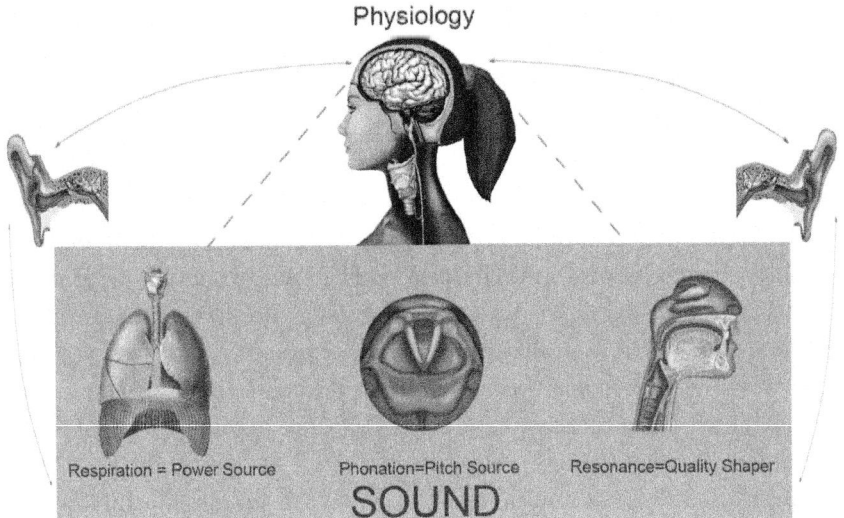

Figure 5.4. Sound production and feedback system. *Blue Tree Publishing*

harmful. For example, grit, growling, screaming, and glottal onsets are stylistic effects found in rock, country, and pop music. These tools must be used with the least amount of tension needed to avert damage. Also, if used too often, a tense onset may become part of one's technique and no longer employed just as a stylistic tool. These habits often creep into the speaking voice as well, compounding a singer's vocal challenges.

It is possible to create a desired vocal tool such as a "grit" or "growl" in more than one way. The key to longevity in one's singing career is finding and understanding the "systems balance" and alignment for singing before making stylistic choices. Balance must be attained before power, agility, or style. This analogy can be clearly seen in sports. For example, a gymnast stretches and finds his or her center of gravity first—whether it be on the balance beam or floor exercise—before doing any flips, turns, or difficult combinations. One might consider a gymnast foolhardy if he or she were to attempt difficult movements before balancing the body and mind. Singers, however, are notorious for ignoring balance and moving immediately to agility, power, and style. They even attempt to warm up by singing what they consider to be an easy song. There are so many variables to be aligned that it is critical for the voice professional to find his or her systems balance and alignment.

In contemporary Christian styles, amplification is used for the singers as well as for the instrumentalists. The volume of energy created by all of this amplification can trick the singer into feeling like he or she needs to sing louder in order to be heard. This happens more when there are no monitors for the singers, but it can happen even with monitors—ear buds as well as "wedge style." Many singers who use ear buds actually prefer to use only one in order to "hear the room" and feel the audience energy.

A point must also be made regarding vibrato. When singers try to create the contemporary sound, they frequently do this by using tension to stop vibrato to create a "straight tone" or "pop style." To sing with less vibrato often takes more airflow, not less. This same issue of inefficient production can be found in churches that ask sopranos to produce a young boy-like sound in order to emulate the "English cathedral" sound. Efficient production and free singing are always desirable.

Balance and alignment of the vocal instrument, comprising the body/mind/spirit connection, is just the beginning for the performer. If one knows where his or her center of balance is, then one can experiment with how far one may go from the central balance point for coloration and effect while still maintaining one's technique. It truly does not matter what style of music someone sings—what matters is the balance of the voice. If a singer knows his or her balance point, then he or she will be able to experiment with breath, resonance, articulation, and even straight tone or delayed vibrato for coloration and effect. It is no different than a painter having a palette with many colors to choose from in order to create nuance in his or her expression.

REPERTOIRE AND RESOURCES

In regard to repertoire and resources, there are large publishing companies, independent artists, and strictly online companies, as well as Christian Copyright License International (CCLI). Many professionals and amateurs involved in church work are familiar with CCLI. One of this resource's main offerings is a church copyright license that permits churches to use everything in its database. This includes use for computer projections, song sheets, bulletin inserts, recording the service, and more. There are options for single ministries, multisite events, and mobile applications. Licensing for music use is not, however, the only thing that CCLI offers. Choices of separate components include the following:

1. SongSelect: Provides transposable chord sheets, lead sheets, and vocal sheets, plus lyrics and audio samples for top CCLI songs.
2. Rehearse License: Allows one to legally copy and share commercial audio recordings and own custom recordings for rehearsal purposes.
3. Stream License: Allows one to legally stream or podcast live worship services over the Internet.
4. ScreenVue: Provides movie clips and clip ideas for sermons and teaching illustrations.
5. Church Video License: Allows one to legally show movies for sermons, Sunday school, classes, and special events. An interesting report is also collected that displays CCLI's top twenty-five songs by churches over the last six-month reporting period.

The website praisecharts.com was established in 1998. This resource sprang from a need for sharing worship music of those such as Louis Giglio where traditional publishers could not handle the need. It started out offering lead sheets and quick charts/chord charts and in recent years has expanded to include orchestration. In November of 2015, the website unveiled "Blessed Assurance—New Hymns from Fanny Crosby," a collection of unfinished and never-before-published Fanny Crosby hymns.

Publishing companies include current houses such as Brentwood Benson, Integrity, Word, and RPM/Dream Worship in addition to well-known houses such as Lillenas, JW Pepper, and Hal Leonard. Brentwood Benson is a division of Capitol Christian Music Group and is considered to be the world's leading Christian choral and worship music company. In November of 2015, Bill Gaither released a new musical, *Let the Glory Come Down*, arranged by Geron Davis and Bradley Knight. The work was premiered by the five-hundred-voice choir of Prestonwood Baptist Church in Dallas. It is also important to note that the publishing industry is currently both consumer driven and institution driven. The consumer-driven aspect relates to what is bought and sold at bookstores, and the institution-driven aspect relates to publishers targeting a particular market.

Another important resource is the Knoxville, Tennessee, Music Library, which has some thirty thousand titles of old stock, or retired print music. It is a resource where churches and composers can send their libraries and/or print music when it is no longer being used. JW Pepper and other publishers also send music samples and demos to this repository.

Published songs by current artists can be more difficult to access. Resources like CD Baby, iTunes, ArtistTrax, and lead sheets found on personal websites can bring new songs to light for the individual. New artists and new music can also be heard at festivals and conferences such as those held at Estes Park, Green Lake Wisconsin, Baylor, Ozarks (Knoxville), Gateway, and SongFest. There are also programs and celebrations geared toward young people. Under the umbrella of the Billy Graham Association, Franklin Graham holds "Youth Festivals." In November 2015, one of these festivals was held in Japan, and the musicians included Michael W. Smith, Hillsong Worship, Tommy Coomes Band, Lena Maria Klingvall, Dennis Agajanian, Night de Light, Saluki, New Wings, and Tomoko and Reiko Shiohama. Other festivals have been held in Brazil, Oklahoma, Alabama, Ukraine, Florida, Spain, and the Faroe Islands. Will Graham (son of Franklin) has hosted celebrations in Canada, West Virginia, Arizona, Tanzania, Kentucky, and the Philippines. There are also many women's conferences such as "Women of Faith" and "Inspire Women," as well as conferences hosted by Beth Moore and Joyce Meyer. These conferences also give a platform to Christian artists who will have influence in the mainstream church. There are other conferences that are led by traveling pastors such as Bishop T. D. Jakes, David Jeremiah, and Tony Evans.

Classic hits from the contemporary Christian music repertoire can be heard on the online radio station "CCM Classic," which features a biography about the featured artist—such as The Archers or Keith Green—as well as songs that have become classics in the genre. An excellent discography of classics can be found in the 2005 book *A City on a Hilltop: A History of Contemporary Christian Music* by Daniel J. Mount. It covers the years from 1961 to 2005 and covers solo artists, groups, choirs, ensembles, organizations, label collections, and praise and worship labels.

FINAL THOUGHTS

Contemporary Christian music, as we have discussed, is a wide umbrella that encompasses many genres and styles. Singers who pursue this profession find themselves in a very demanding and often high-profile field, whether wearing one or several of the hats described above. The level of expectation and output is high and a gold-medal status is anticipated. There is also a high level of visibility, job expectation, and stress to go along with it. Voice balancing is key for vocal health under this level of pressure, voice loading, and overall stress. More about voice balancing may be found in two articles for *VOICEPrints*, the journal of New York Singing Teachers Association (NYSTA), entitled "The SVS and Contemporary Christian Music—Parts I & II."[20]

NOTES

1. Bill Gaither with Ken Abraham, *It's More Than The Music: Life Lessons on Friends, Faith, and What Matters Most* (London: Hodder & Stoughton, 2003), 249.
2. Sharon L Radionoff, "The SVS and Contemporary Christian Music—Part 1: A Brief Overview," *VOICEPrints: The Official Journal of NYSTA* 12, no. 4 (2015): 4–5.
3. Gaither, *It's More Than the Music*, 249.
4. Ralph Carmichael, *He's Everything to Me* (Waco, TX: Word Books Publisher, 1986), 160.
5. Robert H. Mitchell, *I Don't Like That Music* (Carol Stream, IL: Hope Publishing company, 1993), 4.
6. Mitchell, *I Don't Like That Music*, 4.
7. Eugene A. Nida and Charles H. Kraft, *Message and Mission: The Communication of the Christian Faith*, rev. ed. (Pasadena, CA: William Carey Library, 1990), 85.
8. Nida and Kraft, *Message and Mission*, 32.

9. Viv Broughton, *Too Close to Heaven: The Illustrated History of Gospel Music* (London: Midnight Books, 1996), 49.

10. Broughton, *Too Close to Heaven*, 59.

11. Lee Poquette in discussion with the author (October and November, 2015).

12. A word must be inserted here about Hillsong, a new kind of multisite megachurch with international offshoots. What began as Hillsong Australia now has offshoots in London, Kiev, Cape Town, Pretoria, Stockholm, and New York. Hillsong services are also held in Paris, Lyon, Konstanz, Dusseldorf, Amsterdam, Barcelona, Copenhagen, Moscow, Los Angeles, and soon in Buenos Aires and Sao Paulo.

13. Brent Dyer in discussion with the author (October 2015).

14. www.vineyard.org, accessed May 2016.

15. www.vineyardusa.org, accessed May 2016.

16. Carmichael, *He's Everything to Me*, 188.

17. Cindy Cruse Ratcliff in discussion with the author (October 2015).

18. The content of this section draws largely from "Artistic Vocal Styles and Technique" by Sharon L. Radionoff, previously published in *The Performer's Voice*, 2nd ed., edited by Michael S. Benninger, Thomas Murry, and Michael M. Johns (San Diego: Plural Publishing, 2016), 103–112.

19. Buddy Valastro, *Baking with the Cake Boss: 100 of Buddy's Best Recipes and Decorating Secrets* (New York: Atria Books, 2011).

20. Sharon L. Radionoff, "The SVS and Contemporary Christian Music—Part 1: A Brief Overview," *VOICEPrints: The Official Journal of the NYSTA* 12, no. 4 (2015): 4–5; "The SVS and Contemporary Christian Music—Part 2: Voice Balancing Exercises," *VOICEPrints: The Official Journal of NYSTA* 12, no. 5 (2015): 4–6.

6

SINGING AND VOICE SCIENCE

Scott McCoy

This chapter presents a concise overview of how the voice functions as a biomechanical, acoustic instrument. We will be dealing with elements of anatomy, physiology, acoustics, and resonance. But don't panic: the things you need to know are easily accessible, even if it has been many years since you last set foot in a science or math class!

All musical instruments, including the human voice, have at least four things in common, consisting of a *power source, sound source* (vibrator), *resonator*, and a system for *articulation*. In most cases, the person who plays the instrument provides power by pressing a key, plucking a string, or blowing into a horn. This power is used to set the sound source in motion, which creates vibrations in the air that we perceive as sound. Musical vibrators come in many forms, including strings, reeds, and human lips. The sound produced by the vibrator, however, needs a lot of help before it becomes beautiful music—we might think of it as raw material, like a lump of clay that a potter turns into a vase. Musical instruments use resonance to enhance and strengthen the sound of the vibrator, transforming it into sounds we identify as a piano, trumpet, or guitar. Finally, instruments must have a means of articulation to create the nuanced sounds of music. Let's see how these four elements are used to create the sounds of singing.

PULMONARY SYSTEM: THE POWER SOURCE OF YOUR VOICE

The human voice has a lot in common with a trumpet: both use flaps of tissue as a sound source, both use hollow tubes as resonators, and both rely on the respiratory (pulmonary) system for power. If you stop to think about it, you quickly realize why breathing is so important for singing. First and foremost, it keeps us alive through the exchange of blood gases—oxygen in, carbon dioxide out. But it also serves as the storage depot for the air we use to produce sound. Most singers rarely encounter situations in which these two functions are in conflict, but if you are required to sustain an extremely long phrase, you could find yourself in need of fresh oxygen before your lungs are totally empty.

Misconceptions about breathing for singing are rampant. Fortunately, most are easily dispelled. We must start with a brief foray into the world of physics in the guise of *Boyle's Law*. Some of you no doubt remember this principle: the pressure of a gas within a container changes inversely with changes of volume. If the quantity of a gas is constant and its container is made smaller, pressure rises. But if we make the container get bigger, pressure goes down. Boyle's law explains everything that happens when we breathe, especially when we combine it with another physical law: *nature abhors a vacuum*. If one location has reduced pressure, air flows from an area of higher pressure to equalize the two, and vice versa. So if we can create a zone of reduced air pressure by expanding our lungs, air automatically flows in to restore balance. When air pressure in the lungs is increased, it has no choice but to flow outward.

As we all know, the air we breathe goes in and out of our lungs. Each lung contains millions and millions of tiny air sacs called *alveoli*, where gases are exchanged. The alveoli also function like ultra-miniature versions of the bladder for a bag pipe, storing the air that will be used to set the vocal folds into vibration. To get the air in and out of them, all we need to do is make the lungs larger for inhalation and smaller for exhalation. Always remember this relationship between cause and effect during breathing: we inhale because we make ourselves large; we exhale because we make ourselves smaller. Unfortunately, the lungs are organs, not muscles, and have no ability on their own to accomplish this feat. For this reason, your bodies came from the factory with special muscles designed to enlarge and compress your entire thorax (rib cage), while simultaneously moving your lungs. We can classify these muscles in two main categories: any muscle that has the ability to increase the volume capacity of the thorax serves an *inspiratory* function; any muscle that has the ability to decrease the volume capacity of the thorax serves an *expiratory* function.

Your largest muscle of inspiration is called the *diaphragm* (figure 6.1). This dome-shaped muscle originates from the bottom of your sternum (breastbone) and completely fills the area from that point around your ribs to your spine. It's the second-largest muscle in your body, but you probably have no conscious awareness of it or ability to directly control

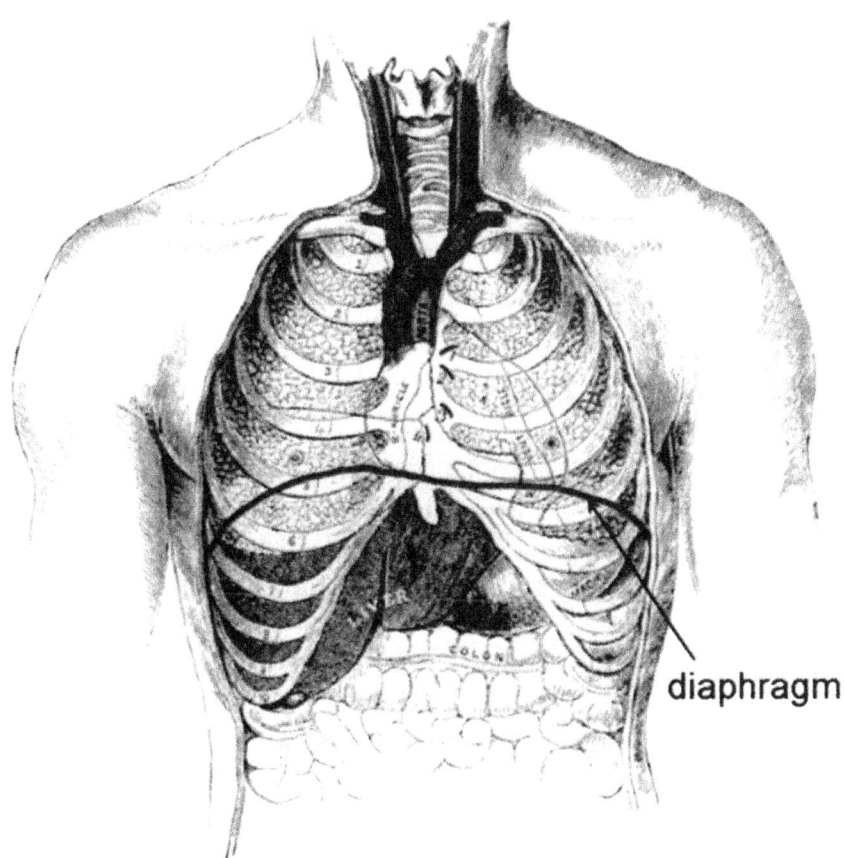

Figure 6.1. Location of diaphragm. *Courtesy of Scott McCoy*

it. When we take a deep breath, the diaphragm contracts and the central portion flattens out and drops downward a couple inches into your abdomen, pressing against all of your internal organs. If you release tension from your abdominal muscles as you inhale, you will feel a gentle bulge in your upper or lower belly, or perhaps in your back, resulting from the displacement of your innards by the diaphragm. This is a good thing and can be used to let you know you have taken a good inhalation.

The diaphragm is important, but we must remember that it cannot function in isolation. After you inhale, it relaxes and gently returns to its resting position through an action called *elastic recoil*. This movement, however, is entirely passive and makes no significant contribution to generating the pressure required to sustain phonation. Therefore, it makes no sense at all to try to "sing from your diaphragm"—unless you intend to sing while you inhale, not exhale!

Eleven pairs of muscles assist the diaphragm in its inhalatory efforts, which are called the *external intercostal* muscles (figure 6.2). These muscles start from ribs one through eleven and connect at a slight angle downward to ribs two through twelve. When they contract, the entire thorax moves up and out, somewhat like moving a bucket handle. With the diaphragm and intercostals working together, you are able to increase the capacity of your lungs by about three to six liters, depending on your gender and overall physical stature; thus, we have quite a lot of air available to power our voices.

Eleven additional pairs of muscles are located directly under the external intercostals, which, not surprisingly, are called the *internal intercostals* (figure 6.2). These muscles start from ribs two through twelve and connect upward to ribs one through eleven. When they contract, they induce the opposite action of their external partners: the thorax is made smaller, inducing exhalation. Four additional pairs of expiratory muscles are located in the abdomen, beginning with the *rectus* (figure 6.2). The two rectus abdominis muscles run from your pubic bone to your sternum and are divided into four separate portions, called *bellies* of the muscle (lots of muscles have multiple bellies; it is coincidental that the bellies of the rectus are found in the location we colloquially refer to as our belly). Definition of these bellies results in the so-called ripped abdomen or six-pack of body builders and others who are especially fit.

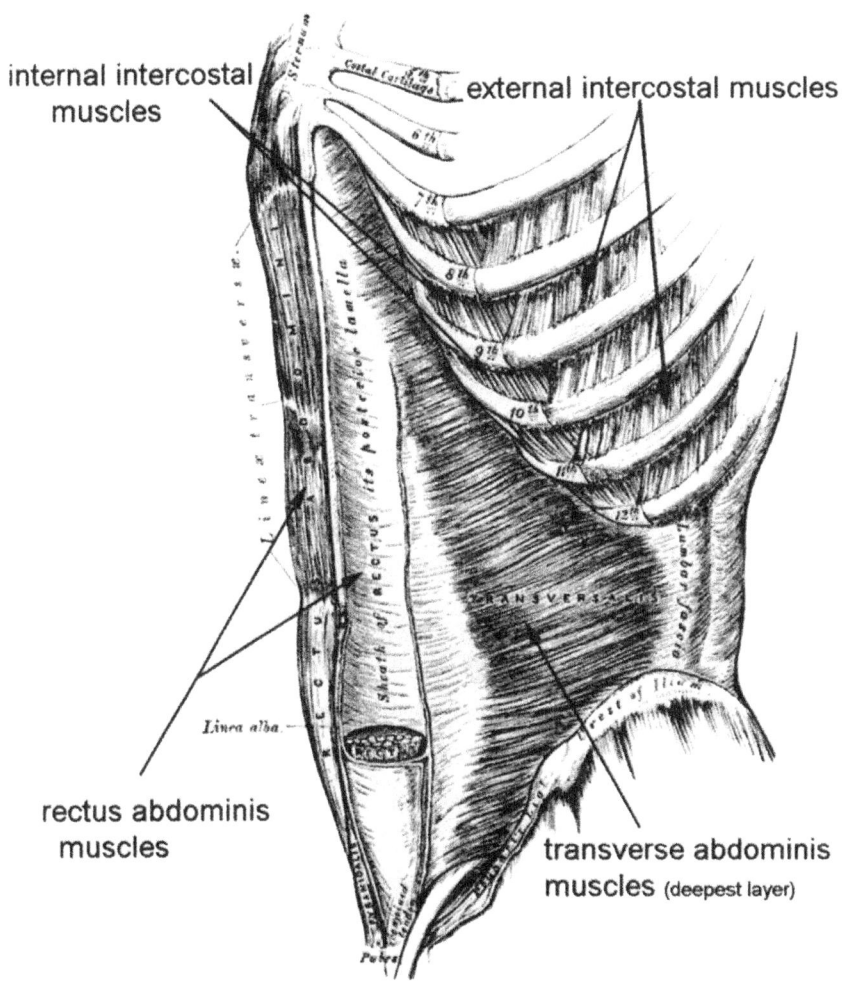

Figure 6.2. Intercostal and abdominal muscles. *Courtesy of Scott McCoy*

The largest muscles of the abdomen are called the *external obliques* (figure 6.3), which run at a downward angle from the sides of the rectus, covering the lower portion of the thorax, and extend all the way to the spine. The *internal obliques* lie immediately below, oriented at an angle that crisscrosses the external muscles. They are slightly smaller, beginning at the bottom of the thorax, rather than extending over it. The deepest muscle layer is the *transverse abdominis* (figure 6.3), which is oriented with fibers that run horizontally. These four muscle

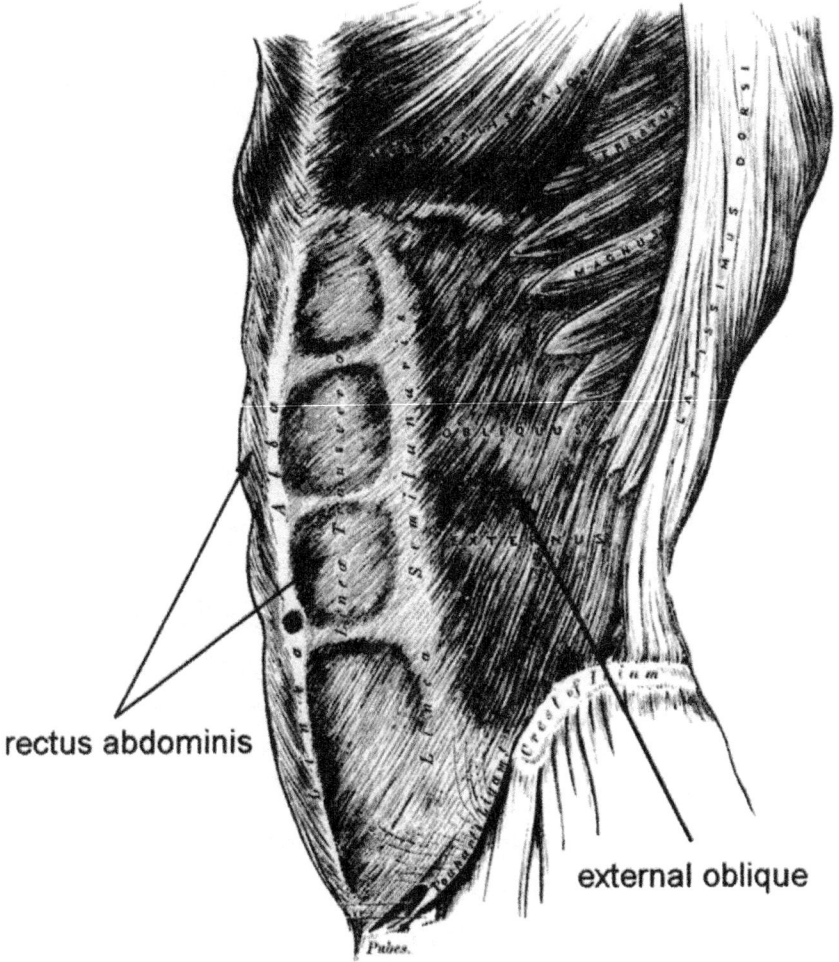

Figure 6.3. External oblique and rectus abdominus muscles. *Courtesy of Scott McCoy*

pairs completely encase the abdominal region, holding your organs and digestive system in place while simultaneously helping you breathe.

Your expiratory muscles are quite large and can produce a great deal of pulmonary or air pressure. In fact, they easily can overpower the larynx. Healthy adults generally can generate more than twice the pressure that is required to produce even the loudest sounds; therefore, singers must develop a system for moderating and controlling airflow and breath pressure. This practice goes by many names, including breath support, breath control, and breath management, all of which rely on the principle of *muscular antagonism*. Muscles are said to have an antagonistic relationship when they work in opposing directions, usually pulling on a common point of attachment, for the sake of increasing stability or motor control. You can see a clear example of muscular antagonism in the relationship between your biceps (flexors) and triceps (extensors) when you hold out your arm. In breathing for singing, we activate inspiratory muscles (e.g., diaphragm and external intercostals) during exhalation to help control respiratory pressure and the rate at which air is expelled from the lungs.

One of the things you will notice when watching a variety of singers is that they tend to breathe in many different ways. You might think that voice teachers and scientists, who have been teaching and studying singing for hundreds, if not thousands of years, would have come to agreement on the best possible breathing technique. But for many reasons, this is not the case. For one, different musical and vocal styles place varying demands on breathing. For another, humans have a huge variety of body types, sizes, and morphologies. A breathing strategy that is successful for a tall, slender woman might be completely ineffective in a short, robust man. Our bodies actually contain a large number of muscles beyond those we've already discussed that are capable of assisting with respiration. For an example, consider your *latissimi dorsi* muscles. These large muscles of the arm enable us to do pull-ups (or pull-downs, depending on which exercise you perform) at the fitness center. But because they wrap around a large portion of the thorax, they also exert an expiratory force. We have at least two dozen such muscles that have secondary respiratory functions, some for exhalation and some for inhalation. When we consider all these possibilities, it is no surprise at all that there are many ways to breathe that can produce beautiful singing. Just remember to practice some muscular antagonism—maintaining a degree of inhalation posture during exhalation—and you should do well.

LARYNX: THE VIBRATOR OF YOUR VOICE

The larynx, sometimes known as the voice box or Adam's apple, is a complex physiologic structure made of cartilage, muscle, and tissue. Biologically, it serves as a sphincter valve, closing off the airway to prevent foreign objects from entering the lungs. When firmly closed, it also is used to increase abdominal pressure to assist with lifting heavy objects, childbirth, and defecation. But if we gently close this valve while we exhale, tissue in the larynx begins to vibrate and produce the sounds that become speech and singing.

The human larynx is a remarkably small instrument, typically ranging from the size of a pecan to a walnut for women and men, respectively. Sound is produced at a location called the *glottis*, which is formed by two flaps of tissue called the *vocal folds* (aka *vocal cords*). In women, the glottis is about the size of a dime; in men, it can approach the diameter of a quarter. The two folds are always attached together at their front point but open in the shape of the letter V during normal breathing, an action called *abduction*. To phonate, we must close the V while we exhale, an action called *adduction* (just like the machines you use at the fitness center to exercise your thigh and chest muscles).

Phonation only is possible because of the unique multilayer structure of the vocal folds (figure 6.4). The core of each fold is formed by muscle, which is surrounded by a layer of gelatinous material called the *lamina propria*. The *vocal ligament* also runs through the lamina propria, which

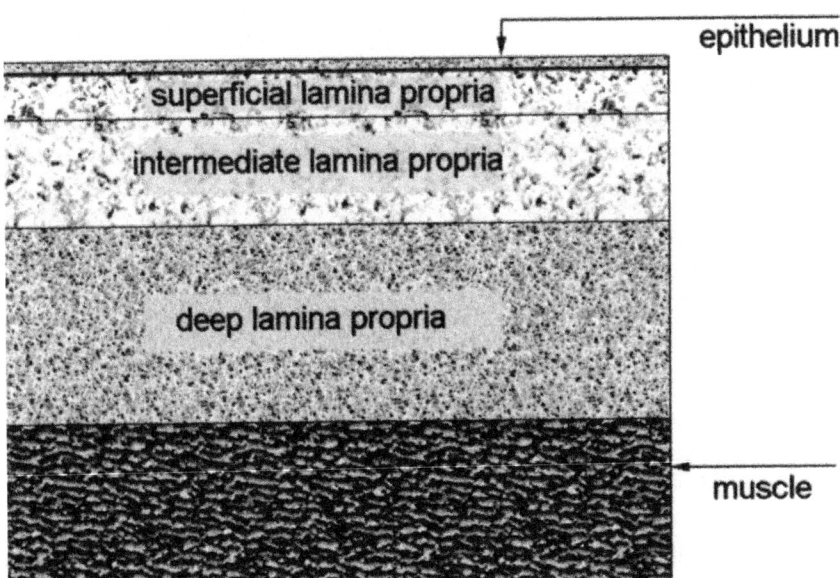

Figure 6.4. Layered structure of the vocal fold. *Courtesy of Scott McCoy*

helps to prevent injury by limiting how far the folds can be stretched for high pitches. A thin, hairless epithelial layer that is constantly kept moist with mucus secreted by the throat, larynx, and trachea surrounds all of this. During phonation, the outer layer of the fold glides independently over the inner layer in a wavelike motion, without which phonation is impossible.

We can use a simple demonstration to better understand the independence of the inner and outer portions of the folds. Explore the palm of your hand with your other index finger. Note that the skin is attached quite firmly to the flesh beneath it. If you poke at your palm, that flesh acts as padding, protecting the underlying bone. Now explore the back of your hand. You will observe that the skin is attached quite loosely—you easily can move it around with your finger. And if you poke at the back of your hand, it is likely to hurt; there is very little padding between the skin and your bones. Your vocal folds combine the best attributes of both sides of your hand. They provide sufficient padding to help reduce impact stress, while permitting the outer layer to slip like the skin on the back of your hand, enabling phonation to occur. When you are sick with laryngitis and lose your voice (a condition called *aphonia*), inflammation in the vocal folds couples the layers of the folds tightly together. The outer layer no longer can move independently over the inner, and phonation becomes difficult or impossible.

The vocal folds are located within the five cartilaginous structures of the larynx (figure 6.5). The largest is called the *thyroid cartilage*, which is shaped like a small shield. The thyroid connects to the *cricoid* cartilage below it, which is shaped like a signet ring—broad in the back and narrow in the front. Two cartilages that are shaped like squashed pyramids sit atop the cricoid, called the *arytenoids*. Each vocal fold runs from the thyroid cartilage in front to one of the arytenoids at the back. Finally, the *epiglottis* is located at the top of the larynx, flipping backward each time we swallow to prevent food and liquid from entering our lungs. Muscles connect between the various cartilages to open and close the glottis and to lengthen and shorten the vocal folds for ascending and descending pitch, respectively. Because they sometimes are used to identify vocal function, it is a good idea to know the names of the muscles that control the length of the folds. We've already mentioned that a muscle forms the core of each fold. Because it runs between the thyroid cartilage and an

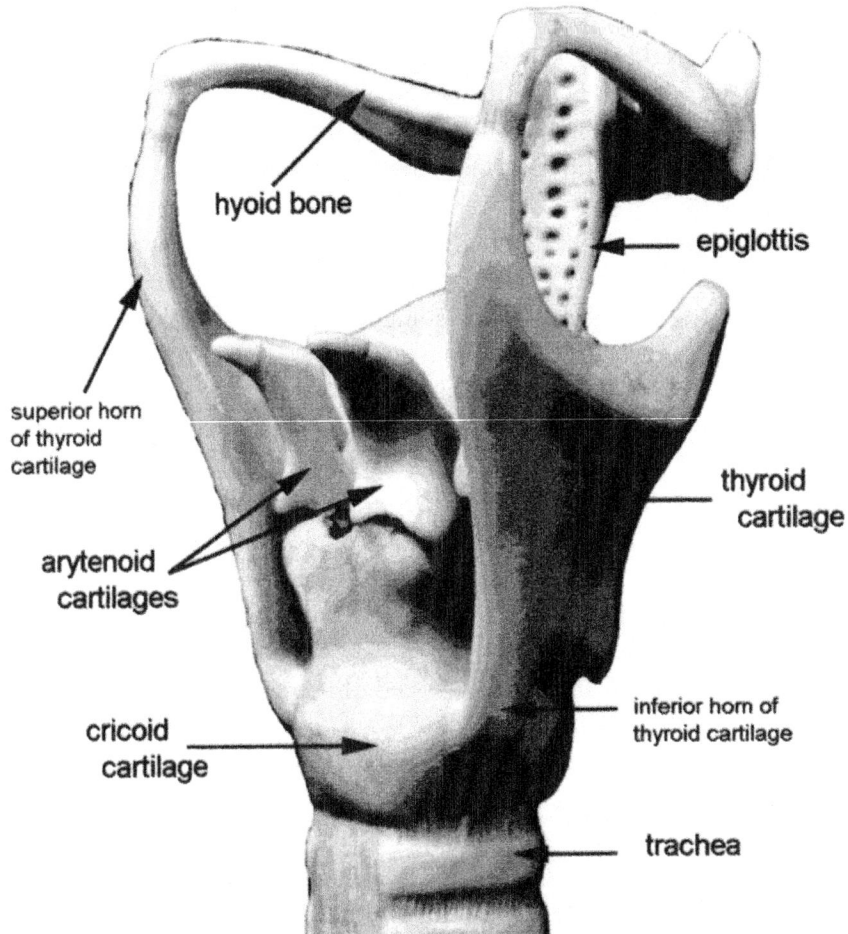

Figure 6.5. Cartilages of the larynx, viewed at an angle from the back. Courtesy of Scott McCoy

arytenoid, it is named the *thyroarytenoid* muscle (formerly known as the *vocalis* muscle). When the thyroarytenoid, or TA muscle, contracts, the fold is shortened and pitch goes down. The folds are elongated through the action of the *cricothyroid*, or CT muscles, which run from the thyroid to cricoid cartilage.

Vocal color (timbre) is created by the combined effects of the sound produced by the vocal folds and the resonance provided by the vocal tract. While these elements can never be completely separated, it is useful to consider the two primary modes of vocal fold vibration and their resulting sound qualities. The main differences are related to the relative thickness of the folds and their cross-sectional shape (figure 6.6). The first option depends on short, thick folds that come together with nearly square-shaped edges. Vibration in this configuration is given a variety of names, including *Mode 1*, *thyroarytenoid* (TA) *dominant*, *chest mode*, or *modal voice*. The alternate configuration uses longer, thinner folds that only make contact at their upper margins. Common names include *Mode 2*, *cricothyroid* (CT) *dominant*, *falsetto mode*, or *loft voice*. Singers vary the vibrational mode of the folds according to the quality of sound they wish to produce.

Before we move on to a discussion of resonance, we must consider the quality of the sound that is produced by the larynx. At the level of the glottis, we create a sound not unlike the annoying buzz of a duck call. That buzz, however, contains all the raw material we need to create speech and singing. Vocal or glottal sound is considered to be *complex*, meaning it consists of many simultaneously sounding frequencies (pitches). The lowest frequency within any tone is called the *fundamental*, which corresponds to its named pitch in the musical scale. Orchestras tune to a pitch called A-440, which means it has a frequency of 440 vibrations per second, or 440 *Hertz* (abbreviated Hz). Additional frequencies are included above the fundamental, which are called *overtones*. Overtones in the glottal sound are quieter than the fundamental. In voices, the overtones usually are whole number multiples of the fundamental, creating a pattern called the *harmonic series* (e.g., 100 Hz, 200 Hz, 300 Hz, 400 Hz, 500 Hz, etc. or G2, G3, C4, G4, B4—note that pitches are named by the international system in which the lowest C of

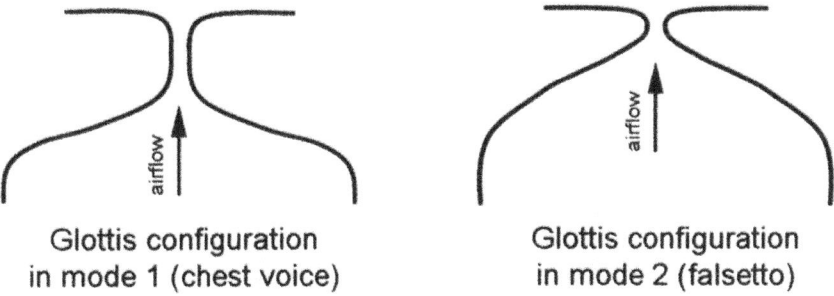

Figure 6.6. Primary modes of vocal fold vibration. *Courtesy of Scott McCoy*

the piano keyboard is C1; middle-C therefore becomes C4, the fourth C of the keyboard) (figure 6.7).

Singers who choose to make coarse or rough sounds as might be appropriate for rock or blues often add overtones that are *inharmonic*, or not part of the standard numerical sequence. Inharmonic overtones also are common in singers with damaged or pathological voices.

Under most circumstances, we are completely unaware of the presence of overtones—they simply contribute to the overall timbre of a voice. In some vocal styles, however, harmonics become a dominant feature. This is especially true in *throat singing* or *overtone singing*, as is found in places like Tuva. Throat singers tune their vocal tracts so precisely that single harmonics are highlighted within the harmonic spectrum as a separate, whistle-like tone. These singers sustain a low-pitched drone and then create a melody by moving from tone to tone within the natural harmonic series. You can learn to do this too. Sustain a comfortable pitch in your range and slowly morph between the vowels [i] and [u]. If you listen carefully, you will hear individual harmonics pop out of your sound.

The mode of vocal fold vibration has a strong impact on the overtones that are produced. In mode 1, high-frequency harmonics are relatively strong; in mode 2, they are much weaker. As a result, mode 1 tends to yield a much brighter, brassier sound.

VOCAL TRACT: YOUR SOURCE OF RESONANCE

Resonance typically is defined as the amplification and enhancement (or enrichment) of musical sound through *supplemental vibration*. What does this really mean? In layman's terms, we could say that resonance makes instruments louder and more beautiful by reinforcing the original vibra-

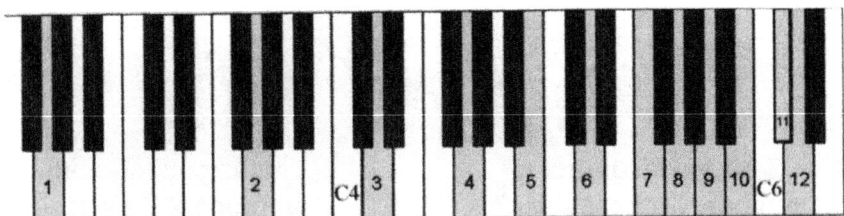

Figure 6.7. Natural harmonic series, beginning at G2. *Courtesy of Scott McCoy*

tions of the sound source. This enhancement occurs in two primary ways, which are known as forced and free resonance (there is nothing pejorative in these terms: free resonance is not superior to forced resonance). Any object that is physically connected to a vibrator can serve as a forced resonator. For a piano, the resonator is the soundboard (on the underside of a grand or on the back of an upright); the vibrations of the strings are transmitted directly to the soundboard through a structure known as the bridge, which also is found on violins and guitars. Forced resonance also plays a role in voice production. Place your hand on your chest and say [a] at a low pitch. You almost certainly felt the vibrations of forced resonance. In singing, this might best be considered your *private* resonance; you can feel it and it might impact your self-perception of sound, but nobody else can hear it. To understand why this is true, imagine what a violin would sound like if it were encased in a thick layer of foam rubber. The vibrations of the string would be damped out, muting the instrument. Your skin, muscles, and other tissues do the same thing to the vibrations of your vocal folds.

By contrast, free resonance occurs when sound travels through a hollow space, such as the inside of a trumpet, an organ pipe, or your vocal tract, which consists of the pharynx (throat), oral cavity (mouth), and nasal cavity (nose). As sound travels through these regions, a complex pattern of echoes is created; every time sound encounters a change in the shape of the vocal tract, some of its energy is reflected backward, much like an echo in a canyon. If these echoes arrive back at the glottis at the precise moment a new pulse of sound is created, the two elements synchronize, resulting in a significant increase in intensity. All of this happens very quickly—remember that sound is traveling through your vocal tract at more than seven hundred miles per hour.

Whenever this synchronization of the vocal tract and sound source occurs, we say that the system is *in resonance*. The phenomenon occurs at specific frequencies (pitches), which can be varied by changing the position of the tongue, lips, jaw, palate, and larynx. These resonant frequencies, or areas in which strong amplification occurs, are called *formants*. Formants provide the specific amplification that changes the raw, buzzing sound produced by your vocal folds into speech and singing. The vocal tract is capable of producing many formants, which are labeled sequentially by ascending pitch. The first two, F1 and F2, are used to create vowels; higher formants contribute to the overall timbre and individual characteristics of a voice. In some singers, especially those who train to sing in opera, formants three through five are clustered together to form a super formant, eponymously called the *singer's formant*, which creates a ringing sound and enables a voice to be heard in a large theater without electronic amplification.

Formants are vitally important in singing, but they can be a bit intimidating to understand. An analogy that works really well for me is to think of formants like the wind. You cannot see the wind, but you know it is present when you see leaves rustling in a tree or feel a breeze on your face. Formants work in the same manner. They are completely invisible and directly inaudible. But just as we see the rustling leaf, we can hear, and perhaps even feel, the action of formants through how they change our sound. Try a little experiment. Sing an ascending scale beginning at B♭3, sustaining the vowel [i]. As you approach the D♮ or E♭ of the scale, you likely will feel (and hear) that your sound becomes a bit stronger and easier to produce. This occurs because the scale tone and formant are on the same pitch, providing additional amplification. If you change to an [u] vowel, you will feel the same thing at about the same place in the scale. If you sing to an [o] or [e] and continue up the scale, you'll feel a bloom in the sound somewhere around C5 (an octave above middle C); [a] is likely to come into its best focus at about G5.

To remember the approximate pitches of the first formants for the main vowels, [i]-[e]-[a]-[o]-[u], just think of a C-major triad in first inversion, open position, starting at E4: [i] = E4, [e] = C5, [a] = G5, [o] = C5, and [u] = E4 (figure 6.8). If your music theory isn't strong, you

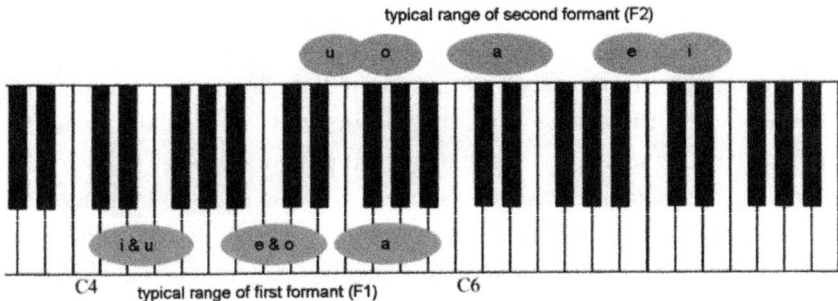

Figure 6.8. Typical range of first and second formants for primary vowels. *Courtesy of Scott McCoy*

could use the mnemonic "every child gets candy eagerly." These pitches might vary by as much as a minor third higher and lower but no farther: once a formant changes by more than that interval, the vowel that is produced *must* change.

Formants have absolutely no preference for what they amplify—they are indiscriminate lovers, just as happy to bond with the first harmonic as the fifth. When men or women sing low pitches, there almost always will be at least one harmonic that comes close enough to a formant to produce a clear vowel sound. The same is not true for women with high voices, especially sopranos, who routinely must sing pitches that have a fundamental frequency *higher* than the first formant of many vowels. Imagine what happens if she must sing the phrase "and I'll leave you forever," with the word "leave" set on a very high, climactic note. The audience won't be able to tell if she is singing *leave* or *love*; the two will sound identical. This happens because the formant that is required to identify the vowel [i] is too far below the pitch being sung. Even if she tries to sing *leave*, the sound that comes out of her mouth will be heard as some variation of [a].

Fortunately, this kind of mismatch between formants and musical pitches rarely causes problems for anyone but opera singers, choir sopranos, and perhaps ingénues in classic music theater shows. Almost everyone else generally sings low enough in their respective voice ranges to produce easily identifiable vowels.

Second formants also can be important, but more so for opera singers than everyone else. They are much higher in pitch, tracking the pattern [u] = E5, [o] = G5, [a] = D6, [e] = B6, [i] = D7 (you can use the mnemonic "every good dad buys diapers" to remember these pitches) (figure 6.8). Because they can extend so high, into the top octave of the piano keyboard for [i], they interact primarily with higher tones in the natural harmonic series. Unless you are striving to produce the loudest unamplified sound possible, you probably never need to worry about the second formant; it will steadfastly do its job of helping to produce vowel sounds without any conscious thought or manipulation on your part.

If you are interested in discovering more about resonance and how it impacts your voice, you might want to install a spectrum analyzer on your computer. Free (or inexpensive) programs are readily available for download over the Internet that will work with either a PC or Mac computer. You don't need any specialized hardware—if you can use Skype or FaceTime, you already have everything you need. Once you've installed something, simply start playing with it. Experiment with your voice to see exactly how the analysis signal changes when you change the way your voice sounds. You'll be able to see how harmonics change in intensity as they interact with your formants. If you sing with vibrato, you'll see how consistently you produce your variations in pitch and amplitude. You'll even be able to see if your tone is excessively nasal for the kind of singing you want to do. Other programs are available that will help you improve your intonation (how well you sing in tune) or enhance your basic musicianship skills. Technology truly has advanced sufficiently to help us sing more beautifully.

MOUTH, LIPS, AND TONGUE: YOUR ARTICULATORS

The articulatory life of a singer is not easy, especially when compared to the demands placed on other musicians. Like a pianist or brass player, we must be able to produce the entire spectrum of musical articulation, including dynamic levels from hushed pianissimos to thunderous fortes, short notes, long notes, accents, crescendos, diminuendos, and so on. We produce most of these articulations the same way instrumentalists do, which is by varying our power supply. But singers have another layer of articulation that makes everything much more complicated; we must produce these musical gestures while simultaneously singing words.

As we learned in our brief examination of formants, altering the resonance characteristics of the vocal tract creates the vowel sounds of language. We do this by changing the position of our tongue, jaw, lips, and sometimes palate. Slowly say the vowel pattern [i]-[e]-[a]-[o]-[u]. Can you feel how your tongue moves in your mouth? For [i], it is high in the front and low in the back, but it takes the opposite position for [u]. Now slowly say the word *Tuesday*, noting all the places your tongue comes into contact with your teeth and palate and how it changes shape as you produce the vowels and diphthongs. There is a lot going on in there—no wonder it takes so long for babies to learn to speak!

Our articulatory anatomy is extraordinarily complex, in large part because our bodies use the same passageway for food, water, air, and sound. As a result, our tongue, larynx, throat, jaw, and palate are all interconnected with common physical and neurologic points of attachment. Our anatomical *Union Station* in this regard is a small structure called the *hyoid bone*. The hyoid is one of only three bones in your entire body that do not connect to other bones via a joint (the other two are your *patellae*, or kneecaps). This little bone is suspended below your jaw, freely floating up and down every time your swallow. It is a busy place, serving as the upper suspension point for the larynx, the connection for the root of the tongue, and the primary location of the muscles that open your mouth by dropping your jaw.

Good singing—in any genre—requires a high degree of independence in all these articulatory structures. Unfortunately, nature conspires against us to make this difficult to accomplish. From the time we were born, our bodies have relied on a reflex reaction to elevate the palate and raise the larynx each time we swallow. This action becomes habitual: palate goes up, larynx also lifts. But depending on the style of music we are singing, we might need to keep the larynx down while the palate goes up (opera and classical) or palate down with the larynx up (country and bluegrass). As we all know, habits can be very hard to change, which is one of the reasons that it can take a lot of study and practice to become an excellent singer. Understanding your body's natural reflexive habits can make some of this work a bit easier.

There is one more significant pitfall to the close proximity of all these articulators: tension in one area is easily passed along to another. If your jaw muscles are too tight while you sing, that hyperactivity will likely be transferred to the larynx and tongue—remember, they all are interconnected through the hyoid bone. It can be tricky to determine the primary offender in this kind of chain reaction of tension. A tight tongue could just as easily be making your jaw stiff, or an elevated, rigid larynx could make both tongue and jaw suffer.

Neurology complicates matters even further. You have sixteen muscles in your tongue, fourteen in your larynx, twenty-two in your throat and palate, and another sixteen that control your jaw. Many of these are very small and lie directly adjacent to each other, and you often are required to contract one quite strongly while its next-door neighbor must remain totally relaxed. Our brains need to develop laser-like control, sending signals at the right moment with the right intensity to the precise spot where they are needed. When we first start singing, these brain signals come more like a blast from a shotgun, spreading the neurologic impulse over a broad area to multiple muscles, not all of which are the intended target. Again, with practice and training, we learn to refine our control, enabling us to use only those muscles that will help, while disengaging those that would get in the way of our best singing.

FINAL THOUGHTS

This brief chapter has only scratched the surface of the huge field of voice science. To learn more, you might visit the websites of the National Association of Teachers of Singing (NATS), the Voice Foundation (TVF), or the National Center for Voice and Speech (NCVS). You can easily locate the appropriate addresses through any Internet search engine. Remember: knowledge is power. Occasionally, people are afraid that if they know more about the science of how they sing, they will become so analytical that all spontaneity will be lost or they will become paralyzed by too much information and thought. In my forty-plus years as a singer and teacher, I've never encountered somebody who actually suffered this fate. To the contrary, the more we know, the easier—and more joyful—singing becomes.

7

VOCAL HEALTH AND THE SINGER OF SACRED MUSIC

Wendy LeBorgne

GENERAL PHYSICAL WELL-BEING

All singers, regardless of genre, should consider themselves as "vocal athletes." The physical, emotional, and performance demands necessary for optimal output require that the artist consider training and maintaining their instrument as an athlete trains for an event. With increased vocal and performance demands, it is unlikely that a vocal athlete will have an entire performing career completely injury free. This may not be the fault of the singer, as many injuries occur due to circumstances beyond the singer's control such as singing through an illness or being on a new medication seemingly unrelated to the voice.

Vocal injury has often been considered taboo to talk about in the performing world as it has been considered to be the result of faulty technique or poor vocal habits. In actuality, the majority of vocal injuries presenting in the elite performing population tend to be overuse and/or acute injury. From a clinical perspective over the past seventeen years, younger, less experienced singers with fewer years of training (who tend to be quite talented) generally are the ones who present with issues related to technique or phonotrauma (nodules, edema, contact ulcers), while more mature singers with professional performing careers tend to present with acute injuries (hemorrhage) or overuse and misuse injuries (muscle tension dysphonia, edema, GERD) or injuries following an illness. There are no current studies documenting use and training in correlation to laryngeal pathologies. However, there are studies that document that somewhere between 35 percent and 100 percent of professional vocal athletes have abnormal vocal fold findings on stroboscopic evaluation. Many times these "abnormalities" are in singers who have no vocal complaints or symptoms of vocal problems. From a performance perspective, uniqueness in vocal quality often gets hired and perhaps a slight aberration in the way a given larynx functions may become quite marketable. Regardless of what the vocal folds may look like, the most integral part of performance is that the singer must maintain agility, flexibility, stamina, power, and inherent beauty (genre appropriate) for their current level of performance taking into account physical, vocal, and emotional demands.

Unlike sports medicine and the exercise physiology literature where much is known about the types and nature of given sports injuries, there is no common parallel for the vocal athlete model. However, because the vocal athlete utilizes the body systems of alignment, respiration, phonation, and resonance with some similarities to physical athletes, a parallel protocol for vocal wellness may be implemented/considered for vocal athletes to maximize injury prevention knowledge for both the singer and teacher. This chapter aims to provide information on vocal wellness and injury prevention for the vocal athlete.

CONSIDERATIONS FOR WHOLE BODY WELLNESS

Nutrition

You have no doubt heard the saying "You are what you eat." Eating is a social and psychological event. For many people, food associations and eating have an emotional basis resulting in either overeating or being malnourished. Eating disorders in performers and body image issues may have major implications and consequences for the performer on both ends of the spectrum (obesity and anorexia). Singers should be encouraged to reprogram the brain and body to consider food as fuel. You want to use high-octane gas in your engine, as pouring water in your car's gas tank won't get you very far. Eating a poor diet or a diet that lacks appropriate nutritional value will have negative physical and vocal effects on the singer. Effects of poor dietary choices for the vocal athlete may result in physical and vocal effects ranging from fatigue to life-threatening disease over the course of a lifetime. Encouraging and engaging in healthy eating habits from a young age will potentially prevent long-term negative effects from poor nutritional choices. It is beyond the scope of this chapter to provide a complete overview of all the dietary guidelines for pediatrics, adolescents, adults, and the mature adult; however, a listing of additional references to help guide your food and beverage choices for making good nutritional choices can be found online at websites such as Dietary Guidelines for Americans, Nutrition.gov Guidelines for Tweens and Teens, and Fruits and Veggies Matter. See the online companion web page on the NATS website for links to these and other resources.

Hydration

"Sing wet, pee pale." This phrase was echoed in the studio of Van Lawrence regarding how his students would know if they were well hydrated. Generally, this rule of pale urine during your waking hours is a good indicator that you are well hydrated. Medications, vitamins, and certain foods may alter urine color despite adequate hydration. Due to the varying levels of physical and vocal activity of many performers, in order to maintain adequate oral hydration, the use of a hydration calculator based on activity level may be a better choice. These hydration calculators are easily accessible online and take into account the amount and level of activity the performer engages in on a daily basis. In a recent study of the vocal habits of musical theater performers, one of the findings indicated a significantly underhydrated group of performers.[1]

Laryngeal and pharyngeal dryness as well as "thick, sticky, mucus" are often complaints of singers. Combating these concerns and maintaining an adequate viscosity of mucus for performance has resulted in some research. As a reminder of laryngeal and swallowing anatomy, nothing that is swallowed (or gargled) goes over or touches the vocal folds directly (or one would choke). Therefore, nothing that a singer eats or drinks ever touches the vocal folds, and in order to adequately hydrate the mucous membranes of the vocal folds, one must consume enough fluids for the body to produce a thin mucus. Therefore, any "vocal" effects from swallowed products are limited to potential pharyngeal and oral changes, not the vocal folds themselves.

The effects of systemic hydration are well documented in the literature. There is evidence to suggest that adequate hydration will provide some protection of the laryngeal mucosal membranes when they are placed under increased collision forces as well as reducing the amount of effort (phonation threshold pressure) to produce voice. This is important for the singer because it means that with adequate hydration and consistency of mucus, the effort to produce voice is less and your vocal folds are better protected from injury. Imagine the friction and heat produced when two dry hands rub together and then what happens if you put lotion on your hands. The mechanisms in the larynx to provide appropriate mucus production are not fully understood, but there is enough evidence at this time to support oral hydration as a vital component of every singer's vocal health regime to maintain appropriate mucosal viscosity.

Although very rare, overhydration (hyperhidrosis) can result in dehydration and even illness or death. An overindulgence of fluids essentially makes the kidneys work "overtime" and flushes too much water out of the body. This excessive fluid loss in a rapid manner can be detrimental to the body.

In addition to drinking water to systemically monitor hydration, there are many nonregulated products on the market for performers that lay claim to improving the laryngeal environment (e.g., Entertainer's Secret, Throat Coat Tea, Greathers Pastilles, Slippery Elm, etc.). Although there may be little detriment in using these products, quantitative research documenting change in laryngeal mucosa is sparse. One study suggests that the use of Throat Coat when compared to a placebo treatment for pharyngitis did show a significant difference in decreasing the perception of sore throat.[2] Another study compared the use of Entertainer's Secret to two other nebulized agents and its effect on phonation threshold pressure (PTP).[3] There was no positive benefit in decreasing PTP with Entertainer's Secret.

Many singers use personal steam inhalers and/or room humidification to supplement oral hydration and aid in combating laryngeal dryness.

There are several considerations for singers who choose to use external means of adding moisture to the air they breathe. Personal steam inhalers are portable and can often be used backstage or in the hotel room for the traveling performer. Typically, water is placed in the steamer and the face is placed over the steam for inhalation. Because the mucus membranes of the larynx are composed of a saltwater solution, one study looked at the use of nebulized saline in comparison to plain water and its potential effects on effort or ease to sound production in classically trained sopranos.[4] Data suggested that perceived effort to produce voice was less in the saline group than the plain water group. This indicated that the singers who used the saltwater solution reported less effort to sing after breathing in the saltwater than singers who used plain water. The researchers hypothesized that because the body's mucus is not plain water (rather it is a saltwater—think about your tears), when you use plain water for steam inhalation, it may actually draw the salt from your own saliva, resulting in a dehydrating effect.

In addition to personal steamers, other options for air humidification come in varying sizes of humidifiers from room size to whole house humidifiers. When choosing between a warm air or cool mist humidifier, considerations include both personal preference and needs. One of the primary reasons warm mist humidifiers are not recommended for young children is due to the risk of burns from the heating element. Both the warm mist and cool air humidifiers act similarly in adding moisture to the environmental air. External air humidification may be beneficial and provide a level of comfort for many singers. Regular cleaning of the humidifier is vital to prevent bacteria and mold buildup. Also, depending on the hardness of the water, it is important to avoid mineral buildup on the device and distilled water may be recommended for some humidifiers.

For traveling performers who often stay in hotels, fly on airplanes, or are generally exposed to other dry-air environments, there are products on the market designed to help minimize drying effects. One such device is called a Humidflyer, which is a face mask designed with a filter to recycle the moisture of a person's own breath and replenish moisture on each breath cycle.

For dry nasal passages or to clear sinuses, many singers use Neti pots. Many singers use this homeopathic flushing of the nasal passages regularly. Research supports the use of a Neti pot as a part of allergy relief and chronic rhinosinusitis control when utilized properly, sometimes in combination with medical management.⁵ Conversely, long-term use of nasal irrigation (without taking intermittent breaks from daily use) may result in washing out the "good" mucus of the nasal passages, which naturally help to rid the nose of infections. A study presented at the 2009 American College of Allergy, Asthma, and Immunology (ACAAI) annual scientific meeting reported that when a group of individuals who were using twice-daily nasal irrigation for one year discontinued using it, they had an increase in acute rhinosinusitis.⁶

Tea, Honey, and Gargle to Keep the Throat Healthy

Regarding the use of general teas (which many singers combine with honey or lemon), there is likely no harm in the use of decaffeinated tea (caffeine may cause systemic dryness). The warmth of the tea may provide a soothing sensation to the pharynx and the act of swallowing can be relaxing for the muscles of the throat. Honey has shown promising results as an effective cough suppressant in the pediatric population.⁷ The dose of honey given to the children in the study was two teaspoons. Gargling with salt or apple cider vinegar and water are also popular home remedies for many singers with the uses being from soothing the throat to curing reflux. Gargling plain water has been shown to be efficacious in reducing the risk of contracting upper respiratory infections. I suggest that when gargling, the singer only "bubble" the water with air and avoid engaging the vocal folds in sound production. Saltwater as a gargle has long been touted as a sore throat remedy and can be traced back to 2700 BCE in China for treating gum disease. The science behind a saltwater rinse for everything from oral hygiene to sore throat is that salt (sodium chloride) may act as a natural analgesic (pain killer) and may also kill bacteria. Similar to the effects that not enough salt in the water may have on drawing the salt out of the tissue in the steam inhalation, if you oversaturate the water solution with excess salt and gargle it, it may act to draw water out of the oral mucosa, thus reducing inflammation.

Another popular home remedy reported by singers is the use of apple cider vinegar to help with everything from acid reflux to sore throats. Dating back to 3300 BCE, apple cider vinegar was reported as a medicinal remedy, and it became popular in the 1970s as a weight loss diet cocktail. Popular media reports apple cider vinegar can improve conditions from acne and arthritis to nosebleeds and varicose veins. Specific efficacy data regarding the beneficial nature of apple cider vinegar for the purpose of sore throat, pharyngeal inflammation, and/or reflux has not been reported in the literature at this time. Of the peer-reviewed studies found in the literature, one discussed possible esophageal erosion and inconsistency of actual product in tablet form.[8] Therefore, at this time, strong evidence supporting the use of apple cider vinegar is not published.

Medications and the Voice

Medications (over the counter, prescription, and herbal) may have resultant drying effects on the body and often the laryngeal mucosa. General classes of drugs with potential drying effects include: antidepressants, antihypertensives, diuretics, ADD/ADHD medications, some oral acne medications, hormones, allergy drugs, and vitamin C in high doses. The National Center for Voice and Speech (NCVS) provides a listing of some common medications with potential voice side effects including laryngeal dryness. This listing does not take into account all medications, so singers should always ask their pharmacist of the potential side effects of a given medication. Due to the significant number of drugs on the market, it is safe to say that most pharmacists will not be acutely aware of "vocal side effects," but if dryness is listed as a potential side effect of the drug, you may assume that all body systems could be affected. Under no circumstances should you stop taking a prescribed medication without consulting your physician first. As every person has a different body chemistry and reaction to medication, just because a medication lists dryness as a potential side effect, it does not necessarily mean you will experience that side effect. Conversely, if you begin a new medication and notice physical or vocal changes that are unexpected, you should consult with your physician. Ultimately, the goal of medical management for any condition is to achieve the most benefits with the least side effects. Please see the companion page on the NATS website for a list of possible resources for the singer regarding prescription drugs and herbs.

In contrast to medications that tend to dry, there are medications formulated to increase saliva production or alter the viscosity of mucus.

Medically, these drugs are often used to treat patients who have had a loss of saliva production due to surgery or radiation. Mucolytic agents are used to thin secretions as needed. As a singer, if you feel that you need to use a mucolytic agent on a consistent basis, it may be worth considering getting to the root of the laryngeal dryness symptom and seeking a professional opinion from an otolaryngologist.

Reflux and the Voice

Gastroesophageal reflux (GERD) and/or laryngopharyngeal reflux (LPR) can have a devastating impact on the singer if not recognized and treated appropriately. Although GERD and LPR are related, they are considered as slightly different diseases. GERD (Latin root meaning "flowing back") is the reflux of digestive enzymes, acids, and other stomach contents into the esophagus (food pipe). If this backflow is propelled through the upper esophagus and into the throat (larynx and pharynx), it is referred to as LPR. It is not uncommon to have both GERD and LPR, but they can occur independently.

More frequently, people with GERD have decreased esophageal clearing. Esophagitis, or inflammation of the esophagus, is also associated with GERD. People with GERD often feel heartburn. LPR symptoms are often "silent" and do not include heartburn. Specific symptoms of LPR may include some or all of the following: lump in the throat sensation, feeling of constant need to clear the throat/postnasal drip, longer vocal warm-up time, quicker vocal fatigue, loss of high frequency range, worse voice in the morning, sore throat, and bitter/raw/brackish taste in the mouth. If you experience these symptoms on a regular basis, it is advised that you consider a medical consultation for your symptoms. Prolonged, untreated GERD or LPR can lead to permanent changes in both the esophagus and/or larynx. Untreated LPR also provides a laryngeal environment that is conducive for vocal fold lesions to occur as it inhibits normal healing mechanisms.

Treatments of LPR and GERD generally include both dietary and lifestyle modifications in addition to medical management. Some of the dietary recommendations include: elimination of caffeinated and carbonated beverages, smoking cessation, no alcohol use, and limiting tomatoes, acidic foods and drinks, and raw onions or peppers, to name a few. Also, avoidance of high-fat foods is recommended. From a lifestyle perspective, suggested changes include not eating within three hours of lying down, eating small meals frequently (instead of large meals), elevating the head of your bed, avoiding tight clothing around the belly, and not bending over or exercising too soon after you eat.

Reflux medications fall in three general categories: antacids, H2 blockers, and proton pump inhibitors (PPI). There are now combination drugs that include both an H2 blocker and proton pump inhibitor. Every medication has both associated risks and benefits, and singers should be aware of the possible benefits and side effects of the medications they take. In general terms, antacids (e.g., Tums, Mylanta, Gaviscon) neutralize stomach acid. H2 (histamine) blockers, such as Axid (nizatidine), Tagamet (cimetidine), Pepcid (famotidine), and Zantac (ranitidine), work to decrease acid production in the stomach by preventing histamine from triggering the H2 receptors to produce more acid. Then there are the PPIs: Nexium (esomeprazole), Prevacid (lansoprazole), Protonix (pantoprazole), AcipHex (rabeprazole), Prilosec (omeprazole), and Dexilant (dexlansoprazole). PPIs act as a last line of defense to decrease acid production by blocking the last step in gastric juice secretion. Some of the most recent drugs to combat GERD/LPR are combination drugs (e.g., Zegrid [sodium bicarbonate plus omeprazole]), which provide a short-acting response (sodium bicarbonate) and a long release (omeprazole). Because some singers prefer a holistic approach to reflux management, strict dietary and lifestyle compliance is recommended and consultation with both your primary care physician and naturopath are warranted in that situation. Efficacy data on nonregulated herbs, vitamins, and supplements is limited, but some data does exist.

Physical Exercise

Vocal athletes, like other physical athletes, should consider how and what they do to maintain both cardiovascular fitness and muscular strength. In today's performance culture, it is rare that a performer stands still and sings, unless in a recital or choral setting. The range of physical activity can vary from light movement to high-intensity choreography with acrobatics. As performers are being required to increase their on-stage physical activity level from the operatic stage to the pop-star arena, overall physical fitness is imperative to avoid compromise in the vocal system. Breathlessness will result in compensation by the larynx, which is now attempting to regulate the air. Compensatory vocal behaviors over time may result in a change in vocal performance. The health benefits of both cardiovascular training and strength training are well documented for physical athletes but relatively rare in the literature for vocal performers.

Mental Wellness

Vocal performers must maintain a mental focus during performance and a mental toughness during auditioning and training. Rarely during vocal performance training programs is this important aspect of performance addressed, and it is often left to the individual performer to develop their own strategy or coping mechanism. Yet, many performers are on antianxiety or antidepressant drugs (which may be the direct result of performance-related issues). If the sports world is again used as a parallel for mental toughness, there are no elite-level athletes (and few junior-level athletes) who don't utilize the services of a performance/sports psychologist to maximize focus and performance. I recommend that performers consider the potential benefits of a performance psychologist to help maximize vocal performance. Several references that may be of interest to the singer include: Joanna Cazden's *Visualization for Singers* (Joanna Cazden, 1992) and Shirlee Emmons and Alma Thomas's *Power Performance for Singers: Transcending the Barriers* (Oxford, 1998).

Unlike instrumentalists, whose performance is dependent on accurate playing of an external musical instrument, the singer's instrument is uniquely intact and subject to the emotional confines of the brain and body in which it is housed. Musical performance anxiety (MPA) can be career threatening for all musicians, but perhaps the vocal athlete is more severely impacted. The majority of literature on MPA is dedicated to instrumentalists, but the basis of definition, performance effects, and treatment options can be considered for vocal athletes. Fear is a natural reaction to a stressful situation, and there is a fine line between emotional excitation and perceived threat (real or imagined). The job of a performer is to convey to an audience through vocal production, physical gestures, and facial expression a most heightened state of emotion. Otherwise, why would audience members pay top dollar to sit for two or three hours for a mundane experience? Not only is there the emotional conveyance of the performance but also the internal turmoil often experienced by the singers themselves in preparation for elite performance. It is well documented in the literature that even the most elite performers have experienced debilitating performance anxiety. MPA is defined on a continuum with anxiety levels ranging from low to high and has been reported to comprise four distinct components: affect, cognition, behavior, and physiology. Affect comprises feelings (e.g., doom, panic, anxiety). Affected cognition will result in altered levels of concentration, while the behavior component results in postural shifts, quivering, and trembling. Finally physiologically the body's autonomic nervous system (ANS) will activate, resulting in the "fight or flight" response.

In recent years, researchers have been able to define two distinct neurological pathways for MPA. The first pathway happens quickly and without conscious input (ANS), resulting in the same fear stimulus as if a person were put into an emergent, life-threatening situation. In those situations, the brain releases adrenaline, resulting in physical changes of increased heart rate, increased respiration, shaking, pale skin, dilated pupils, slowed digestion, bladder relaxation, dry mouth, and dry eyes, all of which severely affect vocal performance. The second pathway that has been identified results in a conscious identification of the fear/threat and a much slower physiologic response. With the second neuromotor response, the performer has a chance to recognize the fear, process how to deal with the fear, and respond accordingly.

Treatment modalities to address MPA include psycho-behavioral therapy (including biofeedback) and drug therapies. Elite physical performance athletes have been shown to benefit from visualization techniques and psychological readiness training, yet within the performing arts community, stage fright may be considered a weakness or character flaw precluding readiness for professional performance. On the contrary, vocal athletes, like physical athletes, should mentally prepare themselves for optimal competition (auditions) and performance. Learning to convey emotion without eliciting an internal emotional response by the vocal athlete may take the skill of an experienced psychologist to help change ingrained neural pathways. Ultimately, control and understanding of MPA will enhance performance and prepare the vocal athlete for the most intense performance demands without vocal compromise.

VOCAL WELLNESS: INJURY PREVENTION

In order to prevent vocal injury and understand vocal wellness in the singer, general knowledge of common causes of voice disorders is imperative. One common cause of voice disorders is vocally abusive behaviors or misuse of the voice to include phonotraumatic behaviors such as yelling, screaming, loud talking, talking over noise, throat clearing, coughing, harsh sneezing, and boisterous laughing. Chronic or less than optimal vocal properties such as poor breathing techniques, inappropriate phonatory habits during conversational speech (glottal fry, hard glottal attacks), inapt pitch, loudness, rate of speech, and/or hyperfunctional laryngeal-area muscle tone may also negatively impact vocal function. Medically related etiologies, which also have the potential to impact vocal function, range from untreated chronic allergies and sinusitis to endocrine dysfunction and hormonal imbalance. Direct trauma, such as a blow to the neck or the risk of vocal fold damage during intubation, can impact optimal performance in vocal athletes depending on the nature and extent of the trauma. Finally, external irritants ranging from cigarette smoke to reflux directly impact the laryngeal mucosa and ultimately can lead to laryngeal pathology.

Vocal hygiene education and compliance may be one of the primary essential components for maintaining the voice throughout a career. This section will provide the singer with information on prevention of vocal injury. However, just like a professional sports athlete, it is unlikely that a professional vocal athlete will go through an entire career without some compromise in vocal function. This may be a common upper respiratory infection that creates vocal fold swelling for a short time, or it may be a "vocal accident" that is career threatening. Regardless, the knowledge of how to take care of your voice is essential for any vocal athlete.

Train Like an Athlete for Vocal Longevity

Performers seek instant gratification in performance sometimes at the cost of gradual vocal building for a lifetime of healthy singing. Historically, voice pedagogues required their students to perform vocalise exclusively for up to two years before beginning any song literature. Singers gradually built their voice by ingraining appropriate muscle memory and neuromotor patterns through development of aesthetically pleasing tones, onsets, breath management, and support. There was an intensive master-apprentice relationship and rigorous vocal guidelines to maintain a place within a given studio. Time off was taken if a vocal injury ensued or careers potentially were ended, and students were asked to leave a given singing studio if their voice was unable to withstand the rigors of training. Training vocal athletes today has evolved and appears driven to create a "product" quickly, perhaps at the expense of the longevity of the singer. Pop stars emerging well before puberty are doing international concert tours, yet many young artist programs in the classical arena do not consider singers for their programs until they are in their mid- to late twenties.

Each vocal genre presents with different standards and vocal demands. Therefore, the amount and degree of vocal training are varied. Some would argue that performing extensively without adequate vocal training and development is ill-advised, yet singers today are thrust onto the stage at very young ages. Dancers, instrumentalists, and physical athletes all spend many hours per day developing muscle strength, memory, and proper technique for their craft. The more advanced the artist or athlete, generally the more specific the training protocol becomes. Consideration of training vocal athletes in this same fashion is recommended. One would generally not begin a young, inexperienced singer on a Wagner aria without previous vocal training. Similarly, in nonclassical vocal music, there are easy, moderate, and difficult pieces to consider pending level of vocal development and training.

Basic pedagogical training of alignment, breathing, voice production, and resonance are essential building blocks for development of good voice production. Muscle memory and development of appropriate muscle patterns happen slowly over time with appropriate repetitive practice. Doing too much, too soon for any athlete (physical or vocal) will result in an increased risk for injury. When the singer is being asked to do "vocal gymnastics," they must be sure to have a solid basis of strength and stamina in the appropriate muscle groups to perform consistently with minimal risk of injury.

Vocal Fitness Program

One generally does not get out of bed first thing in the morning and try to do a split. Yet many singers go directly into a practice session or audition without proper warm-up. Think of your larynx like your knee, made up of cartilages, ligaments, and muscles. Vocal health is dependent upon appropriate warm-ups (to get things moving), drills for technique, and then cool-downs (at the end of your day). Consider vocal warm-ups a "gentle stretch." Depending on the needs of the singer, warm-ups should include physical stretching; postural alignment self-checks; breathing exercises to promote rib cage, abdominal, and back expansion; vocal stretches (glides up to stretch the vocal folds and glides down to contract the vocal folds); articulatory stretches (yawning, facial stretches); and mental warm-ups (to provide focus for the task at hand). Vocalises, in my opinion, are designed as exercises to go beyond warm-ups and prepare the body and voice for the technical and vocal challenges of the music they sing. They are varied and address the technical level and genre of the singer to maximize performance and vocal growth. Cool-downs are a part of most athletes' workouts. However, singers often do not use cool-downs (physical, mental, and vocal) at the end of a performance. A recent study looked specifically at the benefits of vocal cool-downs in singers and found that singers who used a vocal cool-down had decreased effort to produce voice the next day.[9]

Systemic hydration as a means to keep the vocal folds adequately lubricated for the amount of impact and friction that they will undergo has been previously discussed in this chapter. Compliance with adequate oral hydration recommendations is important and subsequently so is the minimization of agents that could potentially dry the membranes (e.g., caffeine, medications, dry air). The body produces approximately two quarts of mucus per day. If not adequately hydrated, the mucus tends to be thick and sticky. Poor hydration is similar to not putting enough oil in the car engine. Frankly, if the gears do not work as well, there is increased friction and heat, and the engine is not efficient.

Speak Well, Sing Well

Optimize the speaking voice utilizing ideal frequency range, breath, intensity, rate, and resonance. Singers generally are vocally enthusiastic individuals who talk a lot and often talk loudly. During typical conversation, the average fundamental speaking frequency (times per second the vocal folds are impacting) for a male varies from 100 to 150 Hz and 180 to 230 Hz for women. Because of the delicate structure of the vocal folds and the importance of the layered microstructure vibrating efficiently and effectively to produce voice, vocal behaviors or outside factors that compromise the integrity of the vibration patterns of the vocal folds may be considered phonotrauma.

Phonotraumatic behaviors can include yelling, screaming, loud talking, harsh sneezing, and harsh laughing. Elimination of phontraumatic behaviors is essential for good vocal health. The louder one speaks, the farther apart the vocal folds move from midline, the harder they impact, and the longer they stay closed. A tangible example would be to take your hands, move them only six inches apart, and clap as hard and as loudly as you can for ten seconds. Now, move your hands two feet apart and clap as hard, loudly, and quickly as possible for ten seconds. The farther apart your hands are, the more air you move and the louder the clap, and the skin on the hands becomes red and ultimately swollen (if you do it long enough and hard enough). This is what happens to the vocal folds with repeated impact at increased vocal intensities. The vocal folds are approximately 17 mm in length and vibrate at 220 times per second on A3, 440 on A4, 880 on A5, and more than 1,000 per second when singing a high C. That is a lot of impact for little muscles. Consider this fact when singing loudly or in a high tessitura for prolonged periods of time. It becomes easy to see why women are more prone than men to laryngeal impact injuries due to the frequency range of the voice alone.

In addition to the amount of cycles per second the vocal folds are impacting, singers need to be aware of their vocal intensity (volume). Check the volume of the speaking and singing voice and for conversational speech and consider using a distance of three to five feet as a gauge for how loud you need to be in general conversation (about an arm's-length distance). Cell phones and speaking on a Bluetooth device in a car generally results in louder than conversational vocal intensity, and singers are advised to minimize unnecessary use of these devices.

Singers should be encouraged to take "vocal naps" during their day. A vocal nap would be a short period of time (five minutes to an hour) of complete silence. Although the vocal folds are rarely completely still (because they move when you swallow and breathe), a vocal nap minimizes impact and vibration for a short window of time. A physical nap can also be refreshing for the singer mentally and physically.

Avoid Environmental Irritants: Alcohol, Smoking, Drugs

Arming singers with information on the actual effects of environmental irritants so that they can make informed choices on engaging in exposure to these potential toxins is essential. The glamour that continues to be associated with smoking, drinking, and drugs can be tempered with the deaths of popular stars such as Amy Winehouse and Cory Monteith who engaged in life-ending choices. There is extensive documentation about the long-term effects of toxic and carcinogenic substances, but here are a few key facts to consider when choosing whether to partake.

Alcohol, although it does not go over the vocal folds directly, does have a systemic drying effect. Due to the acidity in alcohol, it may increase the likelihood of reflux, resulting in hoarseness and other laryngeal pathologies. Consuming alcohol generally decreases one's inhibitions, and therefore you are more likely to sing and do things that you would not typically do under the influence of alcohol.

Beyond the carcinogens in nicotine and tobacco, the heat at which a cigarette burns is well above the boiling temperature of water (water boils at 212° F; cigarettes burn at over 1400°F). No one would consider pouring a pot of boiling water on their hand, and yet the burning temperature for a cigarette results in significant heat over the oral mucosa and vocal folds. The heat alone can create a deterioration in the lining, resulting in polypoid degeneration. Obviously, cigarette smoking has been well documented as a cause for laryngeal cancer.

Marijuana and other street drugs are not only addictive but can cause permanent mucosal lining changes depending on the drug used and the method of delivery. If you or one of your singer colleagues is experiencing a drug or alcohol problem, research or provide information and support on getting appropriate counseling and help.

SMART PRACTICE STRATEGIES FOR SKILL DEVELOPMENT AND VOICE CONSERVATION

Daily practice and drills for skill acquisition are an important part of any singer's training. However, overpracticing or inefficient practicing may be detrimental to the voice. Consider practice sessions of athletes:

they may practice four to eight hours per day broken into one- to two-hour training sessions with a period of rest and recovery in between sessions. Although we cannot parallel the sports model without adequate evidence in the vocal athlete, the premise of short, intense, focused practice sessions is logical for the singer. Similar to physical exercise, it is suggested that practice sessions do not have to be all "singing." Rather, structuring sessions so that one-third of the session is spent on warm-up; one-third on vocalise, text work, rhythms, character development, and so on; and one-third on repertoire will allow the singer to function in a more efficient vocal manner. Building the amount of time per practice session—increasing duration by five minutes per week, building to sixty to ninety minutes—may be effective (e.g., Week 1: twenty minutes three times per day; Week 2: twenty-five minutes three times per day, etc.).

Vary the "vocal workout" during your week. For example, if you do the same physical exercise in the same way day after day with the same intensity and pattern, you will likely experience repetitive strain–type injuries. However, cross-training or varying the type and level of exercise aids in injury prevention. So when planning your practice sessions for a given week (or rehearsal process for a given role), consider varying your vocal intensity, tessitura, and exercises to maximize your training sessions, building stamina, muscle memory, and skill acquisition. For example, one day you may spend more time on learning rhythms and translation and the next day you spend thirty minutes performing coloratura exercises to prepare for a specific role. Take one day a week off from vocal training and give your voice a break. This does not mean complete vocal rest (although some singers find this beneficial), but rather a day without singing and limited talking.

Practice Your Mental Focus

Mental wellness and stress management are equally as important as vocal training for vocal athletes. Addressing any mental health issues is paramount to developing the vocal artist. This may include anything from daily mental exercises/meditation/focus to overcoming performance anxiety to more serious mental health issues/illness. Every person can benefit from improved focus and mental acuity.

SPECIFIC VOCAL WELLNESS CONCERNS FOR THE SACRED MUSIC VOCALIST

From early Gregorian chant to modern-day praise and worship rock bands, the sacred music vocalist has likely encountered almost every type of musical genre throughout history depending on the denomination and church tradition. General vocal wellness guidelines for all singers hold true for the sacred music vocalist. However, pending the setting for the singer (a traditional Catholic mass, temple, or an arena-type praise and worship rock concert), vocal wellness implications will vary.

Vocal Wellness Tips for Traditional Worship

For the traditional worship vocalist (which may include choral music and solo singing), some of the most common vocal injuries tend to be related to inadequate stamina and/or training for a given piece of music. Specifically, many choristers go to rehearsal once a week for several hours and then sing for several hours for services. However, they do not exercise their voice the rest of the week. A physical analogy can be made to this type of singing. If you only go to the gym and exercise for two hours two days a week, then you are more likely to fatigue and get injured than if you spread out your training and condition for the longer workout. Therefore, if you are in a choir, try to sing for twenty to forty-five minutes daily (when you do not have choir practice) to keep your voice conditioned and "in shape" for those long rehearsals.

Another likely time when traditional worship vocalists experience vocal injury is during the holiday seasons (e.g., High Holy Days, Christmas, Easter) because there is often a major uptick in the duration and intensity of the voice. Cantatas, musicals, and long-duration singing activities are typically a part of the holiday season, regardless of religious denomination. Outside of actual rehearsals and performances, there is generally increased family activity during these parts of the calendar, leading to lack of normal sleeping and eating habits. It is important for the vocalist to take care of themselves physically and vocally as the intensity of the season increases. Vocal conservation during long rehearsals, taking vocal naps when possible, and avoiding overindulgence of food and beverages become imperative during heavy voice-use seasons in the church.

Contemporary Christian Singers

Similar to contemporary pop singers, contemporary Christian singers are required to put on high physical-intensity shows. Therefore, both physical and vocal fitness should be foremost in the minds of anyone desiring to perform praise and worship music today. Praise and worship singers should be physically and vocally in shape to meet the necessary performance demands.

Performance of contemporary Christian music requires that the singer have a flexible, agile, dynamic instrument with appropriate stamina. Singers must have a good command of their instrument as well as exceptional underlying intention to what they are singing as it is much more about relaying a message and connecting with the audience as part of the worship experience. The praise and worship music is an integral part of worship in today's contemporary services. It encompasses the first fifteen to twenty minutes of the service, setting the tone for worship, and leaves the congregation in the last five to ten minutes with the music they will sing to themselves as they leave worship. The voices that convey this message must reflect the mood and intent of the worship, requiring dynamic control, vocal control/power, and an emotional connection to the text.

Another unique aspect to contemporary Christian praise and worship bands is often the use of fogs/hazers. In some cases, the chemicals used in the fogs/haze can be irritating to the voice. If the singer takes a spray bottle (such as an empty/washed-out window cleaner bottle) and fills it with water, they can spritz the air on the stage prior to performance to pull the dust to the floor (the water particles will weigh down the dust and pull it to the floor and out of your face). Secondly, the use of a small fan that blows the air toward the congregation will draw haze/fog from the stage and away from the singer. Depending on your stage setup, this fan can be placed either at the singer's feet or on speakers. Multiple fans are fine.

Similar to other commercial music vocalists, praise and worship singers use microphones and amplification. If used correctly, amplification can be used to maximize vocal health by allowing the singer to produce voice in an efficient manner while the sound engineer is effectively able to mix, amplify, and add effects to the voice. Understanding both the utility and limits of a given microphone and sound system is essential for the singer both for live and studio performances. Using an appropriate microphone not only can enhance the singer's performance but can reduce vocal load. Emotional extremes (intimacy and exultation) can be enhanced by appropriate microphone choice, placement, and acoustical mixing, thus saving the singer's voice.

Not everything a singer does is "vocally healthy," sometimes because the emotional expression may be so intense it results in vocal collision forces that are extreme. Even if the singer does not have formal vocal training, the concept of "vocal cross-training" (which can mean singing in both high and low registers with varying intensities and resonance options) before and after practice sessions and services is likely a vital component to minimizing vocal injury.

FINAL THOUGHTS

Ultimately, the singer must learn to provide the most output with the least "cost" to the system. Taking care of the physical instrument through daily physical exercise, adequate nutrition and hydration, and focused attention on performance will provide a necessary basis for vocal health during performance. Small doses of high-intensity singing (or speaking) will limit impact stress on the vocal folds. Finally, attention to the mind, body, and voice will provide the singer with an awareness when something is wrong. This awareness and knowledge of when to rest or seek help will promote vocal well-being for the singer throughout his or her career.

NOTES

1. W. LeBorgne et al., "Prevalence of Vocal Pathology in Incoming Freshman Musical Theatre Majors: A 10-year Retrospective Study," Fall Voice Conference, New York, 2012.

2. J. Brinckmann et al., "Safety and Efficacy of a Traditional Herbal Medicine (Throat Coat) in Symptomatic Temporary Relief of Pain in Patients with Acute Pharyngitis: A Multicenter, Prospective, Randomized, Double-Blinded, Placebo-Controlled Study," *Journal of Alternative and Complementary Medicine* 9, no. 2 (2003): 285–298.

3. N. Roy et al., "An Evaluation of the Effects of Three Laryngeal Lubricants on Phonation Threshold Pressure (PTP)," *Journal of Voice* 17, no. 3 (2003): 331–342.

4. K. Tanner et al., "Nebulized Isotonic Saline versus Water Following a Laryngeal Desiccation Challenge in Classically Trained Sopranos," *Journal of Speech Language and Hearing Research* 53, no. 6 (2010): 1555–1566.

5. C. Brown and S. Graham, "Nasal Irrigations: Good or Bad?" *Current Opinion in Otolaryngology, Head and Neck Surgery* 12, no. 1 (2004): 9–13.

6. T. Nsouli, "Long-Term Use of Nasal Saline Irrigation: Harmful or Helpful?" American College of Allergy, Asthma and Immunology Annual Scientific Meeting, Abstract 32, 2009.

7. M. Shadkam et al. "A Comparison of the Effect of Honey, Dextromethorphan, and Diphenhydramine on Nightly Cough and Sleep Quality in Children and Their Parents," *Journal of Alternative and Complementary Medicine* 16, no. 7 (2010): 787–793.

8. L. Hill et al., "Esophageal Injury by Apple Cider Vinegar Tablets and Subsequent Evaluation of Products," *Journal of the American Dietetic Association* 105, no. 7 (2005): 1141–1144.

9. R. O. Gottliebson, "The Efficacy of Cool-Down Exercises in the Practice Regimen of Elite Singers," PhD dissertation, University of Cincinnati, 2011.

USING AUDIO ENHANCEMENT TECHNOLOGY

Matthew Edwards

In the early days of popular music, musicians performed without electronic amplification. Singers learned to project their voices in the tradition of vaudeville performers with a technique similar to operatic and operetta performers who had been singing unamplified for centuries. When microphones began appearing on stage in the 1930s, vocal performance changed forever since the loudness of a voice was no longer a factor in the success of a performer. In order to be successful, all a singer needed was an interesting vocal quality and an emotional connection to what he or she was singing. The microphone would take care of projection.[1]

Vocal qualities that may sound weak without a microphone can sound strong and projected when sung with one. At the same time, a singer with a voice that is acoustically beautiful and powerful can sound harsh and pushed if he or she lacks microphone technique. Understanding how to use audio equipment to get the sounds a singer desires without harming the voice is crucial. The information in this chapter will help the reader gain a basic knowledge of terminology and equipment commonly used when amplifying or recording a vocalist as well as providing tips for singing with a microphone.

THE FUNDAMENTALS OF SOUND

In order to understand how to manipulate an audio signal, you must first understand a few basics of sound including frequency, amplitude, harmonics, and resonance.

Frequency

Sound travels in waves of compression and rarefaction within a medium, which for our purposes is air (see figure 8.1). These waves travel through the air and into our inner ears via the ear canal. There they are converted via the eardrums into nerve impulses that are transmitted to the brain and interpreted as sound. The number of waves per second is measured in Hertz (Hz), which gives us the frequency of the sound that we have learned to perceive as pitch. For example, we hear 440 Hz (440 cycles of compression and rarefaction per second) as A4, the pitch A above middle C.

Amplitude

The magnitude of the waves of compression and rarefaction determines the amplitude of the sound, which we call its "volume." The larger the waves of compression and rarefaction, the louder we perceive the sound to be. Measured in decibels (dB), amplitude represents changes in air pressure from the baseline. Decibel measurements range from zero decibels (0 dB), the threshold of human hearing, to 130 dB, the upper edge of the threshold of pain.

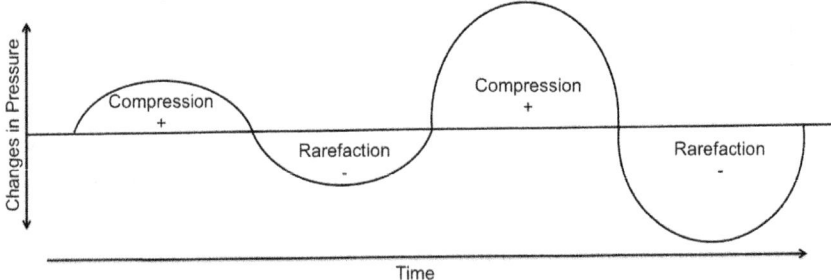

Figure 8.1. Compression and rarefaction. *Creative Commons*

Harmonics

The vibrating mechanism of an instrument produces the vibrations necessary to establish pitch (the fundamental frequency). The vibrating mechanism for a singer is the vocal folds. If an acoustic instrument, such as the voice, were to produce a note with the fundamental frequency alone, the sound would be strident and mechanical like the emergency alert signal used on television. Pitches played on acoustic instruments consist of multiple frequencies, called overtones, which are emitted from the vibrator along with the fundamental frequency. For the purposes of this chapter, the overtones that we are interested in are called harmonics. Harmonics are whole number multiples of the fundamental frequency. For example, if the fundamental is 220 Hz (A3), the harmonic overtone series would be 220 Hz, 440 Hz (fundamental frequency times two), 660 Hz (fundamental frequency times three), 880 Hz (fundamental frequency times four), and so on. Every musical note contains both the fundamental frequency and a predictable series of harmonics, each of which can be measured and identified as a specific frequency. This series of frequencies then travels through a hollow cavity (the vocal tract) where they are attenuated or amplified by the resonating frequencies of the cavity, which is how resonance occurs.

Resonance

The complex waveform created by the vocal folds travels through the vocal tract, where it is enhanced by the tract's unique resonance characteristics. Depending on the resonator's shape, some harmonics are amplified and some are attenuated. Each singer has a unique vocal tract shape with unique resonance characteristics. This is why two singers of the same voice type can sing the same pitch and yet sound very different. We can analyze these changes with a tool called a spectral analyzer as seen in figure 8.2. The slope from left to right is called the spectral slope. The peaks and valleys along the slope indicate amplitude variations of the corresponding overtones. The difference in spectral slope between instruments (or voices) is what enables a listener to aurally distinguish the difference between two instruments playing or singing the same note.

Because the throat and mouth act as the resonating tube in acoustic singing, changing their size and shape is the only option for making

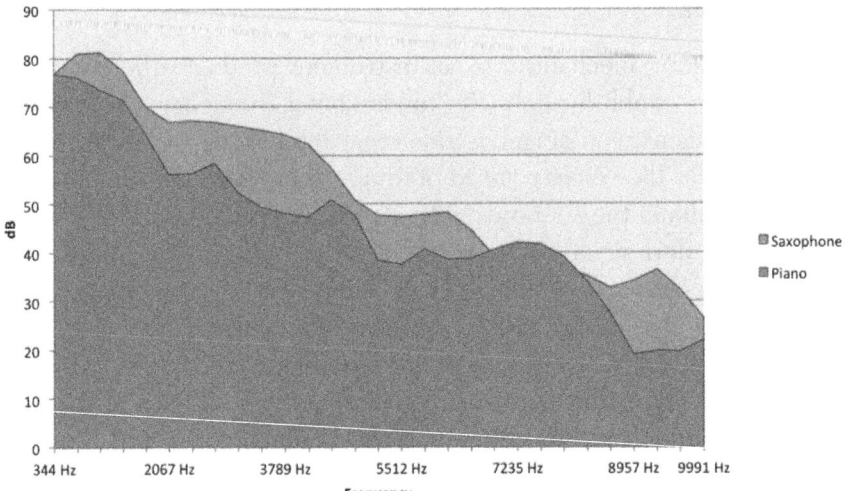

Figure 8.2. The figure above shows two instruments playing the same pitch. The peak at the far left is the fundamental frequency and the peaks to the right are harmonics that have been amplified and attenuated by the instrument's resonator, resulting in a specific timbre. *Courtesy of Matthew Edwards*

adjustments to timbre for those who perform without microphones. In electronically amplified singing, the sound engineer can make adjustments to boost or attenuate specific frequency ranges, thus changing the singer's timbre. For this and many other reasons discussed in this chapter, it is vitally important for singers to know how audio technology can affect the quality of their voice.

SIGNAL CHAIN

The signal chain is the path an audio signal travels from the input to the output of a sound system. A voice enters the signal chain through a microphone, which transforms acoustic energy into electrical impulses. The electrical pulses generated by the microphone are transmitted through a series of components that modify the signal before the speakers transform it back into acoustic energy. Audio engineers and producers understand the intricacies of these systems and are able to make an infinite variety of alterations to the vocal signal. While some engineers strive to replicate the original sound source as accurately as possible, others use the capabilities of the system to alter the sound for artistic effect. Since more components and variations exist than can be discussed in just a few pages, this chapter will discuss only basic components and variations found in most systems.

Microphones

Microphones transform the acoustic sound waves of the voice into electrical impulses. The component of the microphone that is responsible for receiving the acoustic information is the diaphragm. The two most common diaphragm types that singers will encounter are dynamic and condenser. Each offers advantages and disadvantages depending on how the microphone is to be used.

Dynamic Dynamic microphones consist of a dome-shaped Mylar diaphragm attached to a free-moving copper wire coil that is positioned between the two poles of a magnet. The Mylar diaphragm moves in response to air pressure changes caused by sound waves. When the diaphragm moves, the magnetic coil that is attached to it also moves. As the magnetic coil moves up and down between the magnetic poles, it

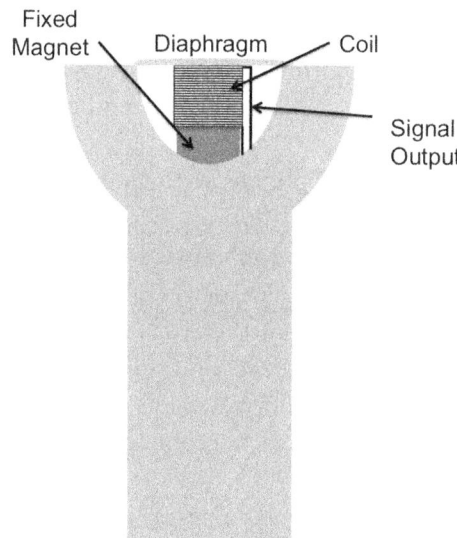

Figure 8.3. This is the basic design of a dynamic microphone. *Courtesy of Matthew Edwards*

produces an electrical current that corresponds to the sound waves produced by the singer's voice. That signal is then sent to the soundboard via the microphone cable.

The Shure SM58 dynamic microphone is the industry standard for live performance because it is affordable, nearly indestructible, and easy to use. Dynamic microphones such as the Shure SM58 have a lower sensitivity than condenser microphones, which makes them more successful at avoiding feedback. Because of their reduced tendency to feedback, dynamic microphones are the best choice for artists who use handheld microphones when performing.

Condenser Condenser microphones are constructed with two parallel plates: a rigid posterior plate and a thin, flexible anterior plate. The anterior plate is constructed of either a thin sheet of metal or a piece of Mylar that is coated with a conductive metal. The plates are separated by air, which acts as a layer of insulation. In order to use a condenser microphone, it must be connected to a soundboard that supplies "phantom power." A component of the soundboard, phantom power sends a 48-volt power supply through the microphone cable to the microphone's plates. When the plates are charged by phantom power, they form a capacitor. As acoustic vibrations send the anterior plate into motion, the distance between the two plates varies, which causes the capacitor to release a small electric current. This current, which corresponds with the acoustic signal of the voice, travels through the microphone cable to the soundboard where it can be enhanced and amplified.

Electret condenser microphones are similar to condenser microphones, but they are designed to work without phantom power. The anterior plate of an electret microphone is made of a plastic film coated with a conductive metal that is electrically charged before being set into place opposite the posterior plate. The charge applied to the anterior plate will last for ten or more years and therefore eliminates the need for an exterior power source. Electret condenser microphones are often used in head-mounted and lapel microphones, laptop computers, and smartphones.

Recording engineers prefer condenser microphones for recording applications due to their high level of sensitivity. Using a condenser microphone, performers can sing at nearly inaudible acoustic levels and

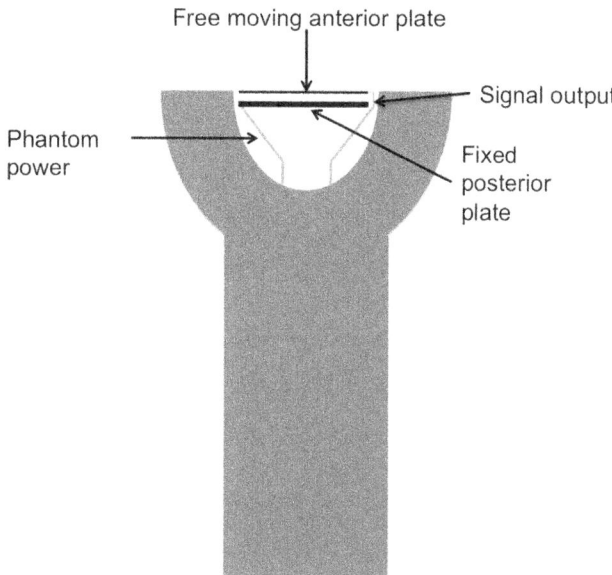

Figure 8.4. This is the basic design of a condenser microphone. *Courtesy of Matthew Edwards*

obtain a final recording that is intimate and earthy. While the same vocal effects can be recorded with a dynamic microphone, they will not have the same clarity as those produced with a condenser microphone.

Frequency Response Frequency response is a term used to define how accurately a microphone captures the tone quality of the signal. A "flat response" microphone captures the original signal with little to no signal alteration. Microphones that are not designated as "flat" have some type of amplification or attenuation of specific frequencies, also known as cut or boost, within the audio spectrum. For instance, the Shure SM58 microphone drastically attenuates the signal below 300 Hz and amplifies the signal in the 3 kHz range by 6 dB, the 5 kHz range by nearly 8 dB, and the 10 kHz range by approximately 6 dB. The Oktava 319 microphone cuts the frequencies below 200 Hz while boosting everything above 300 Hz with nearly 5 dB between 7 kHz and 10k Hz (see figure 8.5). In practical terms, recording a bass singer with the Shure SM58 would drastically reduce the amplitude of the fundamental frequency while the Oktava 319 would produce a slightly more consistent boost in the range of the singer's formant. Either of these options could

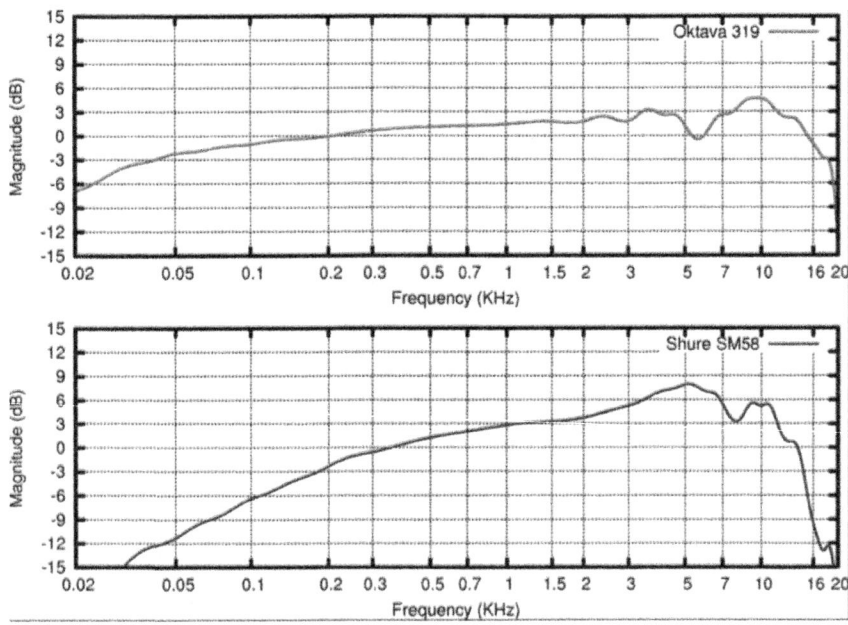

Figure 8.5. Example frequency response graphs for the Oktava 319 and the Shure SM58. *Wikimedia Commons*

be acceptable depending on the situation, but the frequency response must be considered before making a recording or performing live.

Amplitude Response The amplitude response of a microphone varies depending on the angle at which the singer is positioned in relation to the axis of the microphone. In order to visualize the amplitude response of a microphone at various angles, microphone manufacturers publish polar pattern diagrams (also sometimes called a directional pattern or a pickup pattern). Polar pattern diagrams usually consist of six concentric circles divided into twelve equal sections. The center point of the microphone's diaphragm is labeled 0° and is referred to as "on-axis" while the opposite side of the diagram is labeled 180° and is described as "off-axis."

Although polar pattern diagrams appear in two dimensions, they actually represent a three-dimensional response to acoustic energy. You can use a round balloon as a physical example to help you visualize a three-dimensional polar pattern diagram. Position the tied end of the balloon away from your mouth and the inflated end directly in front of your lips. In this position, you are singing on-axis at 0° with the tied end of the balloon being 180°, or off-axis. If you were to split the balloon in half vertically and horizontally (in relationship to your lips), the point at which those lines intersect would be the center point of the balloon. That imaginary center represents the diaphragm of the microphone. If you were to extend a 45° angle in any direction from the imaginary center and then drew a circle around the inside of the balloon following that angle, you would have a visualization of the three-dimensional application of the two-dimensional polar pattern drawing.

The outermost circle of the diagram indicates that the sound pressure level (SPL) of the signal is transferred without any amplitude reduction, indicated in decibels (dB). Each of the inner circles represents a -5 dB reduction in the amplitude of the signal up to -25 dB. Figure 8.7 below is an example.

Figures 8.8, 8.9, and 8.10 show the most commonly encountered polar patterns.

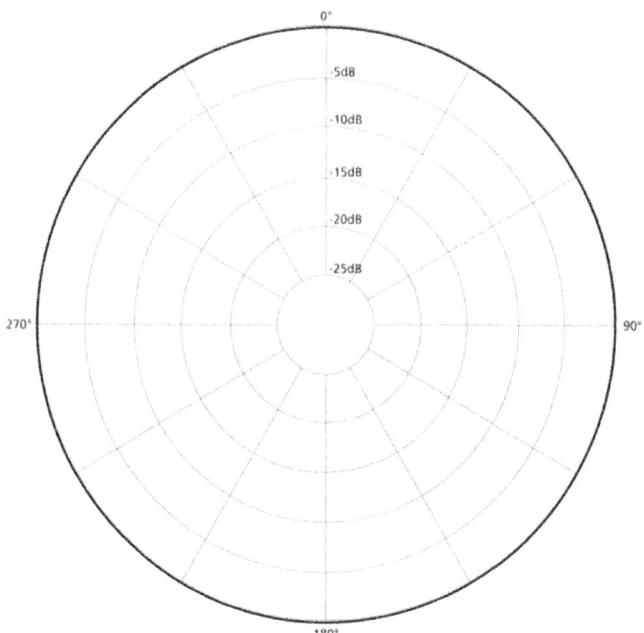

Figure 8.6. An example of a microphone polar pattern diagram. *Wikimedia Commons*

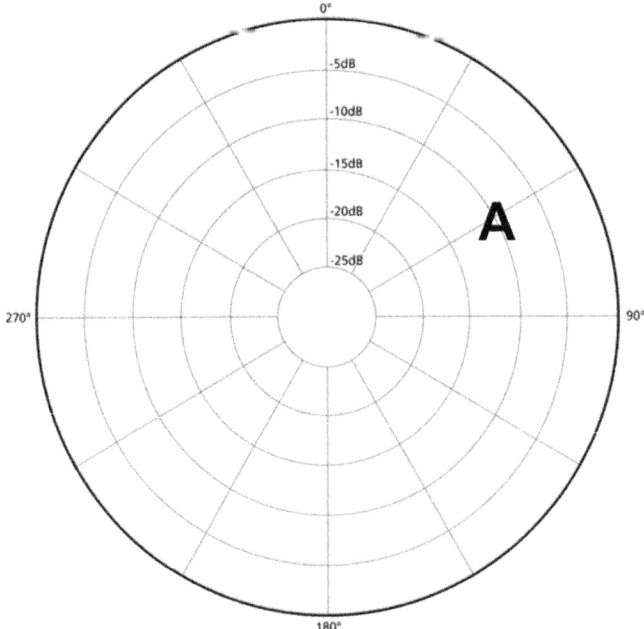

Figure 8.7. If the amplitude response curve intersected with point A, there would be a -10-dB reduction in the amplitude of frequencies received by the microphone's diaphragm at that angle. *Wikimedia Commons*

When you are using a microphone with a polar pattern other than omnidirectional (a pattern that responds to sound equally from all directions), you may encounter frequency response fluctuations in addition to amplitude fluctuations. Cardioid microphones in particular are known for their tendency to boost lower frequencies at close proximity to the sound source while attenuating those same frequencies as the distance between the sound source and the microphone increases. This is known as the "proximity effect." Some manufacturers will notate these frequency response changes on their polar pattern diagrams by using a combination of various lines and dashes alongside the amplitude response curve.

Sensitivity While sensitivity can be difficult to explain in technical terms without going into an in-depth discussion of electricity and electrical terminology, a simplified explanation should suffice for most readers. Manufacturers test microphones with a standardized 1 kHz tone at 94

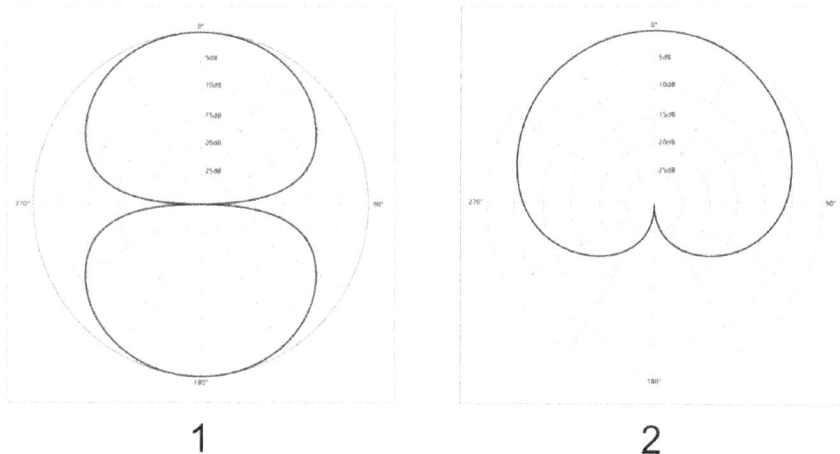

Figure 8.8. Diagram one represents a bidirectional pattern; diagram two represents a cardioid pattern. *Creative Commons*

dB in order to determine how sensitive the microphone's diaphragm will be to acoustic energy. Microphones with greater sensitivity can be placed farther from the sound source without adding excessive noise to the signal. Microphones with lower sensitivity will need to be placed closer to the sound source in order to keep excess noise at a minimum. When shopping for a microphone, the performer should audition several

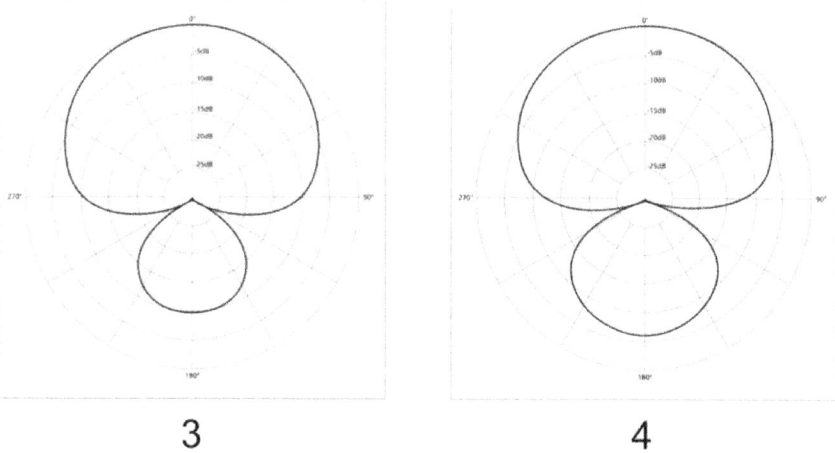

Figure 8.9. Diagram three represents a supercardioid pattern; diagram four represents a hypercardioid pattern. *Creative Commons*

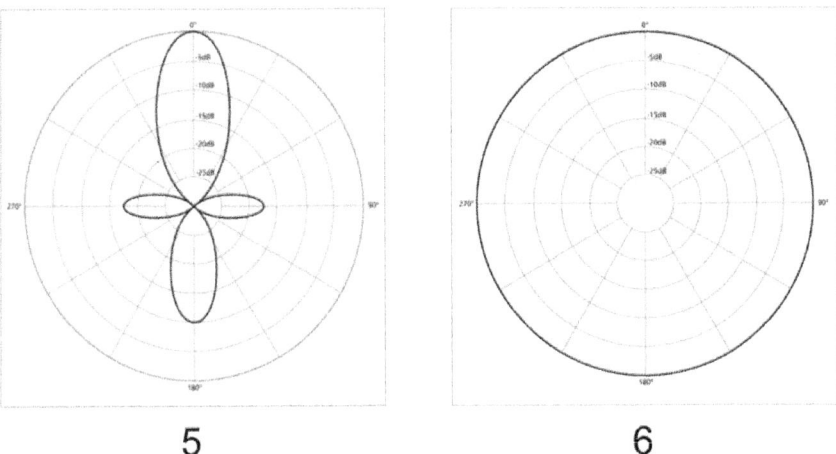

Figure 8.10. Diagram five represents a shotgun pattern, and diagram six represents an omnidirectional pattern. *Creative Commons*

next to each other, plugged into the same soundboard, with the same volume level for each. When singing on each microphone, at the same distance, the performer will notice that some models replicate the voice louder than others. This change in output level is due to differences in each microphone's sensitivity. If a performer has a loud voice, they may prefer a microphone with lower sensitivity (one that requires more acoustic energy to respond). If a performer has a lighter voice, they may prefer a microphone with higher sensitivity (one that responds well to softer signals).

Equalization (EQ)

Equalizers enable the audio engineer to alter the audio spectrum of the sound source and make tone adjustments with a simple electronic interface. Equalizers come in three main types: shelf, parametric, and graphic.

Shelf Shelf equalizers cut or boost the uppermost and lowermost frequencies of an audio signal in a straight line (see figure 8.11). While this style of equalization is not very useful for fine-tuning a singer's tone quality, it can be very effective in removing room noise. For example, if an air conditioner creates a 60-Hz hum in the recording studio, the shelf can be set at 65 Hz, with a steep slope. This setting eliminates frequen-

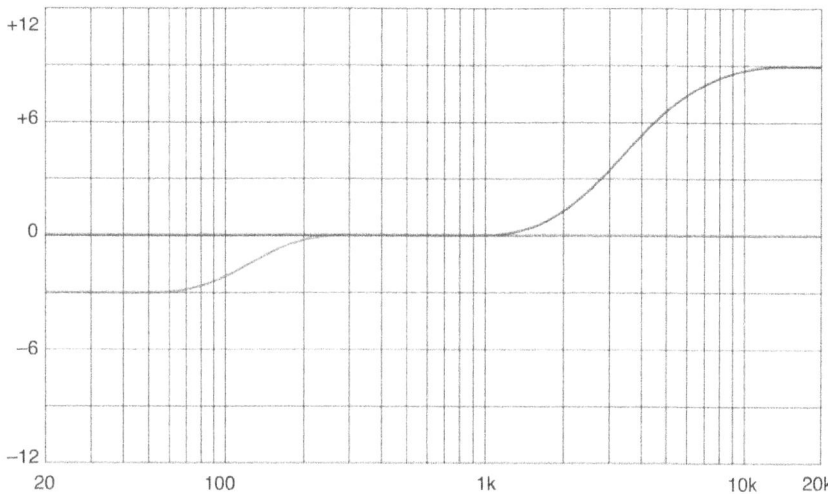

Figure 8.11. The frequency amplitude curves above show the effect of applying a shelf EQ to an audio signal. *Wikimedia Commons*

cies below 65 Hz and effectively removes the hum from the microphone signal.

Parametric Parametric units simultaneously adjust multiple frequencies of the audio spectrum that fall within a defined parameter. The engineer selects a center frequency and adjusts the width of the bell curve surrounding that frequency by adjusting the "Q" (see figure 8.12). He or she then boosts or cuts the frequencies within the bell curve to alter the audio spectrum. Parametric controls take up minimal space on a soundboard and offer sufficient control for most situations. Therefore, most live performance soundboards have parametric EQs on each individual channel. With the advent of digital workstations, engineers can now use computer software to fine-tune the audio quality of each individual channel using a more complex graphic equalizer in both live and recording studio settings without taking up any additional physical space on the board. However, many engineers still prefer to use parametric controls during a live performance since they are usually sufficient and are easier to adjust mid-performance.

Parametric adjustments on a soundboard are made with rotary knobs similar to those in figure 8.13 below. In some cases, you will find a button labeled "low cut" or "high pass" that will automatically apply a shelf

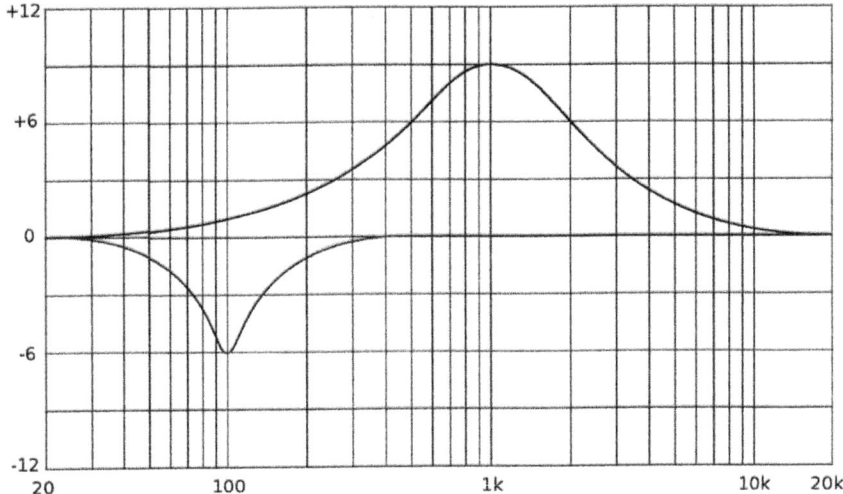

Figure 8.12. The frequency amplitude curves above display two parametric EQ settings. The top curve represents a boost of +8 dB set at 1 kHz with a relatively large bell curve—a low Q. The lower curve represents a high Q set at 100 Hz with a cut of -6 dB. *Wikimedia Commons*

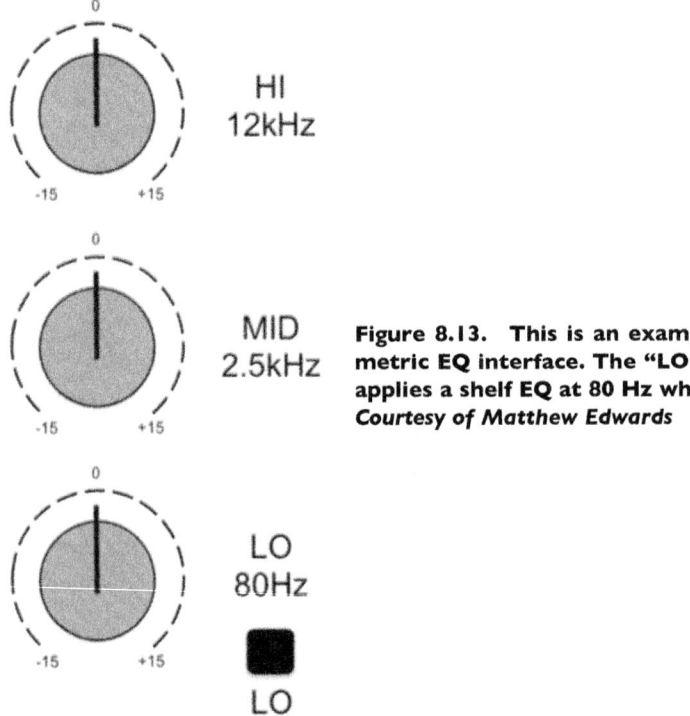

Figure 8.13. This is an example of a parametric EQ interface. The "LO CUT" button applies a shelf EQ at 80 Hz when depressed. *Courtesy of Matthew Edwards*

filter to the bottom of the audio spectrum at a specified frequency. On higher-end boards, you may also find a knob that enables you to select the high pass frequency.

Graphic   Graphic equalizers enable engineers to identify a specific frequency for boost or cut with a fixed frequency bandwidth. For example, a ten-band equalizer enables the audio engineer to adjust ten specific frequencies (in Hz): 31, 63, 125, 250, 500, 1K, 2K, 4K, 8K, and 16K. Graphic equalizers are often one of the final elements of the signal chain, preceding only the amplifier and speakers. In this position, they can be used to adjust the overall tonal quality of the entire mix.

Utilizing Equalization   Opinions on the usage of equalization vary among engineers. Some prefer to only use equalization to remove or reduce frequencies that were not a part of the original sound signal. Others will use EQ if adjusting microphone placement fails to yield acceptable results. Some engineers prefer a more processed sound and may use equalization liberally to intentionally change the vocal quality of the singer. For instance, if the singer's voice sounds dull, the engineer could add "ring" or "presence" to the voice by boosting the equalizer in the 2–10 kHz range.

Compression

Many singers are capable of producing vocal extremes in both frequency and amplitude levels that can prove problematic for the sound team. To help solve this problem, engineers often use compression.

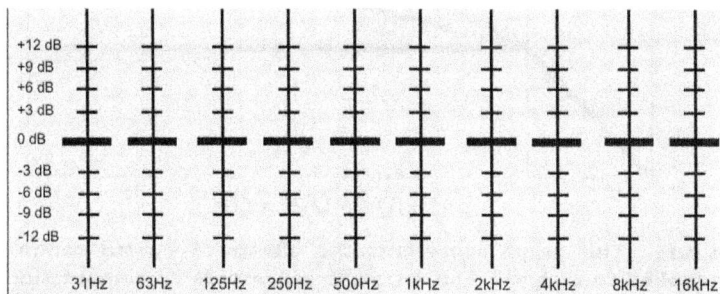

Figure 8.14.   This is an example of a graphic equalizer interface.
Courtesy of Matthew Edwards

Compressors limit the output of a sound source by a specified ratio. The user sets the maximum acceptable amplitude level for the output, called the "threshold," and then sets a ratio to reduce the output once it surpasses the threshold. The typical ratio for a singer is usually between 3:1 and 5:1. A 4:1 ratio indicates that for every 4 dB beyond the threshold level, the output will only increase by 1 dB. For example, if the singer went 24 dB beyond the threshold with a 4:1 ratio, the output would only be 6 dB beyond the threshold level (see figure 8.15 below).

Adjusting the sound via microphone technique can provide some of the same results as compression and is preferable for the experienced artist. However, compression tends to be more consistent and also gives the singer freedom to focus on performing and telling a story. The addi-

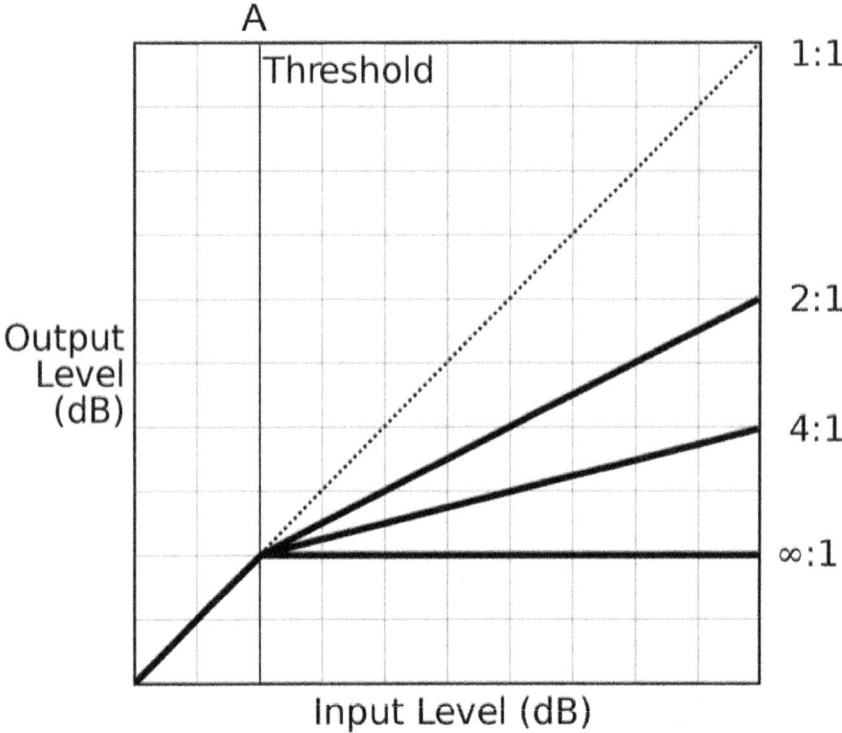

Figure 8.15. This graph represents the effects of various compression ratios applied to a signal. The 1:1 angle represents no compression. The other ratios represent the effect of compression on an input signal with the threshold set at line A. *Wikimedia Commons*

tional artistic freedom provided by compression is especially beneficial to singers who use head-mounted microphones, performers who switch between vocal extremes such as falsetto and chest voice, and those who are new to performing with a microphone. Compression can also be helpful for classical singers whose dynamic abilities, while impressive live, are often difficult to record in a manner that allows for consistent listening levels through a stereo system.

If a standard compressor causes unacceptable alterations to the tone quality, engineers can turn to a multiband compressor. Rather than affecting the entire spectrum of sound, multiband compressors allow the engineer to isolate a specific frequency range within the audio signal and then set an individual compression setting for that frequency range. For example, if a singer creates a dramatic boost in the 4-kHz range every time they sing above an A4, a multiband compressor can be used to limit the amplitude of the signal in only that part of the voice. By setting a 3:1 ratio in the 4-kHz range at a threshold that corresponds to the amplitude peaks that appear when the performer sings above A4, the engineer can eliminate vocal "ring" from the sound on only the offending notes while leaving the rest of the signal untouched. These units are available for both live and studio use and can be a great alternative to compressing the entire signal.

Reverb

Reverb is one of the easier effects for singers to identify; it is the effect you experience when singing in a cathedral. An audience experiences natural reverberation when they hear the direct signal from the singer and then, milliseconds later, they hear multiple reflections as the acoustical waves of the voice bounce off the side walls, floor, and ceiling of the performance hall.

Many performance venues and recording studios are designed to inhibit natural reverb. Without at least a little reverb added to the sound, even the best singer can sound harsh and even amateurish. Early reverb units transmitted the audio signal through a metal spring, which added supplementary vibrations to the signal. While some engineers still use spring reverb to obtain a specific effect, most now use digital units. Common settings on digital reverb units include wet/dry, bright/dark, and options for delay time. The wet/dry control adjusts the amount of

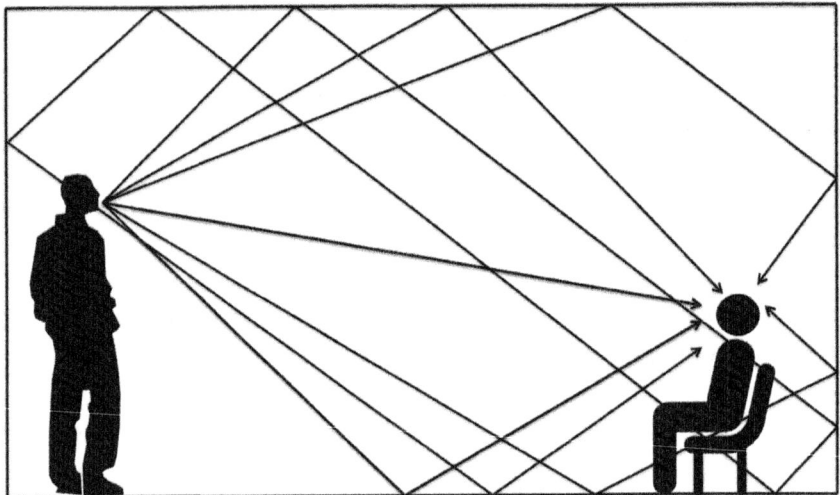

Figure 8.16. This diagram illustrates the multiple lines of reflection that create reverb. *Courtesy of Matthew Edwards*

direct signal (dry) and the amount of reverberated signal (wet). The bright/dark control helps simulate the effects of various surfaces within a natural space. For instance, harder surfaces such as stone reflect high frequencies and create a brighter tone quality while softer surfaces such as wood reflect lower frequencies and create a darker tone quality. The delay time, which is usually adjustable from milliseconds to seconds, adjusts the amount of time between when the dry signal and wet signals reach the ear. Engineers can transform almost any room into a chamber music hall or concert stadium simply by adjusting these settings.

Delay

Whereas reverb blends multiple wet signals with the dry signal to replicate a natural space, delay purposefully separates a single wet signal from the dry signal to create repetitions of the voice. With delay, you will hear the original note first and then a digitally produced repeat of the note several milliseconds to seconds later. The delayed note may be heard one time or multiple times and the timing of those repeats can be adjusted to match the tempo of the song.

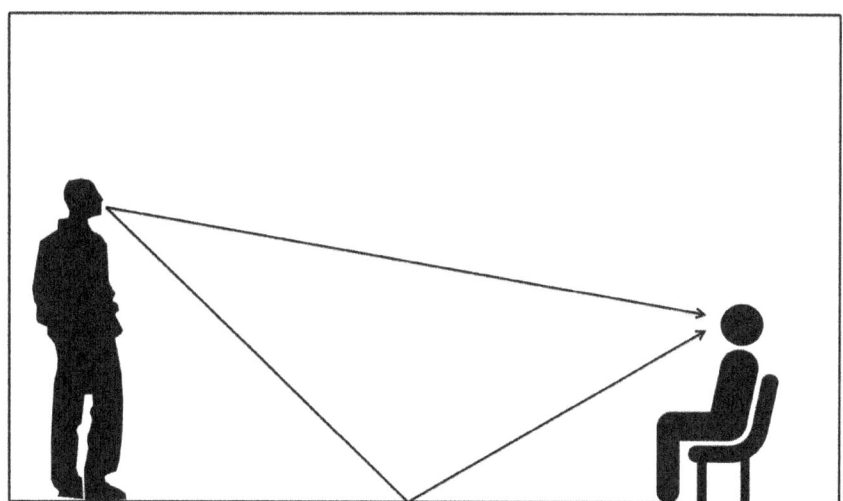

Figure 8.17. This diagram illustrates how a direct line of sound followed by a reflected line of sound creates delay. *Courtesy of Matthew Edwards*

Auto-Tune

Auto-Tune was first used in studios as a useful way to clean up minor imperfections in otherwise perfect performances. Auto-Tune is now an industry standard that many artists use, even if they are not willing to admit it. Auto-Tune has gained a bad reputation in the past few years, and whether or not you agree with its use, it is a reality in today's market. If you do not understand how to use it properly, you could end up sounding like T-Pain.[2]

Both Antares and Melodyne have developed Auto-Tune technology in both "auto" and "graphical" formats. "Auto" Auto-Tune allows the engineer to set specific parameters for pitch correction that are then computer controlled. "Graphical" Auto-Tune tracks the pitch in the selected area of a recording and plots the fundamental frequency on a linear graph. The engineer can then select specific notes for pitch correction. They can also drag selected pitches to a different frequency, add or reduce vibrato, and change formant frequencies above the fundamental. To simplify, the "auto" function makes general corrections while the "graphic" function makes specific corrections. The "auto" setting is usually used to achieve a specific effect (for instance "I Believe" by Cher), while the "graphic" setting is used to correct small imperfections in a recorded performance.

Digital Voice Processors

Digital voice processors are still relatively new to the market and have yet to gain widespread usage among singers. While there are several brands of vocal effects processors available, the industry leader as of this printing is a company called TC-Helicon. TC-Helicon manufactures several different units that span from consumer to professional grade. TC-Helicon's premier performer-controlled unit is called the VoiceLive 3. The VoiceLive 3 incorporates more than twelve vocal effects, eleven guitar effects, and a multi-track looper with 250 factory presets and 250 memory slots for user presets. The VoiceLive 3 puts the effects at the singer's feet in a programmable stomp box that also includes phantom power, MIDI in/out, a USB connection, guitar input, and monitor out. Onboard vocal effects include equalization, compression, reverb, and "auto" Auto-Tune. The unit also offers µMod (an adjustable voice modulator), a doubler (for thickening the lead vocal), echo, delay, reverb, and several other specialized effects.[3]

One of the most impressive features of digital voice processors is the ability to add computer-generated harmonies to the lead vocal. After the user sets the musical key, the processor identifies the fundamental frequency of each sung note. The computer then adds digitized voices at designated intervals above and below the lead singer. The unit also offers the option to program each individual song, with multiple settings for every verse, chorus, and bridge.

THE BASICS OF LIVE SOUND SYSTEMS

Live sound systems come in a variety of sizes from small practice units to state-of-the-art stadium rigs. Most singers only need a basic knowledge of the components commonly found in systems that have one to eight inputs. Units beyond that size usually require an independent sound engineer and are beyond the scope of this chapter.

Following the microphone, the first element in the live signal chain is usually the mixer. Basic portable mixers provide controls for equalization, volume level, auxiliary (usually used for effects such as reverb and compression), and, on some units, controls for built-in digital effects processors. Powered mixers combine an amplifier with a basic mixer, providing a compact solution for those who do not need a complex system. Since unpowered mixers do not provide amplification, you will need to add a separate amplifier to power this system.

The powered mixer or amplifier connects to speaker cabinets, which contain a "woofer" and a "tweeter." The woofer is a large round speaker that handles the bass frequencies while the tweeter is a horn-shaped speaker that handles the treble frequencies. The crossover, a component built into the speaker cabinet, separates high and low frequencies and sends them to the appropriate speaker (woofer or tweeter). Speaker cabinets can be either active or passive. Passive cabinets require a powered mixer or an amplifier in order to operate. Active cabinets have an amplifier built-in and do not require an external amplifier.

If you do not already own a microphone and amplification system, you can purchase a simple setup at relatively low cost through online vendors such as Sweetwater.com and MusiciansFriend.com. A dynamic microphone and a powered monitor are enough to get started. If you would like to add a digital voice processor, Digitech and TC-Helicon both sell entry-level models that will significantly improve the tonal quality of a sound system.

Monitors are arguably the most important element in a live sound system. The monitor is a speaker that faces the performers and allows them to hear themselves and/or the other instruments on stage. On-stage volume levels can vary considerably, with drummers often producing sound levels as high as 120 dB. Those volume levels make it nearly impossible for singers to receive natural acoustic feedback while performing. Monitors can improve aural feedback and help reduce the temptation to oversing. Powered monitors offer the same advantages as powered speaker cabinets and can be a great option for amplification when practicing. They are also good to have around as a backup plan in case you arrive at a venue and discover they do not supply monitors. In-ear monitors offer another option for performers and are especially useful for those who frequently move around the stage.

MICROPHONE TECHNIQUE

The microphone is an inseparable part of the contemporary commercial music singer's instrument. Just as there are techniques that improve singing, there are also techniques that will improve microphone use. Understanding what a microphone does is only the first step to using it successfully. Once you understand how a microphone works, you need hands-on experience.

The best way to learn microphone technique is to experiment. Try the following exercises to gain a better understanding of how to use a microphone when singing:

- Hold a dynamic microphone with a cardioid pattern directly in front of your mouth, no farther than one centimeter away. Sustain a comfortable pitch and slowly move the microphone away from your lips. Listen to how the vocal quality changes. When the microphone is close to the lips, you should notice that the sound is louder and has more bass response. As you move the microphone away from your mouth, there will be a noticeable loss in volume and the tone will become brighter.
- Next, sustain a pitch while rotating the handle down. The sound quality will change in a similar fashion as when you moved the microphone away from your lips.
- Now try singing breathy with the microphone close to your lips. How little effort can you get away with while producing a marketable sound?
- Try singing bright vowels and dark vowels and notice how the microphone affects the tone quality.
- Also experiment with adapting your diction to the microphone. Because the microphone amplifies everything, you may need to underpronounce certain consonants when singing. You will especially want to reduce the power of the consonants [t], [s], [p], and [b].

FINAL THOUGHTS

Since this is primarily an overview, you can greatly improve your comprehension of the material by seeking other resources to deepen your knowledge. There are many great resources available that may help clarify some of these difficult concepts. Most important, you must experiment. The more you play around with sound equipment on your own, the better you will understand it and the more comfortable you will feel when performing or recording with audio technology.

NOTES

1. Paula Lockheart, "A History of Early Microphone Singing, 1925–1939: American Mainstream Popular Singing at the Advent of Electronic Amplification," *Popular Music and Society* 26, no. 3 (2003): 367–385.

2. For example, listen to T-Pain's track "Buy You a Drank (Shawty Snappin')."

3. "VoiceLive 3," TC-Helicon, www.tc-helicon.com/products/voicelive-3/ (accessed May 2, 2016).

GLOSSARY

Acclamation: A liturgical song originally intended for the entire congregation such as the *Sanctus* ("Holy, Holy, Holy") of the Mass.
Advent: One of the major seasons of the Christian church year. Advent begins four Sundays before Christmas and is an anticipatory time preparing for the birth of Christ and the second coming of Christ.
Anthem: A choral composition on a biblical or otherwise religious text that is added to the service to complement the liturgy. Originally an Anglican genre, it is now ubiquitous across numerous denominations and is regarded as the most significant "choral moment" of a worship service. Historically accompanied by the organ.
Antiphon: The liturgical name for a "refrain" that is typically sung before and after each psalm in the office and at various points in the Mass.
Antiphonale: A book with the ordinary and proper chants of the Liturgy of the Hours (Office). The English term is "antiphonary."
Apocrypha: Additional "hidden" or extra books of scripture, sometimes included within the Old Testament (for Catholics) or as an addition between the Old and New Testament or an appendix at the end of the Bible (for liturgical Protestants).
Book of Common Prayer: The prayer book of the Anglican Communion that contains Eucharistic liturgies as well as liturgies for morning

and evening prayer and occasional services. The 1549 first edition introduced English-language liturgy to the Church for the first time

Canticle: A text in the genre of a psalm, usually from another part of the Bible. Famous examples include the Song of Mary (*Magnificat*), Song of Zechariah (*Benedictus*), and Song of Simeon (*Nunc Dimittis*), all from the Book of Luke.

Cantillation: A method for chanting the sacred books of the Jewish and (later) Christian tradition. This method dates back to seventh century and was developed by rabbis in Tiberias, Israel. Cantillation not only provides the text with melody but also provides syntactical understanding. The melody of the text often also serves to highlight specific sections.

Cathedral: The principal church of a diocese (region); where the bishop is seated.

Chazzanut: The general term used for describing the large body of traditional Jewish cantorial music.

Choirmaster: In the Anglican tradition, the principal choir director of a church.

Chorale: A four-part, German-language homophonic composition that sets a poetic religious text. The chorale was developed in Germany during the Reformation era and remains an important genre of hymnody to this day.

Christmas: One of the major seasons of the Christian church year. It is a twelve-day celebration of the birth of Christ that begins with Christmas Day on December 25.

Contemporary Christian Music: An umbrella term that includes a wide gamut of Christian music that is sung in a commercial or nonclassical style. Also refers to the industry as a whole.

Divine Liturgy: See Eucharist.

Divine Office: See Liturgy of the Hours.

Easter: One of the major seasons of the Christian church year. This fifty-day season begins on Easter Sunday, which celebrates the resurrection of Christ, and lasts until Pentecost Sunday.

Easter Triduum: See Triduum.

Epiphany: One of the major seasons of the Christian church year. Begins with the Feast of Epiphany on January 6 and lasts until Ash Wednesday, which marks the beginning of Lent.

GLOSSARY

Eucharist: The celebration of the Lord's Supper instituted by Jesus at the Last Supper; also called Mass, Holy Communion, or Divine Liturgy. The term is also used to refer to the blessed bread and wine.

Evening Prayer: The last major daily office of the Liturgy of the Hours, also known as Vespers, to be distinguished from Eucharist; for Anglican use, see Evensong.

Evensong: A prayer service in English, adapted from medieval Latin Vespers and Compline, featuring choral music as part of the liturgy, including anthems, the *Phos Hilaron*, and the *Magnificat* and *Nunc Dimittis* canticles.

Good Friday: Friday of Holy Week. Recounts the crucifixion of Jesus of Nazareth.

Gospel: (1) The first four books of the New Testament—Matthew, Mark, Luke, and John—which tell the story of the life, death, and resurrection of Jesus of Nazareth. (2) An African American genre of Christian music that is a forerunner of contemporary Christian music.

Graduale: A book with the ordinary and proper chants of the Mass. The English term is "gradual."

High Holidays: The term "high holidays" (or "high holy days") refers to the holidays of Rosh Hashanah (the Jewish New Year) and the holiday of Yom Kippur (the Day of Atonement) that occurs ten days later. In Hebrew the holidays of Rosh Hashanah and Yom Kippur are also known as the *Yamim Noraim*, or Days of Awe.

Holy Communion: See Eucharist.

Holy Triduum: See Triduum.

Holy Week: The week leading up to Easter. Holy Week begins on Palm (Passion) Sunday and includes Maundy Thursday and Good Friday.

Houseplant Church: A church established through the efforts of a missionary group.

Hymn: A poetic religious text set to music, usually in a four-voice homophonic style. The term "hymn" can also refer to just the text alone and not the tune (soprano melody) or harmonization (ATB voices).

Kol Nidre: The name of the Jewish evening service that begins at sundown commencing the holiday of Yom Kippur. It is also the name of the chanted liturgical selection that begins the service. It is one of the most famous pieces of cantorial music.

Lectionary: A calendar of appointed scriptures for worship services. Many liturgical Protestants use the Revised Common Lectionary, which is adapted from the modern Catholic lectionary and offers a three-year cycle of biblical readings.

Lent: One of the major seasons of the Christian church year. Begins on Ash Wednesday, which occurs forty days before Easter Sunday.

Liturgy: The traditions and customs of worship of a specific religion or denomination, including texts, music, and rituals.

Liturgy of the Hours: Also known as the "office" or "divine office," the daily cycle of liturgies throughout the course of the day, celebrated especially in monasteries. The Eucharist (Holy Communion) is distinct from the office.

Mass: A Eucharistic liturgy. As a musical genre, refers to a compositional setting of the five parts of the Mass Ordinary: Kyrie, Gloria, Credo, Sanctus, and Agnus Dei.

Matins: See Morning Prayer.

Maundy Thursday: Thursday of Holy Week. Commemorates the Last Supper.

Megachurch: A large church generally characterized by contemporary music and an informal, nonliturgical evangelical Protestant style. Megachurches usually have an average weekly attendance of two thousand or greater.

Megillot: The sacred texts that are chanted during the year as part of Jewish holiday and festival observances. They include Ecclesiastes, Esther, Song of Songs, Ruth, and Lamentations. Each of these scrolls has a specific chant that is unique to the holiday.

Morning Prayer: A major daily office of the Liturgy of the Hours, also known as Lauds, to be distinguished from Eucharist; sometimes called Matins.

New Testament: The twenty-seven books that constitute the second major part of the Christian Bible. The New Testament discusses the teachings of Jesus and his apostles.

Nusach: The system of Jewish prayer modes and melodic motives that guide traditional prayer services.

Office: See Liturgy of the Hours.

Old Testament: The label that Christians assign to the Jewish scriptures, the first thirty-nine (for Protestants) or forty-six (for Catholics) books of the Bible.

Oratorio: A large-scale and unstaged dramatic work for chorus, orchestra, and soloists, usually on a religious theme. Oratorios often draw their stories from the Old Testament.

Ordinary: An element of the liturgy used in the same textual form throughout the year.

Paschal Triduum: See Triduum.

Passion: A specific subgenre of oratorio that tells the story of the arrest, trial, and crucifixion of Jesus of Nazareth. Unlike most oratorios, Passions are based on a New Testament subject and are often used liturgically (during Holy Week).

Pentecost: The longest of the major seasons of the Christian church year. Begins on Pentecost Sunday (or Whitsunday) and lasts until the first Sunday of Advent. Also known, along with the time between the seasons of Christmas and Lent, as Ordinary Time.

Proper: An element of the liturgy with a text used only on a particular day in the year.

Psalm: A text of praise, confession of sin, lament, or petition found in the psalter, the Book of Psalms from the Old Testament. There are 150 psalms.

Rosh Hashanah: The Jewish New Year.

Schola: A small liturgical choir; from the Latin *schola cantorum*, which means "school of singers" or "song school." In the Middle Ages, the *schola* consisted of men (monks or clerics) and choir boys.

Second Vatican Council: A meeting of the world's Catholic bishops from 1962 to 1965 that simplified and updated the liturgy to make it more accessible and participatory.

Shabbat: The Jewish Sabbath. Shabbat begins on Friday night at sundown and continues until Saturday evening at sundown.

Shaliach Tzibur: Hebrew for "messenger of the congregation." Since ancient times that cantor's role has been seen as one who acts as an emissary for the congregation by chanting and singing prayers and chants.

Solesmes Abbey: The Benedictine monastery in France that has been a leader in the promotion of Gregorian chant since the nineteenth century.

Torah: A handwritten parchment scroll that contains the first five books of the Hebrew Bible: Genesis, Exodus, Leviticus, Numbers, and Deuteronomy.

Triduum: The period of three days that begins on Maundy Thursday and ends with evening prayer on Easter Sunday. Also called the Paschal Triduum, Easter Triduum, or Holy Triduum.

Whitsunday: See Pentecost.

Vespers: See Evening Prayer.

Yamim Noraim: See High Holidays.

Yom Kippur: The Jewish Day of Atonement.

INDEX

abdomen, 148, *149*
abduction, 152
Academy for Jewish Religion (AJR), 10, 12–13
Academy for Jewish Religion California (AJRCA), 10, 13–14
accented syllables, in Gregorian chant, 45, 49, 50
Acclamation, 30
ACDA. *See* American Choral Directors Association
Act of Supremacy, 93
adduction, 152
administrative duties, 111–12
Advent, Season of, 26, 59, 96, 97
Agnus Dei, 28, 30, 31, 33, 63
AGO. *See* American Guild of Organists
AJR. *See* Academy for Jewish Religion
AJRCA. *See* Academy for Jewish Religion California

alcohol, 107, 178
Alleluia, 33, 63
Alleluia of the Mass, 30
allergies, 174
altar, choir and, 62
alveoli, 146
"Amazing Grace," 42
American Choral Directors Association (ACDA), 99, 116
American Conference of Cantors or the Cantor's Assembly, 15, 18
American Guild of Organists (AGO), 115
amplification, 139, 181, 185, 188, 204–5
amplitude, 186
amplitude response, 192–96, *194*
Annunciation, 26
ANS. *See* autonomic nervous system
anthem, 95, 96, 105, 106
Antiphon, 30
antiphonale, 36

215

Antiphonale Monasticum, 51, 76
Antiphonale Romanum, 76
Antiphonale Romanum II, 51, 76
anxiety, 172–73
apple cider vinegar, 168–69
articulation, 145, 160–62
artist-driven culture, 128
The Art of Cantillation: A Step-by Step Guide to Chanting Torah (Wolfe & Portnoy), 20
arytenoids, 153
Ashkenazic, 6
Assembly of God (Pentecostal movement), 127–28
Association of Anglican Musicians, 115
Assumption, 26
audience, 139, 172–73, 181. *See also* congregation
auditioning, 107–9
autonomic nervous system (ANS), 173
Auto-Tune, 203–4

Baking with the Cake Boss (Valastro), 137
Baroque Era, 56–57, 93
beauty, 52–53
Belz School of Jewish Music. *See* Yeshiva University
Benedictine monks, 23
Benediction, 65–66
Benedictus, 62, 63
Benedict XVI (Pope), 83
Bernstein, Michael, 1
Bible, 2–4, 9
bidirectional pattern, of microphones, 195
"The Big Middle," 134
Blessed Sacrament, 62, 65

Blessed Virgin Mary, 65–66
body. *See* physical well-being
body chemistry, 169
Boyle's Law, 146
brain, 161–62
breathing, 49–50, 84, 139, 146–51, 174–75
breathlessness, 172
Brooklyn Tabernacle, 135
Broughton, Viv, 122–23
Bruckner, Anton, 40

CA. *See* Cantors Assembly
Calvin, John, 121
cancer, 178
Canticle, 29
Canticum novum: Gregorian Chant for Today's Choirs (Ruff), 51
Cantillation, 9, 13, 15, 16, 20
cantor: admission, 7–9; congregation and, 3–5; definition of, 5; education, 7, 9–16; first steps in becoming, 8–9; *hazzan*, 2–3; Hebrew and, 2; Heschel on, 4–5; liturgical origins of, 2–5; mentorship, 8; modern, 2, 4–5; musical characteristics of, 5–7; recitals, 10; role of, 2, 4–5; Shulchan Aruch guidelines for, 4; training institutions for, 9–16; training requirements for, 7–9; variety of, 1–2; written application process for, 9. *See also* Jewish music
Cantors Assembly (CA), 14, 18
cantus planus, 47
carcinogens, 178
Cardine, Eugene, 48
cardioid microphones, 194, 195
Carmel Bach Festival, 113

INDEX

Carmichael, Ralph, 120, 123–26
cartilages, of larynx, *154*
cathedrals, 95, 97, 114–15, 139
Catholic Church, 55, 59, 93. *See also* Second Vatican Council
Catholic ethos, 59–60
Catholic identity, 71, 81
Catholic music: choral music, 57–58, 93; concerts, 67–69; contemporary, 82; diversity of, 89; ethnic, 81–82; Evangelical, 82; history and theory of, 88; history of, 55; liturgical origins of, 55–60; Mass in, 62–63; modern classical, 81; musical characteristics of, 61–69; performance skills for liturgy in, 84–86; practical guides to, 88; repertoire and resources of, 87; repertoire of, 61–69; schools of thought in, 80–83; structures and organizations of, 86–87; traditionalist, 80–81
Catholic Reformation, 56–57
Catholic superiority, 71–72
CCLI. *See* Christian Copyright License International
celebration music, Jewish, 5–6
cell phones, 177
Champion Forest Baptist Church, 132
chant, 30, 31, 38. *See also* Gregorian chant; Latin chant
Chapel by the Sea, 127
chazzanut, 7, 12–13
Check the Record, 126
chest mode, 155, *155*
choir, 62, 78–80, 91
chorale, 94–95
choral music, 10, 39, 91; additional resources for, 114–15; administrative duties for, 111–12; auditioning for, 107–9; blend, 84; Catholic, 57–58, 93; conducting, 99, 111, 116; diction, 106–7; directors, 101–2, 109; experience with, 102; further reading on, 116; history of, 93; institutions and universities for, 99; Jewish, 16; language, 106–7; listening to, 114–15; liturgical origins of, 92–97; liturgy and, 65–66; musical characteristics of, 92–97; organ in, 96–97; polyphony, 72; practical skills for career in, 109–10; professional organizations, 115–16; Protestant, 94–95; reading/musicianship in, 100–103, 105–6; recordings of, 114; repertoire of, 61, 79, 92–97; sectionals in, 111; secular, 117n2; singing, 100; skill set diversification for, 111–12; solo opportunities in, 111; style of, 101–2; summer work in, 113–14; technique for, 98–107; traditional, 60; training requirements for, 98–107; venues for, 115; vibrato in, 103–5; vowels in, 106
chord charts, 140
Christian Copyright License International (CCLI), 139–40
Christianity, 24, 39, 82, 93–96, *94*. *See also specific denominations*
Christian radio, 128
Christmas, Season of, 26, 96, 97
Chronicles, Book of, 3
church: contemporary Christian music and, 120–21; high, 96; Houseplant, 132, 134; law, 81, 82–83; liturgy and, 72; megachurches, *131*, 131–32, *133*, 134; musical

tradition of, 75; principal musician of, 108, 109; year, 97
Church of England, 96
Church Video License, 140
civil war, 122
Classical Era, 93
Close to You, 125
Collect of the Mass, 28, *34*
commercial music, 136–37
commitment, 109–10
Common Prayer, Book of, 96
Communio, 33, 63
Communion, 65, 81, 96
compensatory vocal behaviors, 172
The Complete Jewish Songbook for Children, 19
The Complete Shireinu: 350 Fully Notated Jewish Songs (Eglash), 19
Compline, 32, 36, 66
compositional complexity, 39
compression, *186*, 199, *200*, 201
concerts, 67–69
condenser microphones, 190–91, *191*
conducting, 38, 50, 99, 111, 116
congregation, 3–5, 78–80, 85, 86. *See also* audience
consonants, 206
contemporary Catholic music, 82
contemporary Christian music, 119; church and, 120–21; genres, 135; historical context of, 122–31; liturgical origins of, 122–34; musical characteristics of, 134–35; new music, 121–22; 1940–1960, 123; 1961–1989, 123–28; 1990–present, 128–31; repertoire and resources of, 139–42; singers, 181–82; training requirements of, 135–36; vocal technique and, 136–39

cool-downs, 176
coping mechanisms, 172
copyrights, 139–40
Council of Trent, 25, 55–57, 67
counterpoint, of Middle Ages, 39
Counter Reformation, 56
Credo, 33, 63
Creed, 79
cricoid cartilage, 153, *154*
cricothyroid (CT) dominant, 154, 155, *155*
Crosby, Fanny, 140
crossover music, 128
Crouch, Andraé, 119, 125
CT. *See* cricothyroid dominant
culture, 6, 31, 59, 66, 73, 128

Davidson, Charles, 19
Debbie Friedman School of Sacred Music. *See* Hebrew Union College–Jewish Institute of Religion
decibels, 186
delay, 202, *203*
devotional music, Jewish, 5–6
diaphragm, 147, *147*, 148
diction, 84, 106–7
Dies Irae, 64
diet, 164–65, 171, 180
digital voice processors, 204
diphthongs, 106
Dixie Four Quartet, 129
dominant, final, and range, in Gregorian chant, 43–44
Dorsey, Thomas A., 122
drinking, 107, 178
drugs, 178
Duruflé, 58
dust, 181
Dyer, Brent, 132

INDEX

dynamic microphones, *189*, 189–90, 206

ears, 186
Easter, Season of, 26, 68, 96, 97
Easter Triduum, 26
Easter Vigil, 69–70
Eglash, Joel N., 19
elastic recoil, 148
emotions, 172–73, 182
employment contracts, 99–100, 110
English language, 106
Entertainer's Secret, 166
entertainment, Jewish, 5–6
environmental irritants, 178
epiglottis, 153
Epiphany, Time after, 26, 96, 97
Episcopal Church, 92, 96, 115
epithelial layer, *152*, 153
equalization (EQ), 196–99, *197–99*
ethnic Catholic music, 81–82
ethnic groups, of Jewish music, 6–7
Eucharist, 29, 65
Eucharistic prayer, 25, 28, 62, 79, 96
Evangelic Catholic music, 82
Evensong, 32
exercise, 171–72
Exodus, 2
external intercostal muscles, 148, *149*
external obliques, 149, *150*
Extraordinary Form, 83–84
eye contact, with congregation, 86

falsetto mode, 155, *155*
FAU. *See* Florida Atlantic University
fear, 172
feast day, 29
feedback, 205
feedback system, *138*
Ferial Day, 30

"fight or flight" response, 173
first formant, *158*
five-line staff, for Gregorian chant, *46*
Florida Atlantic University (FAU), 17
fogs/hazers, 181
Foley, Edward, 87
folk music, 82, 125, 127
forced resonance, 157
formants, 157–60, *158*
440 Hertz, 155, 186
free resonance, 157
frequency, 155, 176–77, 186, *188*, 201–2, *202*
frequency response, 191–92, *192*, 194
fundamental pitch, 155
funerals, 5
Fux, Johann, 59

Gaither, Bill, 127, 129–30, 140
Gaither, Gloria, 130
gargling water, 168–69
gastroesophageal reflux (GERD), 170–71
Gates of Prayer, 18
Gates of Song (Shaarei Shirah) (Davidson), 19
gender, Gregorian chant and, 50
GERD. *See* gastroesophageal reflux
Giglio, Louis, 140
Gill, Gerald Dennis, 87
globalization, culture and, 59
Gloria, 33, 63, 76–77
glottis, 152, 155
Golden Keys Quartet, 129
Good Friday, 26, 64, 69
Gospel Acclamation, 79
gospel music, 123. *See also* contemporary Christian music

Graduale, 33, 36, 63
Graduale Novum, 51
Graduale Romanum, 51, 75
Graduale Simplex, 75–76
Graduale Triplex, 51
Gradus ad Parnassus, 59
Graham, Billy, 120, 123, 124–25
Grant, Amy, 128
graphic EQ, 199, *199*
Great Depression, 122–23
Gregorian chant, 23; accented syllables in, 45, 49, 50; books about, 52; breathing in, 49–50; Catholic ethos and, 60; conducting, 50; dominant, final, and range in, 43–44; five-line staff for, *46*; gender and, 50; improvisation in, 42; interpretation of, 47–48; intonation in, 50; liturgical origins of, 24–40; melody of, 41–45; modality of, 41–44; musical characteristics of, 40–45; notation, 38, 46, *46*, 48; note lengthening in, 49–50; octaves of, 37, 43, 50; official chant books of, 75; proper Mass in, 63; repertoire and resources of, 51; Second Vatican Council and, 27; tempo of, 49–50; training requirements of, 46–50; transcription of, 46; translation of, 48–49; treatment of text, 45; vocal technique of, 47. *See also* Mass
Gregorian Missal, 51
Gregory the Great (Pope), 25, 37
Guild of Temple Musicians (GTM), 17

Handel, George Frideric, 65
harmonics, 160, 187, *188*
harmonic series, 155–56, *156*, 186
HaSharim, 20

Hasidic songs, 18
Hava NaShira workshop, 16
Hayburn, Robert, 87
Haydn, 57
hazzan, 2–3, 8, 14
health. *See* physical well-being
Hebrew, 2, 6, 13
Hebrew College, 10, 15
Hebrew Union College–Jewish Institute of Religion (HUC-JIR), 10, 11–12
Hebrew University Jewish Music Centre, 17–18
Hebrew University Jewish Music Research Center (JMRC), 17–18
Henry VIII (King), 93
Heschel, Abraham Joshua, 4–5
He's Everything to Me (Carmichael), 124–26
"He's Everything to Me," 125
"He Touched Me," 129
high art music, 59
high church, 96
higher education, in vocal performance, 98–99
high holidays, 9, 11, 13, 16, 20
High Mass, 66–67
high pass EQ, 197
Hillsong, 143n12
H. L. Miller Cantorial School. *See* Jewish Theological Seminary
holidays, 180
Holy Spirit, 37
Holy Week, 26, 65, 111
honey, 168–69
houseplant churches, 132, 134
"How Great Art Thou," 123
HUC-JIR. *See* Hebrew Union College–Jewish Institute of Religion

INDEX

Huff, Ronn, 130
humidification, 166–67
hydration, 107, 165–68, 176
hymns, 95–96, 115
Hymn Society, 115
hyoid bone, 161
hypercardioid pattern, of microphones, *195*

I Don't Like That Music (Mitchell), 121
Immaculate Conception, 26
immigration, Jewish, 6
important feast days, 26
improvisation, 24, 40, 42
inflammation, 168
inharmonic overtones, 156
instant gratification, 174
Institution Narrative, 62
instrumental music, 93
instruments, 60, 145, *188*. *See also* voice
intentions, 181
internal intercostal muscles, 148, *149*
internal obliques, 149
intervals, 44
intonation, 50, 104
Introit, 33, 63
Italian opera, 100–101
It's More Than the Music: Life Lessons on Friends, Faith, and What Matters Most (Gaither), 129–30
Iubilate Deo, 51
"I've Been to Calvary," 129

Jackson, Mahalia, 123
jaw, 161
jazz, 122, 126
Jesus Christ, 66, 68, 72

Jesus festivals, 130
Jesus movement, 127
Jewish choral music, 16
Jewish culture, 6
Jewish festivals, 11
Jewish holidays, 16, 18, 20
Jewish immigration, 6
Jewish law, 4
Jewish music, 5; ethnic groups of, 6–7; modal system, 9, 11; non-cantorial opportunities to sing, 16–17; online sound archives of, 17–18; publishers, 18; repertoire and resources of, 17–20; theory, 9. *See also* cantor
Jewish Theological Seminary (JTS), 10, 14–15
JMRC. *See* Hebrew University Jewish Music Research Center
John Paul II (Pope), 83
Journal of Synagogue Music, 18
JTS. *See* Jewish Theological Seminary
Judaic Sound Archives, 17
Judaism, 1, 11, 14, 17, 18. *See also* Jewish music

Kartsonakis, Dino, 123
Knox, John, 121
Knoxville, Tennessee, 141
Kol Nidre prayer, 1
Kyrie, 33, 63, 76–77, 79

Ladino, 6
laity, 72
Lakewood Church, *131*, *132*, *133*, 135
lamina propria, 152, *152*
language, 106–7
laryngeal cancer, 178

laryngopharyngeal reflux (LPR), 170–71
larynx, 151–56, *154*, 161, 164
Latin chant, 23, 28, 75
Latin liturgy, 61
Latin recitation, 67
Lauds, 32, 36
laughing, 177
lead sheets, 140
Lectionary, 30
legato, 100–101, 104
Lent, Season of, 26, 59, 68, 96, 97
"Let's Just Praise the Lord," 130
Let the Glory Come Down, 140
Liber Hymnarius, 51, 76
Light Records, 125–26
lineless notation, 50
lips, 160–62
listening, to choral music, 114–15
liturgical origins: of cantor, 2–5; of Catholic music, 55–60; of choral music, 92–97; of contemporary Christian music, 122–34; of Gregorian chant, 24–40
Liturgical Year or Church Year, 29
liturgy: active participation in, 73, 75; basic terms of, 29–30; calendar of, 26, 96, 97; choral music and, 65–66; Christianity and, 24; church and, 72; committees of, 82; culture of, 31, 73; definition of, 24, 29; development of, 25; Jesus Christ and, 72; Latin, 61; medieval, 30; musical performance within, 61–62; music history and, 57–58; rites of, 73; role of music in, 70; scripture and, 73; in Second Vatican Council, communal understanding of, 70–71; in Second Vatican Council, regional variety of, 71; of Second Vatican Council, 75–77; structures of, 33; vernacular and, 73
Liturgy Constitution (*Sacrosanctum Concilium*), 72–75
The Liturgy Documents, 87
Liturgy of the Eucharist, 29, 77
Liturgy of the Hours, 29, 30, 51, 61, 64–65, 69, 76
Liturgy of the Word, 29, 77
live sound systems, 204–5
Locus Iste, 40
loft voice, 155, *155*
loudness, 185
"Love Is Surrender," 125
low cut EQ, 197, *198*
Low Mass, 66–67
loyalty, 110
LPR. *See* laryngopharyngeal reflux
Luke, Gospel of, 36
lungs, 146
Luther, Martin, 25, 93, 121
A Lyrical Vision: The Music Documents of the U.S. Bishops (Foley), 87

MacKenzie, Bob, 130
madrigals, 57
major scale, 41
Marian antiphons, 66
marijuana, 178
Mass, 23, 25, 61; in Catholic music, 62–63; elements of, 33; etymology and definition of, 33; funeral, 36; music and, 77; office and, 31–32; ordinary and proper, 32–33; polyphony, 63; reformed order of, 75; structure of, *34–35*
"Mass of Paul VI," 75
Master of Music (MM), 98–99

INDEX

Matins, 32
Mattins, 32
McCoy, Scott, 102
McCracken, Jarrell, 125
medications, 169–70, 171
Medieval Era, 93
megachurches, *131*, 131–32, *133*, 134
Megillot, 9
melismas, 30, 37, 45
melody, of Gregorian chant, 41–45
Memorial Acclamation, 79
mental floss, 179
mental wellness, 172–73, 179–80
message, 181
Message and Mission (Nida), 122
Messiaen, Olivier, 40, 58
microphones: amplitude response of, 192–96, *194*; bidirectional pattern of, *195*; cardioid, 194, *195*; compression and, 199, *200*, 201; condenser, 190–91, *191*; consonants in, 206; dynamic, *189*, 189–90, 206; frequency response of, 191–92, *192*, 194; hypercardioid pattern of, *195*; omnidirectional pattern of, *196*; polar pattern diagram of, 192–94, *193*; proximity effect of, 194; sensitivity of, 194–96; shotgun pattern of, *196*; supercardioid pattern of, *195*; techniques, 137, 181–82, 185, 206; vowels in, 206
Middle Ages, 25, 27, 31, 36, 61–62; counterpoint of, 39; notation in, 38
Milken Archive of Jewish Music, 17
minor scale, 41
missa cantata ("sung Mass"), 66
Missal, 30, 56
missa lecta ("read Mass"), 66

missa solemnis ("solemn Mass"), 66–67
Mitchell, Robert, 121–22
mixers, 205
Mizrahi, 6
MM. *See* Master of Music
Mocquereau, Andre, 47
modality, 41–44, 85
modal voice, 155, *155*
modern classical Catholic music, 81
Modern Era, 93
modern notation, *46*
monitors, 139, 205
Morning Prayer, 32
Moses, 2
mouth, 160–62
Mozart, 57, 58
MPA. *See* musical performance anxiety
mucus, 153, 165–70, 176
muscular antagonism, 151
musical characteristics: of cantor, 5–7; of Catholic music, 61–69; of choral music, 92–97; of contemporary Christian music, 134–35; of Gregorian chant, 40–45
musical performance anxiety (MPA), 172–73
Musicam Sacram, 76–77
music history, liturgy and, 57–58
musicianship skills, 160
Music in Catholic Liturgy: A Pastoral and Theological Companion to Sing to the Lord (Gill), 87
Music Library (Knoxville), 141

NAJCF. *See* North American Jewish Choral Festival
naps, 177
nasal, 160

National Association of Pastoral Musicians, 78
National Religious Broadcasters (NRB), 126
Neti pot, 167–68
neurology, 161
Newman, Karen, 1
new music, 121–22
"new order." *See* "Novus Ordo"
New Testament, 25, 122
Nida, Eugene, 122
night office, 32
North American Jewish Choral Festival (NAJCF), 15–16
notation, 25, 38, *38*, 46, *46*, 48, 50
note lengthening, in Gregorian chant, 49–50
"Novus Ordo" ("new order"), 75
NRB. *See* National Religious Broadcasters
Le nuove musiche, 57
nusach, 12–13, 14, 15
nutrition, 164–65

Offertorium, 33, 63
office, 31–32, 36
Ogilvie, Lloyd, 120
Oldham, Doug, 129
Old Testament, 29, 65, 70, 122
Oling-Sang-Ruby Union Institute (OSRUI), 16
omnidirectional pattern, of microphones, *196*
online sound archives, of Jewish music, 17–18
opera, 57, 100–101
oratorio, 65, 102
Ordinary Form, 83–84
ordinary Mass, 32–33, *34–35*, 62–63

Ordinary Time, 96
Oregon Bach Festival, 113
organ, in choral music, 96–97
organum, 25, 37
ornamentation, 103–5
O Sacrum Convivium, 40
OSRUI. *See* Oling-Sang-Ruby Union Institute
Ostfeld, Barbara, 8
overhydration, 166
overtones, 156, 186

Palestrina, Giovanni Pierluigi da, 58–59, 102
Papal Legislation on Sacred Music: 95 A.D. to 1977 A.D. (Hayburn), 87
parametric EQ units, 197, *198*, 199
Paschal Triduum, 26
passing tones, 42
Passion, 26
Passover Seder, 5
pastoral music, 77–78
The Pathfinder, 129
Paul VI (Pope), 51
Peace of Constantine, 24, 25
Pentecost, 96
Pentecostal movement. *See* Assembly of God
performance, 61–62, 84–86, 98–99, 172–73
pharynx. *See* throat
phonation, 152–53, 166
phonation threshold pressure (PTP), 166
phonatory system, 137
phonotrauma, 163, 174, 177
physical exercise, 171–72
physical well-being, 163; exercise, 171–72; hydration, 107, 165–68,

176; mental wellness, 172–73, 179–80; nutrition, 164–65; of throat, 168–69; vocal longevity, 174–75; vocal wellness, 174–78
physiology, 137
pipe organ, 73
pitch, 85, 103–5, 159, 186, *188*
Pius X (Pope), 69
Pius XII (Pope), 69
polar pattern diagram, 192–94, *193*
polyphony, 25; choral, 72; definition of, 37; Mass, 63; of ordinary Mass, 63; Renaissance, 37, 39, 40, 98; Roman School, 58; traditional, 81. *See also* Gregorian chant
popular music, 82, 126, 139, 175
Poquette, Lee, 123
Portnoy, Marshall, 20
power source, 145–51
practical skills for career, in choral music, 109–10
practice methods, 178–79
praise music movement, 127–28
prayers, 24, 25, 28, 62, 79, 96
"Precious Lord," 123
pressure, 146, 150–51, 166
priest, 61–62
prima prattica, 57
Prime Terce, Sext, None, 32
principal musician, 108, 109
program notes, 68–69
projection, 185
pronunciation, 84, 106–7
proper Mass, 32–33, *34–35*, 62–63
Protestant choral music, 94–95
Protestant hymnody, 81
Protestantism, 56, 71
Protestant Reformation, 25, 27, 55, 93, 121
proximity effect, 194

Psalms, 29, 30, 42, 44; Book of, 2–3; Responsorial, 76, 79, 84–85
psychology, of performance, 172–73
PTP. *See* phonation threshold pressure
published songs, 141
publishers, Jewish music, 18
publishing companies, 140

reading/musicianship, 100–103, 105–6, 109
read Mass. *See missa lecta*
recitatives, 28
recordings, of choral music, 114
rectus, 148, *149*, *150*
reflexive habits, 161
reflux, 170–71, 178
refraction, *186*
rehearsals, 85, 99, 109, 136, 180
Rehearse License, 140
relaxation, 161–62
religious beliefs, 112
Renaissance Era, 25, 57, 93; polyphony, 37, 39, 40, 98
repertoire and resources: of Catholic music, 87; of choral music, 61, 92–97; of contemporary Christian music, 139–42; of Gregorian chant, 51; of Jewish music, 17–20
Requiem, 36
Requiem Aeternam, 63–64
resonance, 101, 137, 139, 186; forced, 157; free, 157; of instruments, 145; private, 157; vocal tract as source of, 156–60
resonator, 145
respiratory system, 137, 168
Responsorial Psalm, 76, 79, 84–85
résumé, 107
reverb, 201–2, *202*

rhythm, 85–86
rock 'n' roll, 125, 127, 134
Roman Catholic Church, 47
Roman Rite Liturgy, 76
Roman School polyphony, 58
Romantic Era, 93
room humidification, 166–67
Rosh Hashanah, 16, 20
Ruff, Anthony, 51

Sabbath, 5, 9
Sacrosanctum Concilium. See Liturgy Constitution
saliva production, 169
saltwater rinse, 168
Salve Regina, 31, 32
Sanctus, 28, 30, 31, 33, 62, 63, 79
Santa Fe Desert Chorale, 113
Schaeffer, Frances, 119
Schola, 30, 36–37, 50
schola cantorum (song school), 36–37, 111
School of Jewish Music. See Hebrew College
score, 38
scripture, liturgy and, 73
scripture readings, 27–28
seasons, 97
second formant, *158*
Second Vatican Council (Vatican II), 31, 56, 61, 67; communal understanding of liturgy in, 70–71; documents issued by, 71–72; documents of, 70; Gregorian Chant and, 27; interpretation of, 74; interpreting, 28; liturgy of, 75–77; openness to dialogues with others in, 71; origin of, 69–70; reformed liturgy of, 78; regional variety in liturgy of, 71; secular music and, 71. *See also* Catholic music
sectionals, in choral music, 111
secular music, 57–59, 71, 78, 117n2
seminaries, offering education of cantor, 9–16
sensitivity, of microphones, 194–96
Shabbat, 1, 11, 18
Shabbat Anthology (published in six volumes), 19
Shaliach Tzibur, 3
Shapiro, Scott, 1–2
shelf equalizers, 196–97, *197*
Shema Yisrael, 2
Shivoitz, Jeffrey, 19–20
shotgun pattern, of microphones, *196*
Shulchan Aruch, 4
sickness, 109
signal chain, 188–89, 204
Sign of the Cross, 65
singer's formant, 158
Sing to the Lord: Music in Divine Worship, 53, 77, 87
skill development, 178–79
skill set diversification, 111–12
sleep, 180
Smith, Chuck, 127
smoking, 178
sneezing, 177
social media, 120
solemn Mass. *See missa solemnis*
Solesmes Abbey, 76
"Solesmes Method," 48
solo singing, 100, 102, 111
song school. *See schola cantorum*
sound, 137, *138*, 145, 186–88
sound systems, 181–82, 188–89, 204–5
speakers, 205
speaking voice, 176–77

spectrum analyzer, 159–60
stamina, 180, 181
Stamps Quartet, 129
steam inhalers, 166–67
sternum, 147, 148
stile antico, 57
straight-tone singing, 99, 103–4, 139
Stream License, 140
stress, 172
stylistic diversity, 60
summer work, in choral music, 113–14
Summorum Pontificum, 83
sung Mass. *See missa cantata*
supercardioid pattern, of microphones, *195*
supplemental vibration, 156–57
supraglottic vocal tract, 137
Symmes, Thomas, 121

TA. *See* thyroarytenoid dominant
Tara Publications, 18
TC-Helicon, 204
tea, 168–69
Te Deum, 64
Tell It Like It Is, 125
tempo, of Gregorian chant, 49–50
Tenebrae, 64
tension, 161
tessituras, 105
text, of Gregorian chant, 45
"There's Something about That Name," 130
thinking ahead, 84
thorax, 147
throat, 166, 168–69
throat singing, 156
through-composed pieces, 30
thyroarytenoid (TA) dominant, 155, *155*

thyroarytenoid muscle, 154
thyroid cartilage, 153, *154*
timbre, 188
tongue, 160–62
Too Close to Heaven (Broughton), 122–23
Torah, 9, 11, 20
traditionalist Catholic music, 80–81
traditional worship, vocal wellness for, 180
training: for cantor, 7–9; for choral music, 98–107; of contemporary Christian music, 135–36; of Gregorian chant, 46–50; institutions for cantor, 9–16
Transcontinental Music, 18, 19
transcription, of Gregorian chant, 46
transverse abdominis, 149
Tridentine Low Mass, 67
Triduum, 26

Union for Reform Judaism (URJ), 16–17

Valastro, Buddy, 137
Vatican II. *See* Second Vatican Council
vernacular, liturgy and, 73
Vernacular Hymnody, 66–67
Vespers, 32, 36, 64
Vespers of the Blessed Virgin Mary, 64
vibration, *155*, 155–57
vibrato, 103–5, 137, 139
Vigils, 32
Virgin Mary, 65–66
visualization techniques, 173
vocal folds, 152–53, 164–66, 176; damage to, 174; structure of, *152*, *177*; vibration, 155, *155*

vocalise, 174, 176
vocal tract, 137, 156–60
voice: articulators of, 160–62; athletic demands of, 163–64, 171–72, 174–75; balancing, 142; beauty of, 52–53; challenges of, 138; conservation, 178–79; cross-training, 182; development of, 175; disorders, 174; fatigue of, 107, 180; fitness program for, 175–76; forced resonance and, 157; habits, 161, 163, 174; health of, 136, 176, 177; hygiene education, 174; improvisation with, 40; injury of, 163–64, 174–78; instruments and, 145; intensity of, 177; larynx, vibrator of, 151–56, *154*, 164; ligament, 152–53; loft, 155, *155*; longevity, 174–75; medications and, 169–70; misuse and abuse of, 174; modal, 155, *155*; performance, higher education in, 98–99; problems with, 164; processors, 204; production, 84; pulmonary system as power source of, 146–51; qualities, 185, 206; reflux and, 170–71; side effects, 169; speaking, 176–77; styles, 137–38; technique, 47, 107, 136–39, 163; training, 174–75; vibrato, 103–5; vocal naps, 177; vocal tract as source of resonance of, 156–60; wellness, 174–78, 180–82
A Voice Still Heard (Werner), 3–4
vowels, 106, 137, *158*, 160, 206

warm-up, 85, 138, 176
Werner, Eric, 3–4
We Speak to Nations, 135
whole body wellness. *See* physical well-being
Wolfe, Josee, 20

Yeshiva University, 10, 15–16
Yom Kippur, 1, 20

Zamru Lo (Shivoitz), 19–20

ABOUT THE EDITOR AND CONTRIBUTORS

Matthew Hoch is associate professor of voice and coordinator of voice studies at Auburn University, as well as choirmaster and minister of music at Holy Trinity Episcopal Church in Auburn, Alabama. His extensive experience as a professional chorister includes eight seasons with the Oregon Bach Festival, two seasons with the Santa Fe Desert Chorale, and recordings with the Spoleto Festival Choir (Italy). From 2003 to 2005 he was the baritone soloist at historic Trinity Church on Copley Square in Boston. Dr. Hoch is the author of several books, including *A Dictionary for the Modern Singer* and *Voice Secrets*, coauthored with Linda Lister. He holds a BM degree from Ithaca College, MM degree from the Hartt School, and DMA degree from the New England Conservatory. He is the 2016 winner of the Van L. Lawrence Fellowship, awarded jointly by the Voice Foundation and NATS.

○ ○ ○

Matthew Edwards is associate professor of voice and voice pedagogy at Shenandoah Conservatory and artistic director of the CCM Voice Pedagogy Institute. His current and former students have performed on and off-Broadway as well as on national and international tours, major motion picture soundtracks, and have appeared on Billboard music charts. Edwards is the author of *So You Want to Sing Rock 'n' Roll* and has contributed chapters to *Manual of Singing Voice Rehabilitation*, *The Vocal Athlete*, *Get the Callback*, and *A Dictionary for the Modern Singer*. He has authored articles for *Journal of Singing*, *Journal of Voice*, *American Music Teacher*, *VOICEPrints*, and *Southern Theatre*. Edwards regularly presents workshops on functional training for the CCM singer at conferences and universities throughout the United States.

Evan Kent is an *oleh chadash* ("new immigrant") to Israel, having moved in the summer of 2013. Previously, he was the cantor at Temple Isaiah in Los Angeles for twenty-five years, also serving on the faculty of Hebrew Union College (the seminary for the Reform movement of Judaism) for fifteen years. Dr. Kent's publications have appeared in the *Journal of Reform Judaism*, *Sh'ma Magazine*, and *Conservative Judaism*. He also holds a doctorate in music education from Boston University. He is currently on the faculty of Hebrew Union College in Jerusalem, where he teaches classes in both contemporary and historic Jewish music. In addition to his musical and educational pursuits, Evan is an avid runner, having completed multiple marathons and ultra-marathons.

Wendy LeBorgne is a voice pathologist, speaker, author, and master class clinician. She actively presents nationally and internationally on the professional voice and is the clinical director of two successful private practice voice centers: the ProVoice Center in Cincinnati and BBIVAR in Dayton. Dr. LeBorgne holds an adjunct professorship at University of Cincinnati College–Conservatory of Music as a voice consultant, where she also teaches voice pedagogy and wellness courses. She completed a BFA in musical theater from Shenandoah Conservatory and her graduate and doctoral degrees from the University of Cincinnati. Original peer-reviewed research has been published in multiple journals, and she is a contributing author to several voice textbooks. Most recently, she coauthored *The Vocal Athlete* textbook and workbook with Marci Rosenberg. Her patients and private students currently can be found on radio, television, film, cruise ships, Broadway, off-Broadway, national tours, commercial music tours, and opera stages around the world.

ABOUT THE EDITOR AND CONTRIBUTORS

Scott McCoy is a noted author, singer, conductor, and pianist with extensive performance experience in concert and opera. He is professor of voice and pedagogy, director of the Swank Voice Laboratory, and director of the interdisciplinary program in singing health at Ohio State University. His voice science and pedagogy textbook, *Your Voice: An Inside View*, is used extensively by colleges and universities throughout the United States and abroad. McCoy is the associate editor of the *Journal of Singing* for voice pedagogy and is a past president of the National Association of Teachers of Singing (NATS). He also served NATS as vice president for workshops, program chair for the 2006 and 2008 national conferences, chair of the voice science advisory committee, and a master teacher for the intern program. Deeply committed to teacher education, McCoy is a founding faculty member in the NYSTA Professional Development Program, teaching classes in voice anatomy, physiology, acoustics, and voice analysis. He is a member of the distinguished American Academy of Teachers of Singing (AATS).

Sharon L. Radionoff is director of the Sound Singing Institute, as well as singing voice specialist and voice technologist at the Texas Voice Center in Houston. She is an active clinician, lecturer, researcher, and author. She is the author of two books—*The Vocal Instrument* and *Faith and Voice*—as well as many articles and book chapters. Dr. Radionoff earned her BME from Eastern Michigan University, MM from Southern Methodist University, and PhD from Michigan State University. She also completed a professional fellowship at the American Institute for Voice and Ear Research Center in Philadelphia under the direction of Robert T. Sataloff.

Fr. Anthony Ruff, OSB, is a monk of St. John's Abbey and associate professor of theology at St. John's University School of Theology and Seminary in Collegeville, Minnesota. He is the founding director of the National Catholic Youth Choir. He chaired the international committee that wrote the English chant for the 2011 Roman Missal. He has published several books and articles in his specialties of hymnody, Gregorian chant, liturgy, and liturgical music. He is moderator of the popular liturgy blog Pray Tell.

CPSIA information can be obtained
at www.ICGtesting.com
Printed in the USA
BVOW11s0010081216
470154BV00001B/3/P